LEGISLATIVE SYSTEMS IN DEVELOPING COUNTRIES

PUBLICATIONS OF THE CONSORTIUM FOR COMPARATIVE LEGISLATIVE STUDIES

Malcolm E. Jewell,
General Editor

1. G. R. Boynton and Chong Lim Kim, Editors. *Legislative Systems in Developing Countries*

Forthcoming titles to be announced.

LEGISLATIVE SYSTEMS
IN
DEVELOPING COUNTRIES

G. R. BOYNTON and CHONG LIM KIM, Editors

Duke University Press, Durham, North Carolina 1975

© 1975, Duke University Press
L.C.C. card no. 75-13342
I.S.B.N. 0-8223-0344-2
Printed in the United States of America

FOREWORD

This is the first publication in the Duke University Press Comparative Legislative Studies Series, and consequently it seems appropriate to explain the purposes of this series. The field of comparative legislative studies is relatively new, but it is attracting increasing attention from scholars. Although we obviously cannot publish all of the significant scholarly work that is being done in this field, we hope to provide some direction to the comparative study of legislatures and to publish studies that raise provocative questions and will stimulate research by other scholars. The series will include studies of legislative systems, institutions, behavior, and outputs that are cross-national in scope as well as studies of single nations that test and develop hypotheses which are significant for comparative research.

The entire publishing program in comparative legislative research is sponsored by the Consortium for Comparative Legislative Studies, which has been organized by scholars at Duke University, the University of Hawaii, the University of Iowa, and the State University of New York at Albany. The Consortium is the outgrowth of efforts over several years by a group of scholars to promote the systematic and extensive study of legislative systems and processes in a comparative perspective. The Consortium plans to continue sponsoring conferences on legislative studies, which will be one source of volumes in the Duke University Press series.

This present study is actually the product of the fourth in a series of conferences held since 1967 on various aspects of comparative legislative studies and sponsored by scholars who have been associated with the development of the Consortium for Comparative Legislative Studies. Each of these conferences has led to the publication of a volume, and these volumes have contributed significantly to the subfield of comparative legislative studies. The first of these conferences was held in Planting Fields, New York, in December 1967, under the sponsorship of the Comparative Administration Group of the American Society for Public Administration. The focus of that conference was on the relationships between legislative institutions in both developed and developing countries. The conference led to publications of a volume, *Legislatures in Developmental Perspective,* edited by Allan Kornberg and Lloyd D. Musolf and published by Duke University Press (1970).

The second conference in the series was the Shambaugh Conference on Comparative Legislative Behavior Research, held at the University of Iowa in May 1969. This conference brought together scholars from the United States and Europe, and the geographic focus of the papers was on these two areas. The topics included the recruitment of legislators and their roles, patterns of decision-making, the activities of legislative parties, and problems of measuring legislative outputs and feedback. The papers were published in a volume entitled, *Comparative Legislative Behavior: Frontiers of Research,* edited by Samuel C. Patterson and John C. Wahlke and published by John Wiley (1972).

The third conference was the Quail Roost Conference on the Concepts and Methods of Comparative Legislative Study held in February 1970. This conference was particularly concerned with the concept of institutionalization and the relationships between legislative institutions and other components of political systems in both developed and developing countries. There was also particular attention given to the development of better methods for comparative analysis. The papers provide a rich and varied resource for students to use in studying other legislative and political systems. The papers were published in a volume, *Legislatures in Comparative Perspective,* edited by Allan Kornberg and published by David McKay (1973).

The 1971 Shambaugh Conference resulted in the present volume, the geographic focus of which is on Asia, Africa, and Latin America. In most of the countries covered by these papers the legislature is not a powerful decision-making or law-making body. Consequently, most of the papers are concerned with other functions performed by the legislatures. One of the major contributions of this volume is the attention that it focuses on the legislators' role in mediating between government and the citizenry. It suggests that in the future much more attention needs to be given to the roles and activities of individual legislators and not just the formal activities of the legislative body. This volume, like those that preceded it, challenges some traditional assumptions about legislatures and relates legislatures to broader political systems and problems of political development. Like its predecessors, it offers legislative students new insights and hypotheses that can be examined and tested in future research.

Malcolm E. Jewell
General Editor, Comparative
Legislative Studies Series

ACKNOWLEDGEMENTS

For a number of years the Department of Political Science at the University of Iowa has been able to present lecture and conference programs because of a fund created in memory of Professor Benjamin F. Shambaugh, who for many years was Chairman of the Department and Superintendent of the State Historical Society. The first Department executive officer, he served for some forty years, including service as President of the American Political Science Association.

A series of distinguished lectures have been presented through this program, including presentations by Karl Deutsch, Herman Finer, Charles Hyneman, Dayton McKean, Arnold Rogow, and Sheldon Wolin. In 1967 the first Shambaugh Conference was held—a Conference on Judicial Research, which led to the publication of essays entitled *Frontiers of Judicial Research* (Wiley, 1969). The second Conference, held in 1969, was on Comparative Legislative Behavior Research. The papers of this Conference were later published in a volume entitled *Comparative Legislative Behavior: Frontiers of Research* (Wiley, 1972).

The present volume represents a collection of research papers presented at the Third Shambaugh Conference held at the University of Iowa in November 1971. With the exceptions of the introductory chapter and the chapter by Chong Lim Kim and Byung-kyu Woo, all the chapters in this book were presented in preliminary drafts and discussed extensively at the Conference. Thus, what we have here are the results of the extended discussion and criticisms of each research paper given at the Iowa City Conference. In addition to those who presented papers, there were many other scholars who made valuable contributions to the Conference by their participation in conference discussion: Abdo I. Baaklini, State University of New York—Albany; Michael R. King, Pennsylvania State University; Gerhard Loewenberg, University of Iowa; Donald McCrone, University of Iowa; Peter G. Snow, University of Iowa; and Joel G. Verner, Illinois State University.

For financial support of the Conference we are grateful to the Trustees of the Shambaugh Fund, and we are especially indebted to Allin W. Dakin, Administrative Dean of the University. Finally, we would like to acknowledge the editorial comments that Malcolm E. Jewell, general editor of the Comparative Legislative Research Series, has so generously provided us.

G. R. Boynton
Chong Lim Kim

Iowa City, Iowa
May 1974

CONTENTS

LEGISLATIVE SYSTEMS IN DEVELOPING COUNTRIES

Chapter 1

INTRODUCTION

G. R. BOYNTON
CHONG LIM KIM

University of Iowa

Legislatures have been key institutions in the political development of the West for the past two hundred years. While our knowledge of the role played by legislatures in these polities is not as great as it might be, it is very considerable when compared with our knowledge of legislatures in other parts of the world. The postwar development of scholarly interest in non-Western nations has not produced a large number of legislative studies. There are several reasons why scholars have paid less attention to legislatures than to other political institutions. First, very little was known about the countries, and it was necessary to get a general understanding of their politics before doing more specialized research. Second, legislatures did not seem very important to the political scientists observing the political processes of these countries. Legislatures seemed to be rather ineffective institutions. For the most part they were less important centers of power than the executive, the bureaucracy, and the military. In countries where the most basic institutional arrangements were unstable, legislatures were the most unstable of the governmental institutions. This was taken as an additional sign of their relative unimportance. For these reasons political scientists paid little systematic attention to legislative institutions, and as a consequence we know very little about them.

For the past several years a number of political scientists have been doing research to fill this lacuna in our understanding of politics in non-Western or developing countries. This book is one product of that research effort. The papers are, for the most part, based on research in one country, and each author approaches his research from a somewhat different perspective. However, most of the authors employ research strategies and concepts that have been developed in previous studies of legislatures, and it is often possible to make comparisons between research results in the country being studied and research conducted in Western environments.

Each of the research reports in this volume describes, and attempts to explain, the functioning of a specific legislature in its polity. In this introductory essay we attempt to draw together these observations under three broad themes: the legislature as a goal-setting agency for society, the legislature and the management of conflict in society, and the legislature and the integration of the polity. However, two points should be made before proceeding to this effort. First, in no society is the legislature the only political institution carrying out these functions. All political institutions serve these functions in a variety of ways. Thus, in looking at the contributions of legislatures, we will be getting only a partial view of how each function is accomplished in the societies examined. Second, these nine studies are an inadequate base for any substantial generalizations about these three legislative functions. These are important dimensions of legislative activity, and the research reported in this volume will permit us to better understand the functioning of legislatures in governing, but it is only a beginning. There is much work to be done if we are to have adequate understanding of the role of legislatures in the governing process.

LEGISLATURES AS GOAL-SETTING
AGENCIES FOR SOCIETY

The most obvious thing that legislatures do is to pass laws. Each of the legislatures that is described in the following essays has formal responsibility for passing the laws of the country. Since laws are important mechanisms for setting goals for a society, one anticipates that legislatures will be important agencies in the goal-setting of a society. It is clear, however, that formal responsibility for passing legislation is not equivalent to exercising influence in goal-setting. Michael Mezey recounts an incident in which the Thai army was put

on alert during debate on the government tax bill in 1970. The
government leaders made it clear that unless the measure was passed
a coup would take place. What seems really remarkable is that, in the
face of even this dramatic threat, the bill passed by only one vote.
This is only one of a large number of given examples that indicate
the lack of influence of the Thai legislature in setting goals for the
society.

There are two facets to legislative influence in general goal-setting.
One is the source of legislation. Who writes the laws? At one extreme
all legislation might be drafted by members of the legislature. At the
other extreme all legislation may be drafted by the executive branch.
Young C. Kim's account of the operation of committees in the
Japanese Diet indicates that the great majority of bills and treaties
considered by the two committees that he studied were not drafted
by the committee itself. While the other papers are not so explicit as
Kim's, it seems clear that the power of drafting legislation is in the
hands of the executive in most cases.

The second aspect of the legislature's influence in setting goals for
society is its ability to amend and change legislation, in particular, its
ability to make changes in legislation proposed by the executive.
Even if the executive drafts most bills, the legislature may exercise
significant influence if it is able to make meaningful changes in the
legislation. While the legislatures which have been studied appear to
exercise some influence in modifying executive proposed legislation,
these appear to be exceptional acts on the part of the legislatures
rather than the general norm. For example, Raymond Hopkins
reports that the Kenyan legislature was able to block government
initiatives on several matters and force revision on others during the
1963-65 period; in the two subsequent periods (1965-68 and
1969-71) this initiative was substantially curtailed. Marvin Weinbaum's review of the history of the Iranian legislature is a
particularly vivid portrayal of the changing relationships between the
legislature and the executive that characterize many countries. From
1906 through 1923 (with a few interruptions) the Iranian legislature
exercised considerable influence in the government. However, there
was a complete loss of autonomy in 1925 and executive domination
continued through 1941. From 1941 to 1953 the legislature
exercised more influence, but a series of impotent cabinets (founded
on shifting majorities), corruption, and crises brought about by the
unwillingness of the legislature to approve the government budget led
to executive intervention. Since 1953 the legislature has been a

relatively impotent body that exercises little influence on government policy. The Japanese Diet is a rather different case even though the members of the legislature exercise little influence on policy-making. It is a parliamentary system in which the prime minister has the support of a sizable majority and in which party voting is very high. Thus, the minority parties exercise little influence because they do not have enough votes. The majority party votes as a bloc and therefore even individual members of the majority party exercise little influence. Because this style of party government is carried into the committee system, there is little room for legislative autonomy even at this level.

This review of the research reported in this volume confirms the initial estimates of political scientists who have been conducting research in the developing countries for setting goals for the society. If one wants to find their significance in these political systems, one must look elsewhere.

LEGISLATURES AND THE STRUCTURE OF
POLITICAL CONFLICT

After concluding that legislatures play a relatively minor role in the formulation of government policy, it seems mildly paradoxical to think that they might play an important role in structuring political conflict. However, these two things are not as incompatible as one might at first think. It is clear that legislatures are threatening to those who want to suppress controversy. The leaders of political coups almost always disband the legislature as a first step. Our task is to determine how an institution that is relatively impotent in imposing its will on the government may at the same time play an important role in structuring political conflict.

There are two prerequisites for political controversy: first, opposing political elites; and second, an arena in which debate is legitimate. Without these two conditions conflict will necessarily be sporadic or completely inarticulate, or else will be carried on outside political institutions—perhaps in the streets.

Opposition to government programs is ubiquitous. The very nature of any political decision is that it benefits some and not others or that it benefits some more than others. Thus, there is always a basis for political controversy. However, the opposition must establish some individuals who speak for them, that is, some individuals within the opposing groups must be established as an elite that speaks for a broader constituency opposed to the actions of government. The process of recruiting legislators is the most available means of entry into the political system for an opposing group. The electoral process, whether it be election from districts or proportional representation, offers the most open avenue into the political system for opposition groups.

Gary Hoskin describes this process of recruitment of new elites through the legislature in Colombia. During the nineteenth century and early in the twentieth century, politics was dominated by two oligarchical groups. However, the economic crisis of the 1930s and subsequent economic change in the country have led to an opening of the political system. The new groups have found their place in the political system through the legislature. The executive remains in control of the original oligarchical groups, but they have been forced to open the legislature to other groups. He then shows that the controversy in the Colombian legislature can be directly attributed to two basic sources of disagreement between the newer and older elite groups. The older groups are more supportive of the present political arrangements in which the presidency is rotated between the two traditional parties, and the newer groups are opposed to this system of rotation. The older groups are ideologically more conservative, while the newer groups are liberal. However, a major consequence of opening the legislature to new elite groups has been centering political influence in the hands of the executive and reducing the influence of the legislature. Thus, the changing pattern of recruitment was making the legislature an arena for opposition and controversy at precisely the same time that it was losing its influence in policy-making.

Three other countries provide evidence which reinforces this point. Michael Mezey suggests that the Thai legislature is politically influential only during periods of executive instability. But for this argument it is not necessary that the legislature be influential in establishing the policies of government, but only that the recruitment of legislators should provide a sustaining institutional base for opposition. The fact that opposing groups can elect individuals to the legislature who view their function as one of overseeing the government and the implementation of its program indicates that legislative recruitment is important in establishing opposing elites. South Vietnam is a second example in which election to the legislature becomes a base for opposition groups. While Allan

Goodman concentrates on the constituency work of Vietnamese legislators, his description of their activities within the legislature indicates that opposition to the Thieu government is possible in the legislature. Kenya is a one-party state and therefore may be a tougher test of the argument that the recruitment of legislators can provide an institutionalized base for opposition. The candidates are screened by the party to insure that opposition to the government is precluded. Raymond Hopkins suggests that the political influence of the legislature has declined sharply since 1963, but he also reports that the screening process is not so restrictive as to restrain all opposition.

It is, of course, possible to completely suppress opposition. Marvin Weinbaum suggests that in Iran since 1953 the executive has not permitted the election of individuals to the legislature who would oppose the government. Lester Seligman discusses this at some length in his paper on recruitment, and suggests a number of countries in which the executive has taken this action.

It is not enough that potential opposition candidates be elected to the legislature. The legislature must also be an arena in which debate is legitimate if it is to structure controversy. Seligman suggests it is easier for the executive to suppress opposition even after it has reached the legislature in economically less developed countries because of the high risk of political careers in such a country. Achieving political office not only sets one off from the citizenry politically but in important social and economic ways as well. The political office holder participates in a social and economic system which is highly restricted in countries that are principally agricultural and in which per-capita income is very low. If one opposes the executive too strenuously one not only loses political office; one also loses the social and economic benefits that come with that office. There are no careers to which one can return from political office which offer equal amenities. Raymond Hopkins describes the political elite of Kenya in just these terms. One would then expect that opposition to the government would be muted by the obvious consequences of too vocal an opposing stand.

While there are clearly differences in the latitude afforded legislators in opposing the government, it is also clear that in all of the legislatures described in the following papers legislators do call into question the actions of government. The boundaries of opposition may be more narrowly or more broadly defined, but in each country there is room within the legislature for debate and opposition to the government. Thus, the legislature is a legitimate arena for (more or less) political debate.

LEGISLATURES AND THE INTEGRATION OF
POLITICAL SYSTEMS

The concept of political integration has been used in a variety of ways. In this paper we are going to use it to mean interconnection. If behavior in one part of a political system affects behavior in other parts in the system, then the system is, to that extent, integrated. If behavior in one part of the system does not affect behavior in another part of the system, then the system is, to that extent, not integrated.

One way to illustrate what is meant by political integration is to describe what an unintegrated political system would be like. In some countries substantial segments of the population are almost totally disconnected from the national political system. They are physically isolated and have no communication with the larger system of which they are presumably a part. They know nothing of the laws of the country and therefore they do not obey them. They receive no services from the government. They pay no taxes. They participate in the national system not at all. A country which has a segment of its population in this condition is not totally politically integrated. For such a country penetration by the national government into these segments of the population may be an important and difficult problem.

There are two aspects of political integration; one is symbolic and the other behavioral. "United States" symbolizes an interconnection of two hundred million people. Since they think of themselves as one people, they are politically integrated. Thus, beyond the behavioral interconnection described above is the symbolic interconnection—the sense that these people have something in common which structures the way they think and act. The behavioral interconnection of a population and their government is twofold; the connections running from the citizens to the government and the connections from the government to the citizens. Elections and communication of demands for government action are connections running from the citizens to government. Government policies and programs are connections running the other way. Our question is, what role does the legislature play in the political integration of the countries studied in this book? Before trying to answer this question it will be necessary to summarize one of the primary themes that runs through the nine research reports.

Reading these papers leaves one with two very distinct impressions. The first is the relative ineffectiveness of the legislatures in exercising influence on policy matters within their political systems. The second is the frequency with which the authors cite the role of legislators in mediating between government and the citizenry. Allan Goodman makes this the central focus of his paper. He found that one-third of the members of the South Vietnamese legislature were actively engaged in constituency service work. He catalogues some of the types of constituency service activities which they performed and the style in which they accomplished this activity.

> During 1969-70, for example, deputies sought to have constituents released from imprisonment under the Phoenix program, to combat corrupt and change ineffective administrative procedures, to facilitate the processing of emergency and regular relief petitions, and to have public works projects funded on the basis of priorities set within the village rather than the provincial government. While deputies' modes of operation differed greatly, their activities shared a common concern to make local and provincial government responsive to public interests. Each deputy approached individual problems with detachment; the reliance upon or the image of reliance upon personal favoritism as the only way to get things done was de-emphasized. Each believed that the only rights the population had were those they learned to demand.

While Allan Goodman was the only author who made this the central focus of his paper, it is a theme that recurs in many of the papers. Chong Lim Kim and Byung-kyu Woo investigate the role orientation of members of the Korean legislature. They contrast the verbal responses of Korean legislators on a commonly used "role orientation" question with the actual behavior of the legislators. One gets the distinct impression that the verbal responses are little more than that, i.e., they are only verbal with little behavioral implication. At the same time they find a significant percentage of the Korean legislators who are actively involved in serving their constituencies.

Young C. Kim's analysis of two committees in the Japanese legislature touches only peripherally on constituency service, but it is alluded to at two key points in the analysis. In discussing the motivation of legislators in their choice of committee assignments he suggests that one of the most important criteria used is the importance of the work of the committee to the legislator's constituents. Thus, committee assignment is sought in terms of the effects that it will have on one's ability to assist his constituents, resulting in improved chance of his reelection. The assistance that the legislator can provide to his constituents is not, however, in drafting legislation. It is found in the access to and influence with the bureaucracy that this position provides for the legislator. If the legislator is on a committee supervising a ministry he will be able to influence the ministry to assist his constituency.

Raymond Hopkins presents an analysis of constituency service from the other side, from the perspective of the constituents. The respondents interviewed in his survey were much more likely to believe that legislators were interested in and willing to assist them than were civil servants. He also characterizes the electoral process as being affected by constituency service. Many of the politicians run for office on the basis of what they can and have been able to do for their constituents.

It is worth reinforcing this point by citing other research which has found this same phenomenon. In a paper previously published on the Thai legislature Michael Mezey (1972) found that constituency service was an important role played by many of the legislators. Raymond Hopkins' study (1970) of the Tanzanian legislature also found constituency service to be an important part of what those legislators did. M. K. Mohapatra (1971) studied the legislature of the state of Orissa in India and found that most of these state legislators felt that this was an important part of their job. Richard Styskal provides evidence of the existence of this same phenomenon in the Philippines. Allan Goodman makes the point that this kind of work is not confined to legislators in less economically developed countries. In fact, constituency service activity has been found to be an important part of the work of legislators in the United States, France, and England.

If this activity of legislators is as widespread as it appears to be, then it is important to ask why it is so widespread and what effects it has. The question—why is constituency service done?—needs to be subdivided into three questions to be answered effectively.

First, why is there a need for constituency service? If there were no need for constituency service, then no one would be doing it; one must, therefore, try to decide why there is such a need. Government programs are implemented as general rules. When these general rules are implemented selectively for political reasons (to favor one political group over another) or because of bribery and corruption, some citizens will be shortchanged. This creates a need for constituency service. Constituency service is also likely to be needed in almost the opposite case. When a citizen believes that a general rule is being applied to him in a way that is detrimental to his interests or is unfair, he may want someone to serve as his advocate. Finally, citizens may seek advocates because of the timing of the implementation of government programs. For example, a government may set up a five-year plan for rural development. But not every community will have a well dug at the same time. It will be done in some communities before it is in others. Thus, the need for constituency service grows out of the implementation of government policy through general rules. Citizens may object that the rules are not being applied generally. They may seek assistance for making their case an exception. And they may seek assistance to influence the time of the application of the general rule.

The second aspect of the question is: why is it that legislators are predominantly involved in constituency service? The kinds of problems outlined above which lead to the need for constituency service grow out of attempts to influence the bureaucracy in its implementation of government programs. Thus, one seeks a source of influence to exert leverage on the bureaucracy. Legislators are particularly likely to see this as something which is part of their role because of their relationship to the citizenry. The electoral process is the structural base of their influence, while appointment by the government is the structural base of authority of bureaucrats. Thus, legislators are more likely to feel that their relationship to the citizens of the country and the citizens of their district (in district electoral systems) is one that implies providing assistance to citizens in their relationship to government. At this general level, then, we are arguing that the structural relationship between legislators and citizens (the electoral process) provides the general motivating force for constituency service. The data from the study of the Korean legislature provides a partial test of this argument. Some of the legislators are elected at large and some are elected from districts. If the argument about the structural effects of the electoral process is correct, then one would expect a difference in the constituency service behavior of these two types of legislators. This turned out to be the case. In fact, type of election was the strongest independent predictor of constituency service. While this is only very partial validation of the argument, it does suggest the importance of the electoral process in motivating legislators to engage in this kind of activity.

Not all legislators are involved in constituency service. Thus, one must ask: why some legislators and not others? Goodman, and Kim and Woo address themselves to this question most explicitly. In addition to type of election Kim and Woo found that less senior legislators, those who won their election by smaller margins, those who aspire to higher office, and legislators in the majority party are more likely to perform constituency service in Korea. Goodman found a somewhat different set of variables that characterized those who performed constituency service. Those who were anti-government, those whose districts had been most affected by the war, and those who were reelected to the next session of the legislature were more likely to take an active role in assisting their constituents. Mohapatra (1971) found that those legislators with less seniority, those less involved in the work of the legislature, and those in the majority coalition were more involved in constituency service. No very clear pattern emerges from these analyses. Perhaps we must conclude with Goodman that we have only begun to study this phenomenon and a good deal more work is necessary before we will be able to explain it more adequately. Although there were substantial differences in the analysis procedures used, even a re-analysis of these data might shed more light on the phenomenon than this summary is able to do.

Now back to the question, what role does the legislature play in the political integration of the countries covered in this book? Political integration is defined as the interconnection of citizens and government, linkages running between citizens and government, and between government and citizens. Goodman argues very persuasively that the linkages running from citizens to government are very tenuous in South Vietnam. Governmental actions affect the lives of citizens, but actions by citizens have little effect on government. He further argues that the service work of legislators helps build connections between citizens and government:

Creating political power thus requires both the expansion of political participation and the creation of national interests ... I had failed, however, to take quite literally the lesson implied in the comments of those who suggested that political organizations in Vietnam were bankrupt: The people no longer believed in politics or trusted political organizations. . . . The trust so lacking between the people and the government and the people and the political organizations was instrumental to this relationship [constituency service]. Indeed, the amount of trust developed reflected the degree to which deputies were able to convert the needs and demands of their constituents into interests that fostered linkages between the people and that portion of the government acknowledged as legitimate.

Legislators were building the political integration of Vietnam by showing their constituents that their needs could become demands on government; that their actions could affect government policies and government programs. In political systems with higher levels of trust in government the work that legislators do to assist their constituents reinforces this trust by giving citizens the feeling that their actions can affect government. Thus constituency service, which (as Goodman points out) American legislators largely discount, plays a critical role in the process of political integration in developing countries.

The election of legislators is a second linkage between citizens and government. To the extent that citizens believe that their connection to government through electing legislators makes a difference in the way government acts, the electoral process becomes an important symbol of political integration. It is possible to determine citizens' beliefs about the effect of the electoral process only in Kenya. There the citizens believe that legislators are likely to be responsive to their needs, and bureaucrats are not likely to be responsive to their needs. It is, however, possible to ask whether elections make a difference. On the basis of the research reports included in this volume, we have concluded that legislators play a relatively minor role in determining government policy. Thus, elections may not play a central role in determining policy. However, we have also concluded that elections do play a major role in setting the agenda of political controversy. If the election system is open enough to allow some opposition, then the electoral process does structure political conflict. Also elections constitute a structural basis for constituency assistance. They therefore produce a segment of the political elite which is particularly sensitive to the needs of the citizenry. It is clear that elections are no panacea for integrating a polity. At the same time they do contribute to political integration in important ways.

CONCLUSION

The research papers in this volume have been summarized by examining the contribution of each to our understanding of the role

of the legislature in the countries being studied. Three important
for understanding the working of the legislature in a political sys____
have structured this summary. These themes have been: the
legislature as a goal-setting agency for society, the legislature and the
management of conflict, and the role played by the legislature in the
integration of the polity. The question that remains to be addressed
is—where do we go from here?

Research on legislatures in countries that are less industrialized is
just beginning. There are two strategies that might be followed as this
research thrust gathers momentum. One strategy would be to follow
the lead of researchers who have investigated legislatures in the past.
The research is voluminous; the potential leads for research in that
literature are great. Most of the research, however, has assumed that
legislatures are important and then proceeded to investigate the
internal workings of the legislature. Thus, we know a great deal
about recruitment of legislators, the operation of committee systems,
the leadership structures, voting by legislators, and other facets of
the processes which are important as the legislature acts as a major
agency for setting policy for the society. However, the assumption
that underlies this kind of research is an assumption that cannot be
made about legislatures in the countries that are described in this
volume.

A second strategy, and the one that we consider preferable, is to
examine the assumption of the importance of legislatures in
economically less developed countries. What are the important
linkages between the actions of the legislature and other parts of the
political system? What does it do or what aspects of its existence
make a difference in the ongoing system? This is a rather different
task than the ones legislative researchers have usually set for
themselves in the past. It requires new and broader conceptual-
izations and somewhat different kinds of data and analysis. The three
themes which have been used to integrate the research in this volume
could serve as at least part of the conceptual handle for dealing with
these broader questions. They raise to attention at least some of the
broader questions that must be answered if we are to understand the
importance of the legislature in any given political system.

There is one other question that has not been explicitly dealt with
in this introduction, but is a problem of very considerable importance. In what way do legislatures contribute to the stability or
durability of political systems? Major change in the basic political
institutions is as common, if not more common, than the ability of

regimes to survive. One researcher (Gurr, 1972) has estimated that the "life expectancy" of political regimes is approximately 33 years and that half of the regimes studied underwent fundamental transformation by their twelfth year. In what ways have legislatures contributed to this instability? This is both a question of great importance and one about which we know practically nothing.

The challenge is to make research on legislatures an important part of understanding the operation of political systems. This challenge is particularly important in studying legislatures in countries where they have not been important policy-making bodies. The importance of the institution is not obvious in these countries, yet they do contribute to the dynamics of political change. It is only by addressing this broader set of questions that the appropriate groundwork can be laid for investigating topics that researchers of developed countries have been studying.

REFERENCES

GURR, T. (1972) "Persistence and change in political structures, 1800-1971: a comparative study." Unpublished paper.
HOPKINS, R. F. (1970) "The role of the M.P. in Tanzania." Amer. Pol. Sci. Rev. 64 (September): 754-771.
MEZEY, M. L. (1972) "The functions of a minimal legislature: role perceptions of Thai legislators." Western Pol. Q. 25 (December): 686-701.
MOHAPATRA, M. K. (1971) "Administrative value patterns of legislators in an Indian state: conflicting demands on bureaucracy in Orissa." Paper presented at annual meeting of American Political Science Assn., Chicago.

G. R. BOYNTON is Professor of Political Science at the University of Iowa. He recently served two years as Program Director for Political Science at the National Science Foundation. Co-editor of *Political Behavior and Public Opinion* (1974), he has done research on public opinion and political parties. Currently, he is engaged in research on roles of legislatures in mediating societal conflict.

CHONG LIM KIM is Associate Professor of Political Science and Associate Director of the Comparative Legislative Research Center at the University of Iowa. His publications include a co-authored book, *Patterns of Recruitment: A State Chooses Its Lawmakers* (1974), and numerous journal articles in American Political Science Review, Midwest Journal of Political Science, Comparative Political Studies, Comparative Politics, and Journal of Developing Areas.

Part I

LEGISLATURES AND GOAL-SETTING FUNCTION

Chapter 2

CLASSIFICATION AND CHANGE IN LEGISLATIVE SYSTEMS: WITH PARTICULAR APPLICATION TO IRAN, TURKEY, AND AFGHANISTAN

M A R V I N G. W E I N B A U M

University of Illinois

Parliaments rank among the most ubiquitous and venerable institutions of modern government. Aside from a diminishing few traditional monarchies, representative assemblies have made an appearance in every nation during the past half-century. Most legislatures are at least as old as constitutionalism, national unification, and independence. Many had precursors in aristocratic or tribal councils and church assemblies, or were previewed under colonial regimes. Parliaments were erected wherever governments found it necessary to institutionalize their consultations with elites or sought the consent of the masses to legitimize their rule. Though fragile, legislatures have demonstrated impressive recovery powers. Over a third of the world's parliaments have experienced some discontinuity since 1945, and better than sixty percent of all legislatures in Asia and the Middle East have undergone suspensions. Significantly, though, periodic elections and a working parliament are rarely rejected as ideals. In democracies and dictatorships alike, the restoration of a legislature customarily signifies a return to political normalcy, evidence that a period of crisis or transition has passed.

Parliaments outwardly bear a remarkable sameness. Members of congresses, national assemblies, diets, shuras, and so on are typically engaged in speech-making, reviewing legislation in committees, performing constituent services, and casting votes on general laws. In most chambers, political parties or their equivalents direct legislative activities and provide leadership. The formal rules and precedents and informal norms that regulate legislators' behavior are often indistinguishable across systems. These similarities are hardly accidental; nearly every modern legislature is heavily indebted to a Westminster, continental European, or American model. Such pervasive principles as bicameralism, parliamentary immunity, areal representation, and majoritarianism give evidence of minimal structrual inventiveness.

From another perspective, legislatures strike us as more disparate. Despite customary homage to parliamentary sovereignty, legislative powers vary widely from constitutional prescriptions. A notably few chambers are preoccupied with policy formation and provide forums for national debate; many more assume at best only superficial decisional and deliberative roles. What for some legislators is their most meaningful task—the monitoring and direction of administrative acts—is almost unknown in other chambers. Understandably, then, the United States House of Representatives, the French Fifth Republic's National Assembly, the Supreme Soviet, and Afghanistan's House of the People, for example, often seem unlike sister institutions.

Evidence of cross-national correspondence is more readily detected in the latent functions of legislatures. By symbolizing the continuous assent of non-elites in government decisions, parliaments almost universally vest policies and processes—especially leadership succession—with a kind of legitimacy not found elsewhere in a political system. Active legislatures give societal groups a unique sense of participation and frequently best cater to their needs for symbolic recognition. Few regimes, moreover, overlook the potential contribution of parliaments to elite recruitment and socialization, or the utility of elected representatives as intermediaries between government administrators and distant constituencies. The existence of such common denominators thus suggests analytically comparable institutions and the value of comparative studies.

Yet very often what passes for a systematic comparison of legislatures is merely a catalogue of constitutional authorizations and formal procedures. Thematic approaches are often dominated by normative questions or such peripheral issues as the advantages of bicameralism. More ambitious comparative studies are rarely longitudinal and are frequently limited to a subnational focus.[1] Legislative research has thus largely ignored the comparative scholars' penchant, so common to studies of political parties, for developmental analysis and multinational codification. This estrangement from a contemporary analytic idiom, and the associated depreciation of legislatures, has several explanations.

First, the leading scholars of comparative politics have discouraged the study of legislative institutions. As conceived in the familiar systems approach, parliaments are defined as essentially rule-making bodies.[2] Because the pioneering studies focused mainly on developing areas, where they observed many suspended parliaments and few at the centers of power, researchers naturally concluded that legislatures were probably irrelevant (Sisson, 1973). Attention was instead directed to party structures and bureaucratic elites, sectors that had seemingly appropriated the legislative functions. At best this comparative literature admits to a parliamentary contribution to system legitimization. But more exhaustive examination of parliaments in developing nations often seems inhibited by a fear of somehow exposing a Western or democratic bias.

The slight to legislatures as a cross-national phenomenon thus reflects arguments that they are alien grafts on most non-Western countries. A once almost euphoric view of elections and legislatures has been replaced by widespread cynicism and disillusionment throughout much of the Third World. Many parliaments had in fact been created in the belief that they were necessary accoutrements of modern government. They were more often written into constitutions in the hope of gaining the approval of Western powers and their indigenous admirers than in response to impelling national forces. In practice, of course, parliaments have neither brought the anticipated respectability nor contributed notably to political stability or economic growth. Indeed, there is much evidence that liberal legislatures in developing countries have regularly fallen under the sway of traditional elites bent on slowing reforms (Huntington, 1968: 388-392, 402).

The dearth of comparative investigations can be further traced to what David Truman (1965: 1-2) has termed the "parliamentary crisis" in the West. Truman and others call attention to the continuing and near-universal shift of policy initiative from the legislature to the executive, and the apparent yielding of representative and intelligence tasks to political parties, organized interests, the ombudsman, and the mass media. By contrast to an earlier era, legislators strike most scholars, and the public as well, as men of lesser stature, of doubtful competence to deal with the problems of a technological age. The well-ensconced parliaments of the West are unlikely to fade away, but their undeniable metamorphosis leads very naturally to a hesitation to fix their place in a modern polity or try to define their role in more transitional nations.

Finally, broadly comparative legislative research has been retarded by the absence of a framework for analysis. Despite improved research techniques and the growing scholarship on parliaments in Asia and Latin America, we have made small headway toward a paradigm for the study of legislatures (Loewenberg, 1972: 3-21). American state research perhaps shows the way to a more comprehensive, theoretical design. Wahlke and his associates' application of the concept of "role" has already furnished a conceptual reference point for a host of empirical studies of legislators' perceptions and behavioral predispositions.[3] Yet role studies remain too narrowly descriptive and culturally bound to offer a major contribution to cross-national analysis.

A single paradigm for comparative research is probably premature in the absence of any serious codification of legislatures. Except for a few restrictive and highly impressionistic attempts at classification, we have established no reliable, systematic basis on which to differentiate contemporary legislatures.[4] There is a natural temptation to designate as benchmarks in a classification scheme those parliaments that inspired most of the rest. By this approach, legislatures are measured by their proximity to or deviation from ideal types. The halcyon days of parliaments, usually placed during the mid- to late nineteenth century, supposedly saw legislatures possessed of a strong policy initiative. The executive—in effect a committee of the parliament—was continuously accountable to legislative majorities, and members stood in a strong fiduciary relationship to their constituents. Yet as Bracher points out, ascendant parliamentary democracy was short-lived; almost immediately with the introduction of the mass electorate, parliaments entered a crisis of adaptation from which they have not yet recovered (1964: 245-246). The twentieth-century trends toward specialization, centralized leadership, and collective responsibility have already altered democratic expectation about legislatures. To speak of counterfeit or pseudo-parliaments is therefore misleading, especially if we agree that representative institutions have a role to play in non-democratic systems. In short, any classification of legislatures must take them as we find them, not as we might want them.

The typology presented in this paper is, hopefully, a step in this direction. Our point of departure is simply that legislatures must be evaluated relative to adjacent political institutions. An ineffectual, unstable parliament in a fragile political system must be judged differently from one in a nation with strong institutions. Similarly, a legislature that fails to cope with problems of political integration should be contrasted with the integrative performances of structures in the same system. Fortunately, a classification scheme may be uncomplicated by the close and often reciprocal relationship of legislatures to executive institutions. Legislative histories loom large with the efforts of parliamentarians to gain autonomy from monarchs, or to protect their prerogatives from the encroachments of bureaucrats and elected officials. These struggles are not always dramatic. The expansion and contraction of a legislature's powers can be subtle and gradual. Even the most radical and abrupt changes often occur in crises and coups in which the parliament may appear to be a bystander. Still, as the nomenclature below suggests, a legislature's characteristic posture toward executive institutions identifies reasonably distinctive behavioral and structural patterns.[5] This paper posits the existence of five classes of legislatures: the coordinate (Type I), the subordinate (Type II), the submissive (Type III), the indeterminate (Type IV), and the competitive-dominant (Type V). All five are modal types into which any legislature is more or less a good fit.

A TYPOLOGY

The coordinate character of Type I legislatures describes a relationship with the executive less of parity than of cooperation and interdependence. At the cornerstone of their relations is a process of mutual consultation in which the prerogatives of both are well defined and carefully observed. Although the legislative initiative nearly always rests with the government, Type I chambers are not challenged in their right to amend bills, either prior to or during parliamentary consideration. The parliament regularly sets its own working agenda, but only after the views of the executive have been sought. For its part, the executive very rarely proposes important legislation without first testing for rank-and-file sentiment. Except as deputies voluntarily bind themselves by party principles, they have wide latitude as legislators and are likely to resent any suggestion that they are puppets of a government or party. The give-and-take of the coordinate chamber does not preclude legislative-executive disagreements. However, it does assure a reasonably orderly and responsible set of procedures. Should these break down, the coordinate legislature can continue to exist only if the parliament or, more commonly, the government is reconstituted.

Type I legislatures are usually cabinet governments where an executive is responsible both in form and substance to a partisan majority. At the same time, coordinate chambers are rarely possessed of a single, cohesive majority party. Mutual consultation occurs, therefore, not simply as a matter of custom or convenience, but as a practical necessity. Particularly in systems where parliamentary majorities are fluid and parties less disciplined, regular communication between party leaders and their rank and file sustains a viable coalition. It is uncharacteristic of deputies to impose binding agreements on their leaders in a government's formation. Notions of executive independence, often as legacy from the past, may persist. They are occasionally formalized in laws prohibiting a minister from holding membership in the parliament, or in customs allowing the selection of ministers without parliamentary experience. But the practical need for cooperative action undermines any meaningful separation of the executive from the legislature. Whatever the appearances, ministers can survive only so long as parliamentary majorities will tolerate them.

Legislatures that make a meaningful contribution to policy formation find that their own resources for political and technical information are indispensable. As a rule, coordinate legislatures are committed to a parliamentary division of labor and the acquisition of expertise by individual members. Although Type I legislatures are not uniformly well equipped, their standing committees or commissions, especially those responsible for a budgetary policy, are likely to be enterprising and even aggressive. Bolstered by a sense of their own competence and an institutional solidarity that occasionally transcends simple party loyalties, committees will regularly call government and other witnesses and engage them in serious dialogue. Votes on committees may follow party lines, but the deliberations of parliamentary committees can have a strong impact on full parliamentary debate. And while party caucuses often take much of the spontaneity out of debates, plenary sessions tend to be less predictable than in most Type II and Type III legislatures. Of the three, the coordinate legislature is most likely to offer an arena for national issue controversy and to contribute to mass opinion making.

Type I legislatures can flourish in varying degrees of government stability. So long as a new set of ministers is obliged to respect the prevailing modus operandi, executive-parliamentary relations will survive even sharp ideological shifts. The ordinary continuity of personnel leading coalition governments improves chances that ministers are socialized to appropriate norms, are familiar with established channels of communication, and hold the confidence of the deputies. The presence in parliamentary ranks of many former cabinet officials can further strengthen existing precedents. Still, it is questionable whether coordinate legislatures can withstand too rapid government change. Parliamentary mandates that become highly restrictive or uncertain can in time destroy meaningful executive autonomy. Alternately, persistent cabinet instability may increase pressures within a legislature for wholesale delegations of power to a more independent executive.

Type II legislatures contain an element conspicuously absent in coordinate chambers: a disciplined majority (or near-majority) party. The consequences of this difference are far-reaching. A party's pre-eminence guarantees a legislature's subordination. As an instrument of the executive, the party usually becomes a functional substitute for the parliament on several fronts. Through the party, effective parliamentary and national leadership overlap, making the legislative agenda and the government program one. Parliamentary modification of cabinet-sponsored bills, often possible in Type I legislatures, is ruled out. The deputy's personal judgments of policy are irrelevant and his stature diminished. Only as a member of the majority party, and then solely in the privacy of party councils, can the member's views be counted. A bad misreading of party rank-and-file opinion may bring revision of parliamentary strategies or even of the particulars of government bills. Far more often, what passes for consultation with party members is merely explanation and injunction.

The primacy of the executive in subordinate legislatures produces several other noteworthy departures from Type I legislatures. For one, the parliament largely gives way as an intermediary institution to agencies of the majority party and, in some systems, to organized interests. The good offices of individual deputies and interventionist parliamentary committees, often useful allies in coordinate legislatures, are either absorbed or allowed to atrophy as individual petitioners and groups find more direct lines of access to the bureaucracy. Specialized party structures to process grievances and to mediate group demands withdraw from the legislator his claim to a unique constituent relationship. Unable to acquire performance debts, legislators also have difficulty sustaining locally-oriented representative roles. Some interests enjoy built-in access to government through regular party affiliation. In systems where group access predates the emergence of a dominant party and the bureaucracy retains some autonomy from the party, organized groups may regularly bypass the party apparatus. In this case the parliamentarian "may be among the last to know."

Parliamentary recruitment to government posts also declines under the weight of a majority party. Pressures on the executive to draw ministers from legislative ranks are less compelling in the absence of coalition allies demanding that cabinet divisions be honored. Traditions in some subordinate legislatures inhibit outside recruitment. More often, legislators will compete with nonparty technocrats, extra-parliamentary party functionaries, and interest group leaders. Specialized legislative committees and protracted debates are an additional luxury in Type II legislatures. Where the latter is permitted, it is usually to placate an opposition. The occasional presence of influential committees and prestigious chairmen in subordinate chambers testifies to the tenacity of committees as vehicles for group catharsis and public education, and the suitability of chairmen as mediators in the absence of strong party stands on issues. Yet it is rare in any Type II legislature that committees and open debates are allowed to escape party control: they exist, after all, at the sufferance of the executive.

The electoral responsibilities of subordinate legislatures are often indistinguishable in form from those in coordinate chambers. Where the Type II legislature coincides with cabinet government, ministers and their policies are subject to the same confirmation and continuing confidence of parliamentary majorities. It is a familiar contention, however, that a parliamentary system with automatic majorities, high leadership visibility, and party discipline transfers the real mandate to an electorate. The choice left in a parliamentary vote may in fact be hardly different than the latitude of the American electoral college. Yet it would be misleading to conclude that the Type II legislature in a parliamentary system is consequently a body devoid of a meaningful electoral role. The deputies of the majority party do on occasion replace their leaders (and the government's) without recourse to elections. Further, the possibility that party defections will topple a government and require new elections is real, even if remote. Even in a unitary presidential system whose chief executive is personally insulated from legislative removal, a legislative party revolt can sorely undermine the institution's usefulness and jeopardize the administration's reelection. The point is that Type II legislatures cannot be taken for granted. Despite an accustomed regimentation of like-minded parliamentarians, the executive cannot regularly defy its stalwarts in the legislature and still remain in office.

Type III legislatures stand in contrast to subordinate chambers for precisely their inability to set limits on executive discretion. As submissive legislatures, they hold no reserve or ultimate sanctions; aside from what the executive provides, Type III legislatures are without purpose or program. By appearance alone, the key to government control rests, as in Type II legislatures, in a cohesive majority. But the submissive chamber is a consequence rather than the source of executive power. It comes into being because a government restricts access to nominations, manipulates balloting, monopolizes rewards, or physically coerces deputies. Governments may rule through a legislative party, but they are not in fact dependent on a parliamentary majority. If required, an executive can dispense with its party and conceivably the legislature as well. Although not all submissive legislatures ban an opposition, none permits dissident voices to seriously threaten government designs. On the contrary, an opposition can serve executive interests (for example, by relieving governments of responsibility for statements of policy, or as a harmless "safety valve" for dissident groups). In sum, deputies in submissive legislatures neither modify laws nor provide a setting for the careful consideration of alternative policies.

Variance from traditional legislative and deliberative roles by no means marks Type III legislatures as superfluous institutions. Much recent scholarship on parliaments in developing countries calls attention to the latent functions of "weak" or "rubber stamp" legislatures.[6] A good case is made for their ancillary contribution as educational and socializing agents in mobilizing national consent. Submissive legislatures often seem at their best when they provide a ceremonial platform for prime ministers, presidents, and generals. Type III legislatures still more often receive credit for fostering regime legitimacy. For this purpose the chamber needs only to meet on occasion and observe such constitutional formalities as representation for ethnic minorities. Studies suggest, moreover, how legislatures may screen members for a limited recruitment to the national elites. Of course, education, legitimization, and recruitment are hardly exclusive to Type III legislatures. If they sometimes seem less salient elsewhere, it is because other, more manifest and traditional functions obscure them.

Judged by Type I and Type II standards, legislators in submissive chambers are characteristically amateurs. Opportunities to acquire and exercise parliamentary and political skills are minimal in the absence of committee responsibilities, instrumental legislative tasks, and compromise politics. The centralized structure of submissive chambers leaves little room for competent legislative committees. The job of a committee is to educate and exhort rather than to produce a set of experts to parallel those in the ministries. Whether because of membership turnover or assignment procedures, most submissive legislatures turn out few committee veterans.

Often enough, members capitalize on their office for personal or even constituent gains; as individuals, however, Type III legislators are not expected to press group interests or, much less, to help aggregate them. Finally, a low order of professionalism is not always indicative of weak institutionalization. Many Type III legislatures are fortified with elaborate and well defined behavioral norms and formal rules. These emerge over time to meet the chambers' maintenance requirements, but all are of demonstrable compatibility with executive interests.

Type IV legislatures display a pattern of interactions with an executive that can best be described as fragile and mutable. Behind this indeterminacy lies a deficiency of structures and values necessary to stabilize executive-legislative relations. In the legislative types discussed above, one or more parties organized the chamber and supplied strong cues for members to follow. Type IV legislatures, characteristically exposed to non-party factionalism or rampant multipartyism, defy integration and control. Legislators are largely preoccupied with sectarian or local concerns in chambers that neither prize nor provide the mechanisms for compromising divergent interests. Leaders of the kind who might rise above parliamentary divisions seldom emerge and, under cabinet systems, are likely to remain outside the government. Cooperation with a government is naturally weaker where a prime minister owes his appointment to a superior executive (for example, a monarch), or a president is independently elected. In parliamentary and presidential systems alike, the estrangement between Type IV legislatures and their executives frequently reflects their different constituencies.

Indeterminate legislatures rarely take the initiative from an executive. Their fragmentation precludes the formulation of coherent, alternative programs or the tackling of those major issues requiring mutual concessions. Type IV legislatures are far better equipped, through powers of investigation and parliamentary interpellation, to harass and obstruct governments. Lacking the capacity to act decisively on their own, indeterminate legislatures would seem to hold a veto power sufficient to immobilize the policy process. In practice, and in part in recognition of their low efficacy, Type IV legislators acquiesce in strategies that bypass the legislature on issues it is incompetent to resolve. Emergency decrees, administration orders, and the referendum are familiar palliates for legislative paralysis. What results is a blurring of functional lines that satisfies neither institution. On an interpersonal basis, Type IV legislators seek friendly ties to administrators in order to expedite their narrow claims against the bureaucracy. In payment, administrators may exact pledges of limited support. On an institutional basis, however, the relationship is one of mutual suspicion and distrust, creating tensions across the political system.

Type V legislatures possess several basic components of Type IV chambers. Both feature a wide diffusion of power and fluid parliamentary majorities. In each, parochially-minded legislators are under no severe sanctions from parties. A like absence of powerful executive levers and the probability of divergent policy priorities set the stage for legislative-executive deadlock. But here the parallels with Type IV legislatures end. Conflict within Type V legislatures is by comparison highly routinized. Legislative-executive differences do not threaten immobilization, for relationships are constantly subject to readjustment. Governments that have lost touch with parliamentary majorities in a cabinet system may be quickly reconstituted to reflect legislative realities. Elsewhere, the renegotiation of differences with legislative leaders is likely to bring eventual agreement. The weak yet less fragmented party systems of Type V legislatures may play a central role in these processes. First, by producing parliamentary leaders, not merely partisan or factional ones, the parties furnish acceptable people to assume ministerial posts and to serve as liaison with the executive. Second, the parties' regulation of internal conflict allows the emergence of a legislative esprit de corps. Third, party loyalties sufficiently overlap the executive and the legislature to mitigate the worst institutional enmities.

Legislators in competitive-dominant chambers are often described as individual entrepreneurs. Unburdened by party or heavy programmatic commitments, they are largely free to pursue local and constituent aims, as well as to champion their own interests. As legislators, their relative high political stature attests to their success as conduits to decisional centers and to their personal influence. Executive influence with these legislators is in no small way dependent on a willingness to deal with members individually and to share resources—usually in the form of pork barrel and patronage. But the Type V legislature is not without its separate resources. The high functional specialization of its standing committees makes the parliament a worthy competitor of government—especially well armed to humble a bureaucracy. Committees are frequently mini-legislatures where rival groups, administrators, and key legislators mingle. As such, committees specifically and the parliament in general share substantially in the system's capacity for interest aggregation. The societal supports available to competitive-dominant legislatures are another matter. Acceptance varies, as in all legislatures, with the nature and level of expectations these institutions raise, and how well they meet them. By its high visibility alone, the Type V legislature is a good bet to become a focal point of controversy.

The variable functional responsibilities of Type V legislatures are a far cry from the ambiguity and defensiveness found in Type IV chambers. The periodic, often crisis-motivated, extensive delegation of legislative powers to the executive by Type V legislatures, and an occasionally overbearing supervision of the executive, do not portend the absorption of one institution by the other. Although long-term trends may be discernible, deviations from traditional roles are usually viewed as temporary expedients, as legitimate, if unfortunate, responses to special circumstances. Type V legislatures concede the indispensability of executive policy initiatives. These bodies retain, however, important powers of response, not the least of which is their control over the content and pace of their own proceedings. In their ability to regularly alter the text and spirit of government bills, Type V legislatures are distinctive. Overall, relations with the executive and other system institutions are on a competitive footing; such processes as law-making, government oversight, and interest mediation occur in an atmosphere of negotiation and compromise. Only a government under constant threat to its survival and lacking supportive extraparliamentary constituencies need fear legislative dominance. The ascendant legislature is a rare phenomenon in the twentieth century.

A SCHEME FOR CLASSIFICATION

Figure 1 offers a means for locating modern parliaments within the fivefold classification. It posits that a legislature's relative performance of decisional and integrative functions affords a parsimonious and sufficiently sensitive way to identify specific legislatures with the modal types described above. Although just over two dozen chambers are located in Figure 1, the scheme is intended to accommodate the universe of national legislatures. The parliaments identified include those whose literature is most extensive and analytic.[7] Despite an effort to provide a geographic spread, the overrepresentation of some regions reflects the author's research interests and acquaintance. Aside from the three countries considered below, no effort is made to independently validate judgments in Figure 1. As such the classifications must be viewed as tentative, perhaps only suggestive.

Decisions on the placement of legislatures do rest on fairly explicit criteria, however. Although assessment of a parliament's decisional and integrative performance is system-relative, comparative analysis requires that our functional measures have a cross-national equivalence and mutual exclusiveness. Of the two functions, the decisional is the more manifest and familiar. Specifically, it refers to the contribution of a legislature and any of its subsystems to the substance of public policy, either directly or by modifying the acts of others. The casual observer is easily misled by empty delegations of authority or may be prone to overlook indirect, informal influences. At a minimum, evidence of a decisional role should be discernible in a legislature's capacity (1) to initiate legislation; (2) to modify, delay, or defeat bills; (3) to influence administration actions through parliamentary questions, interpellations, and investigations; and (4) to alter departmental (ministerial) budgets, authorizations, and personnel.[8] These criteria are not limited to "legislating" in the customary sense; nor are they so broad as to encompass all forms of "problem solving," from which few legislative activities can be excluded. Further, the decisional capacity of a single legislature is unlikely to be uniform. Formal and normative restrictions may, for example, limit a parliament's ability to shape general laws but will

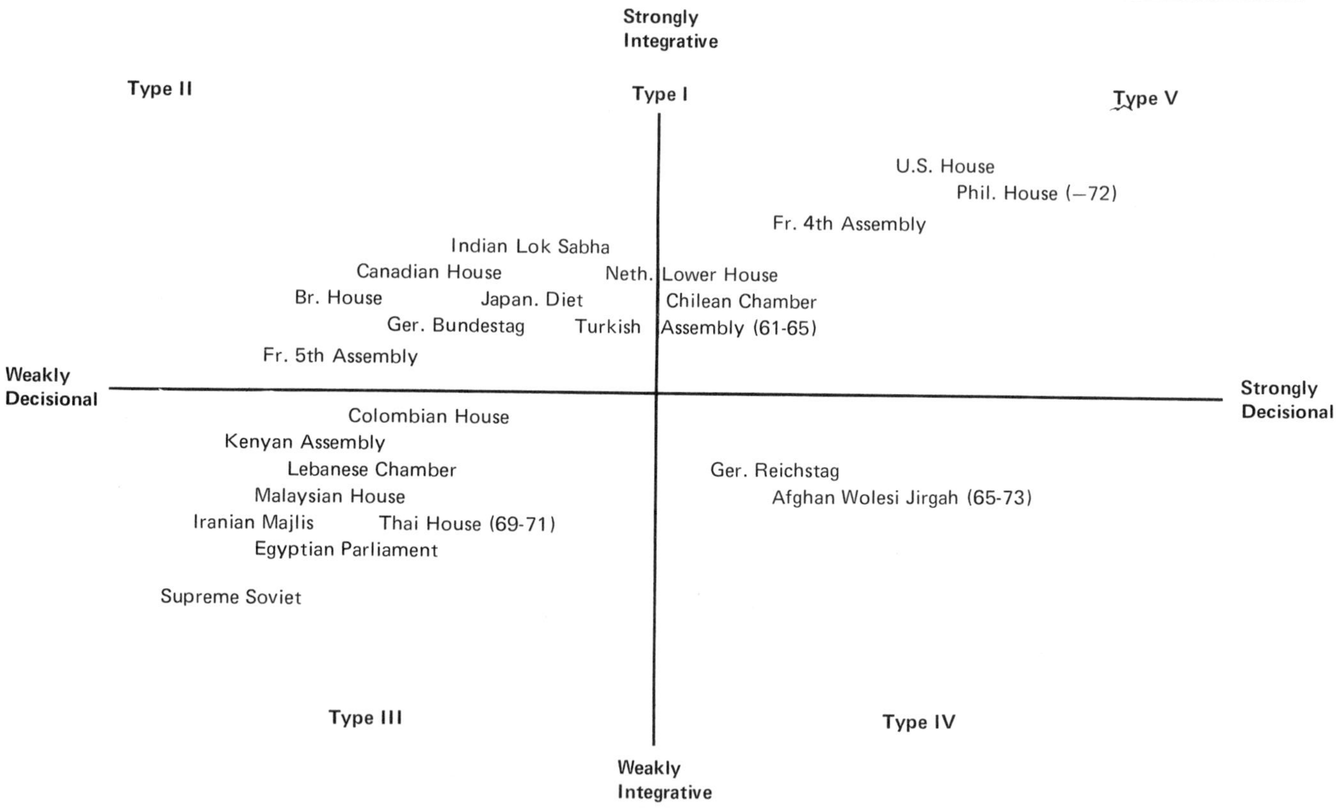

Figure 1: SELECTED LEGISLATURES CLASSIFIED BY DECISIONAL AND INTEGRATIVE FUNCTIONS

fail to inhibit severely its sway over administrative actions. Figure 1 tells us what we already suspect—that the performance of legislatures as decisional bodies is decidedly skewed. That some spread exists, however, figures critically in a classification of legislatures.

The integrative function is more open-ended. Most observers would agree that it involves "a process leading to political cohesion and sentiments of loyalty toward political institutions" (Grossholtz, 1970: 93-113). Less obvious is the contribution legislatures make to this process, and the relevant criteria for determining performance levels. Accordingly, three tests are suggested: (1) *Does the legislature help create and/or disseminate symbols and goals that identify common interests?* This criterion recognizes in particular the educational and socializing role legislatures may have in heightening the perception of mutual interest among regional, ethnic, and other societal groups. The propagation of issues that transcend prevailing group differences serve the same end (Grossholtz, 1970: 111). (2) *Does the legislature adequately focus competing interests and furnish mechanisms leading to the containment and resolution of conflict?* The opportunities for inter-group communication are raised by this criterion. Certainly, the absence of a parliamentary opposition casts doubt on the chamber's capacity for comprehensive political integration. Where parliamentary and sub-parliamentary norms encourage bargaining and compromise, a prima-facie case exists for successful interest aggregation. Evidence of a legislative brokerage role is frequently found in standing committees, party caucuses, and informal parliamentary groupings. (3) *Does the legislature facilitate the control of disintegrative elements, actual and potential?* This is another way of asking whether the legislature adds appreciably to the government's authority to apply sanctions against societal groups that fail to respond to integrative appeals. We find that legislatures do not rank uniformly high or low on the three tests. Most probably fail the second. On the evidence, however, Figure 1 offers an aggregate assessment of the selected chambers, suggesting their wide variance as agencies for political and social integration.

THREE CASES OF LEGISLATIVE CHANGE

The above classification, whatever its utility for labeling con-temporary or recent legislative systems, is necessarily static. The descriptions of the five modal types have, to be sure, hinted at

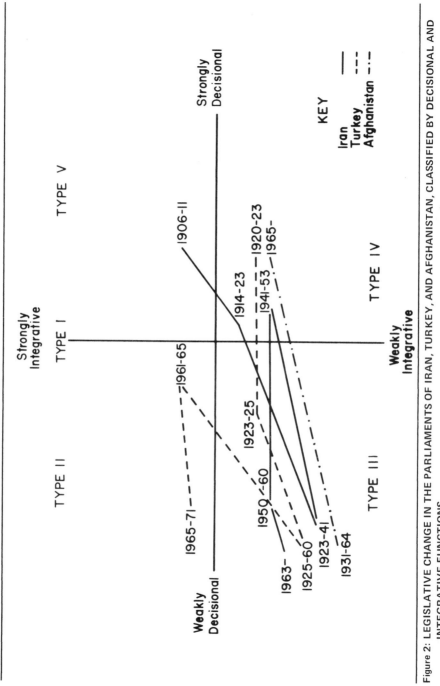

Figure 2: LEGISLATIVE CHANGE IN THE PARLIAMENTS OF IRAN, TURKEY, AND AFGHANISTAN, CLASSIFIED BY DECISIONAL AND INTEGRATIVE FUNCTIONS

several contributory variables in legislative change. Plainly, shifts in executive power, alterations in party systems, and constitution-legal parameters are implicated in the emergence and transformation of legislatures. Nevertheless, a better appreciation of the factors involved in legislative change probably requires the kind of evidence found in longitudinal studies of single systems. To this end, we have selected the twentieth-century parliaments of Iran, Turkey, and Afghanistan, neighboring countries of the Middle East's northern tier. All have experienced wide legislative mutation and together they illustrate all five legislative types (see Figure 2). At a minimum, then, the detailed case materials on Iran and the briefer examinations of Turkey and Afghanistan can be expected to demonstrate the adequacy of the classification scheme. More important, historical descriptions of the three parliaments in their larger system contexts should help to generate and refine hypotheses about legislative change.

IRAN

The 23 Iranian parliaments between 1906 and 1971 cover five and conceivably six legislative eras and fall within three of our five modal types. Parliaments of the first period, 1906 to 1911, display most of the hegemonic and integrative features associated above with Type V legislatures. First convened as a constituent assembly to draft the Fundamental Laws, the Majlis (parliament) culminated a nationalist movement that had allied European-oriented reformists, a traditionalist merchant class, and a conservative clergy against an autocratic monarch. The 1906-07 constitution sought a limited monarchy and ministerial accountability by vesting impressive powers in the Majlis to deal with the economy, foreign treaties and agreements, and succession to the crown.

The first Majlis got off to an impressive start. Smooth adoption of formal rules and a consciousness of precedents paved the way for orderly and productive sessions. The country's fiscal controls, delegated to a committee of twelve deputies, improved almost immediately. The lower house passed measures dealing with municipalities, provincial councils, the press, the administration of justice, and penalties for bribery.[9] It rejected a proposed joint Anglo-Russian loan and forced Mohammad Ali Shah (who had succeeded to the throne on the death of his father Muzaffaru'd Din Shah early in 1907) to dismiss a Belgian Chief of Customs. The popularity of the

Majlis was enhanced by its broadly representative membership. The constitution prescribed that the chamber include landlords, nobles, merchants, clerics, artisans, and farmers, all directly elected from their various classes or guilds.

The Shah's antipathy to this parliament mounted steadily with fears for his life and his throne. Finally in June 1908, the Shah ordered his Russian-officered Cossack brigade to bombard the Majlis building. In subsequent weeks hundreds of constitutionalists were rounded up and many executed. Not until November 1909 was a second Majlis able to convene, and then only after a popular uprising had forced the Shah's abdication. The new parliament was different in two critical respects. The adoption of an areal form of representation reduced the chamber's heterogeneity, virtually eliminating its lower-status deputies while increasing the landlords from 21% to 30% of the membership (Shaji'i, 1965: 180). Second, the earlier informal division between progressives and traditionalists became formalized with the emergence of distinct, if also loose, party groups—the Democrats and the more numerous Moderates. The deputies' continued assertiveness in wide areas of policy-making nevertheless gave the chamber much of the character of the first Majlis. Legislators framed laws on health, education, taxes, opium cultivation, and elections. The reorganization and modernization of the bureaucracy was perhaps the parliament's most notable achievement. But when the deputies almost unanimously rejected an ultimatum from Czarist Russia in December 1911 demanding the expulsion of an American advisor they had engaged, a pliable Qajar Regent approved the dissolution of the Majlis. Once again, many progressive deputies were forced to flee in face of a brutal repression.

A return to a pre-1906 regime was precluded, however. Constitutionalism and the Majlis it embodied had grown steadily as symbols of popular resistance to Russian and British imperialism. Nationalism aside, many elites otherwise disadvantaged in the now vigorous competition for power viewed the Majlis as a necessary base of operation. The crowning of the young Ahmed Shah in late 1914 thus occasioned elections to a new parliament. Significantly, less than 10% of the deputies of the Second Majlis were returned to the Third, and the quality of members noticeably declined (Avery, 1965: 189). The parliament resumed an active role in forming a series of weak cabinets and furnished leading spokesmen for economic reforms. However, measured by diminished effectiveness and the strong evidence of institutional decay, the abbreviated Third—it lasted less than a year, dissolving in the confusion of a Russian invasion of Tehran in November 1915—and a delayed Fourth Majlis appear as transitional Type IV legislatures.

The inauguration of a postwar parliament in November 1921 revived a proud and contentious Majlis. Its membership, much of it pro-Soviet, roundly rejected a treaty negotiated with the British in 1919 that promised to badly dilute Iranian sovereignty. The deputies also returned to their preoccupation with administrative and fiscal reorganization. But the chamber's many independent-minded legislators confronted a newly decisive and expansive executive. Early in 1921, Reza Khan, an officer in the Cossack Brigade, partnered a government coup that elevated him within two years to the post of prime minister.

Reza Khan's ambitions were hardly satisfied, for his larger aim was to create an Iranian republic and to assume its presidency. He reasoned, however, that so radical a constitutional change could be shored by a parliament's sanction. Accordingly, Reza Shah engineered the election of a large pro-government bloc of candidates for the Fifth Majlis. Despite this, the intractable opposition of religious leaders to a republic eventually forced Reza Khan to adopt a more traditional route to supreme power. On December 12, 1925, he deposed Ahmed Shah and, with only four Majlis votes in dissent, was elected to head a new dynasty.

Beginning with the Fifth and certainly the Sixth Majlis, Iran entered a period of characteristic Type III legislatures. Parliamentary autonomy disappeared as the Majlis, previously the national forum, became an obedient arm of Reza Shah. Determined to give no sanctuary to an opposition, the monarch employed his ministry of interior to prepare lists of approved candidates whose elections were then arranged by local election officials. All political parties were banned, as were any political organizations not officially sponsored by the regime.

The tenure of deputies lengthened under Reza Shah; indeed, in one election the turnover fell to under 7%. By contrast to previous parliaments, however, few men of national prominence served. Nor did the Majlis offer opportunities for ambitious men anxious to build a national reputation. The Majlis' decline as a promotional ladder to high office did not obviate its value as a source of rewards for lesser government officials and their families. Nearly 40% of the Majlis' membership from the sixth through the thirteenth terms had held government jobs (Shaji'i, 1965: 180). Over the same period the number of businessmen also increased steeply (Nezami, 1968: 286). The dwindling representation of clerics reflected their disfavor with the imperial court. And the submission of several once largely autonomous tribes to Reza Shah's militia was marked by the elimination of special tribal constituencies in the electoral law revisions of 1934.

A different tact was taken to disarm the numerous landowning deputies. While those openly antipathic to the regime were simply dropped in rigged elections, the rest were bought off. As long as the monarch refrained from seriously pursuing a policy of land reform, the landlords—they averaged 56% of the membership during the 1925-41 period (Shaji'i, 1965: 180)—acquiesced in far-reaching industrialization and modernization programs. For his part, the Shah was willing to placate the landed elite and keep the Majlis in session as a demonstration that his regime rested on more than brute force.

Reza Shah's abdication in August 1941, following a British and Russian ultimatum, abruptly altered Iranian politics and reinstituted a Type IV legislature. Political interest and ambitions long penned up under the Shah's authoritarian rule immediately surfaced and deputies shed their deferential ways. A young monarch, Reza Shah's son, Mohammad Reza Shah Pahlavi, was helpless to impede a kaleidoscopic clash of political factions. Over the next 12 years as many as 30 political parties emerged, most of them personalistic and transient. Although nearly every party claimed nationalist aims, few were ideological. Only the communist Tudeh (Masses) party managed, with progressive appeals, to build a broadly popular and enduring base outside the legislature. Within the Majlis, animated and unwieldy sessions usually disguised the members' essentially conservative predilections. On occasion the legislators adopted an aggressive posture—defying the British on currency reforms, refusing to allow the Russians oil concessions, and, finally, nationalizing the oil industry. But most of the time deputies were busily looking after their personal or group interests, a preoccupation that precluded constructive law-making.

Wartime elections to the Fourteenth Majlis were the freest in many years. Nearly half the deputies elected were freshmen and the chamber was more disparate than any since the first two parliaments.[10] Government interference at the polls returned after 1944, but even sanctioned candidates were usually unreliable once they had entered the Majlis. While members could frequently force their choice of prime minister on the Shah, the chamber regularly failed to support governments of its own making.[11] Often, the more capable the minister the more likely he was to engender deputies' suspicions and jealousies (Avery, 1965: 370).

Bickering ministers and the government's repeated budget defeats in the Majlis prompted the Shah in early 1949 to convene a constituent assembly in hopes of taming the parliament's powers. The monarch's hands were strengthened by a wave of public sympathy after an attempted assassination at Tehran University and by the increasing aggressiveness of his security forces. With loyalists in command of the assembly, it approved an amendment formalizing the Shah's authority to dissolve the parliament. The body also implemented the provision in the constitution for a partly appointed upper house where excesses of the lower chamber could presumably be checked. A mandate on both houses to formulate a set of procedural rules, it was hoped, would help end chaotic Majlis sessions and improve chances for government leadership. But it was the nation's rising nationalist fervor and the related appointment in April 1951 of veteran Majlis deputy Mohammad Mosaddiq that finally brought, if only briefly, executive ascendance and a more unified parliament.

Mosaddiq's leverage with the Majlis rested on a broad but loose coalition of nationalist parties. He erred in believing, however, that his personal popularity would assure a sympathetic Majlis in the elections of March 1952. Without the benefit of government contrivance, many Majlis supporters were defeated by anti-Mosaddiq landlords and clerics. In the tense months that followed, Mosaddiq resigned, returned to office in triumph after bloody street clashes, and then bullied the deputies and the Shah into approval of extensive powers to legislate by decree for six months. He also pushed through a bill that in effect closed down the Senate.

A refusal by the Majlis the following year to extend the decree authority or to help in curbing the Shah's powers also placed that chamber in jeopardy. Mosaddiq used the results of an August 1953 referendum to declare the Majlis dissolved. By this time, however, the Prime Minister's imperious and dogmatic ways had alienated many of his political allies. An international boycott of Iranian oil resulted in a worsening economic crisis and had cost Mosaddiq much of his popular adulation. Thus there was only minor resistance to a government coup and the arrest of Mosaddiq by pro-royalist troops under General Fazollah Zahedi.

The ensuing military government outlawed political parties and restored the Majlis to a Type III legislature. Once again, speedy approval of legislation was largely guaranteed, and the Majlis committees surrendered their claims to expertise, mainly to the government technocrats of the Plan Organization and the National Iranian Oil Company. Prime Minister Zahedi personally supervised and screened candidates for the Eighteenth Majlis. Less than half of the deputies elected in early 1954 had served in the previous lower house, although many were veterans of earlier parliaments. At 60% of the membership, the landlords were never better represented numerically. With large segments of the urban middle class either opposed to the regime or cynically apathetic, the Shah found himself deeply in debt to the landed aristocracy. In return for their loyalty, the landlords gained improved access to government ministries and retained their limited veto over legislation. Thus a bill that would have eroded the landlords' electoral base by requiring peasants to meet literacy requirements and a modest proposal for land redistribution were both defeated by the deputies.

With the regime more secure, the Shah moved to consolidate his powers. General Zahedi was replaced as prime minister in 1955 by a civilian, Manuchehr Eqbal, who boasted before the Majlis that he was the Shah's servant and in no sense accountable to the parliament (Binder, 1962: 277). The Shah's agreement to the revival of a party system, mostly to please the regime's American advisors, left his plans uncompromised. Deputies were invited to join one of two court-sponsored parties, the government's Melliyun (Nationalist) and the "opposition" Mardom (Peoples) party. To no one's surprise, neither party labored to construct a national organization, and their impact on parliamentary activities was minimal.

It is ironic, then, that the Melliyun and Mardom parties precipitated a constitutional crisis in their first electoral competition. The connivance of the two parties on a division of Majlis seats in the summer of 1960 was audacious only in light of the party leaders' elaborate pretense of free elections.[1][2] When disappointed candidates and the regime's critics exposed the bipartisan collusion, an embarrassed Shah felt compelled to call new elections. Renewed complaints of rigged contests and intimidation the following winter induced the Shah to dissolve the parliament indefinitely. In its absence he grasped the long-awaited opportunity to depoliticize the encumbering landed aristocracy and to accelerate plans for social and economic change. Over the next two and a half years, more than 600 decree laws were promulgated. A symbolic few reforms—known collectively as the White Revolution, and including a comprehensive land reform program—were submitted for approval in a national referendum.

By 1963 the parliament's suspension had become an inconvenience to the regime. Western bankers were thought reluctant to conclude development loans without the Majlis' ratification. The Shah was desirous, moreover, for the return of intermediaries who could deflect public demands and serve as "whipping boys" in cases of policy failure. But new elections were risky without a mechanism to screen out candidates opposed to the White Revolution or to assure ministerial dominance of the Majlis. To meet this need, the Shah authorized a group of ambitious technocrats, most with no prior partisan affiliation, to fashion a comprehensive, disciplined party, and then form the government. For election to the Majlis in September 1963, leaders of the party—soon to be called Iran Novin—recruited mainly middle-level civil servants, most of them young careerists.[13]

Under Iran Novin governments, all ministry-sponsored legislation has passed initially to the party's central organization and then to its caucuses in the Majlis and Senate.[14] Government officials are often called to explain bills to party members whose occasional discovery of errors or omissions require legislation to be returned to a ministry. But once a draft is finally agreed to by the prime minister and sanctioned by the Shah, party criticism of legislation in Majlis debate is proscribed. Amendments proposed by deputies of one of the small opposition parties are rarely treated seriously and, in any case, the practice of assigning members to committees by lot allows for little subject matter expertise.[15] Opposition deputies seldom stray outside the well-defined boundaries of permissible debate. While they are free to direct barbs at individual administrators or to criticize the details and implementation of most programs, members refrain from questioning domestic legislative priorities or foreign policy—both the personal province of the Shah.

The regime's enduring suspicion of the Majlis makes it naturally reluctant to invite expanded parliamentary responsibilities or to admit more independent members. At the same time, government leaders despair at the cynical view most educated Iranians hold toward political authority (Zonis, 1971: 192, 314). Officials also seem perplexed and embarrassed by the stubborn indifference to electoral politics visible in every stratum of the society (Weinbaum, 1974). After seven years of impressive economic growth, this low esteem for representative institutions now appears as a growing threat to intelligent and effective planning. Official policy calls for increased but well-modulated participation of the masses in more authentic popular institutions. Undoubtedly, the parliament and recently formed town and provincial councils have a potential contribution to improved political education and a more sensitive monitoring of demands. Yet any appreciable accretion of their decisional powers is probably contingent on deeper penetration of the electorate by a mass party. And at every step, change will require explicit directives from the Shah.

TURKEY

Over the more than half century since the inauguration of a Grand National Assembly, Turkey has been exposed to four of the five legislative types described earlier, including three separate periods of submissive parliaments (see Figure 2). The National Assembly succeeded an Ottoman Assembly founded in 1908 by the triumphant Young Turk movement and dissolved in the Allies invasion of 1918. A still earlier encounter with a parliament, the first in the Muslim world, was rudely suppressed by Sultan Abdulhamid in 1878 after only one year. The chamber convened in 1920 embodied the transfer of authority from the declining sultanate to a rump government headed by Mustafa Kemal (later Ataturk). It brought together a broad array of nationalist elements, united mainly in their opposition to the Istanbul regime and the struggle against invading Greek armies. The legislators included many provincial notables and clerics relishing their first opportunity to wield national power (Kinross, 1965: 269). Rampant factionalism and the members' jealousies and suspicions of Kemal thus rendered the parliament's sessions disorganized and disruptive. Even Kemal's convincing oratory and his prestige as national liberator guaranteed him no more than the support of a minority in the Assembly.

Kemal's military command left him in control of the machinery for the June 1923 elections and gave the means of putting to an end the unmanageable "convention government." Determined to pursue a radical course of industrialization and secularization in the framework of a republic, Kemal arranged for the defeat or retirement of the Assembly's independent members and the seating of more urban, secular legislators (Frey, 1965: 178, 181, 185), all members of the newly organized People's party. While the National Assembly quickly passed from a Type IV to a Type III status, the parliament did not fall entirely under executive sway until mid-1925 when a once-favored group of legislators, opposed to Kemal on personal and programmatic grounds, were abruptly silenced. During the next two decades—after 1938 under Kemal's successor Ismet Inonu—the unicameral parliament was little more than an arm of the People's party. Its members ratified Kemalist principles in the continuous flow of legislation with which the governing elite of bureaucrats, intelligentsia, and military officers indoctrinated Turkey's largely village population.

The compliant National Assembly seemed likely to be undermined as a result of Inonu's announcement in 1945 inviting competition to his People's party. The formation of a Democratic party, catering to peasants, businessmen, and religious elements, assured that segments of the population ignored or muzzled during the one-party period would be well represented in the Assembly. The extent of the dissatisfaction with the Kemalists was revealed by the Democratic party's capture of all but 79 of the 487 seats contested in the 1950 elections—Turkey's first honest count. The new legislators, younger and more inexperienced, many of them locally-minded lawyers and tradesmen (Frey, 1965: 171, 182), submitted readily to the discipline of Prime Minister Adnan Menderes.

The government's intolerance of criticism subjected civil and political liberties increasingly to attack during the 1950s. Hard-pressed opposition legislators voiced continuous dissent, but the chamber was hardly more able to influence executive actions than it had been under the Kemalists. Notwithstanding rigged elections in 1957, anti-Menderes strength in the Assembly rose to 186 seats. However, with the prime minister at the zenith of his power, his Assembly majority in the same year approved rules that restricted the number and scope of parliamentary questions, weakened parliamentary immunities, and circumscribed the coverage of the chamber's proceedings in the press (Weiker, 1963: 11).

The military officers who overthrew Menderes in 1960 sponsored a constitution aimed at preventing future dictatorships through generous grants of power to the nation's universities, press and radio, military, and constitutional court. In order to perpetuate the values of the revolution and deter legislators from either a theocratic or Marxist course, an upper house was added to the parliament, and the coup's leaders were designated as permanent senators. Party primaries were strengthened to allow local activists a greater say in the choice of candidates. Most important, future one-party dominance was presumably eschewed by the introduction of proportional representation in a form preferential to small parties. The parliament elected in 1961 was therefore designed to articulate all but the extremes of Turkish society's plural interests.

Under the exigencies of weak coalition politics, where legislators helped to define the limits and priorities of government policy, the parliament assumed a largely coordinate (Type I) status. Committee members often worked closely with ministers, especially in budgetary decisions. Although legislators were largely disciplined, party leaders in the coalition partnership regularly took the pulse of their rank and file. But legislative-executive relations acquired a new footing after the elections of 1965. The Justice party, inheritor of the Democratic party's loyal constituencies, carried safe majorities in both houses. In the fashion of party government, the decision processes shifted to the cabinet and party caucuses, and the National Assembly was relegated to the role of concerned spectator (Type II).

The Justice party under moderate Suleyman Demirel, renewed its mandate in the 1969 elections, but right-wing desertions during 1970 and 1971 eroded its working majorities in the lower house. Meanwhile, the People's party had also split. A majority faction, led by its general secretary, Bulent Ecevit, alienated many veteran party leaders in an endeavor to carve out a new electoral base with class-based, socialist appeals. Beset with organizational and personal difficulties, Prime Minister Demirel's inability to act decisively in face of mounting street violence by students and anarchists prompted the military's demand for his resignation in March 1971. A slowness in normalizing relations with subsequent military-imposed "above party" governments as well as the parties' resistance to reform legislation left the future course of parliamentary development in Turkey in doubt during the next two-and-one-half years. But the revival of a Type I parliament was presaged by the fall 1973 elections in which resurgent People's party fell short of a parliamentary majority.

AFGHANISTAN

Figure 2 indicates a bifurcated history of the Afghan parliament. The first period, 1931 to 1964, witnessed a Type III legislature under the tutelage of a traditional monarch. During the second, 1965-73 period, a Type IV legislature undermined a liberal, constitutional monarchy. Afghan rulers had summoned consultative assemblies long before the 1931 Constitution, but King Nadir Shah's parliament was the first successful attempt to institutionalize Western parliamentary forms. While royal assent was required for every bill and the king could legislate by decree during a parliamentary recess, the 116-member lower house was delegated broad powers to initiate and approve legislation and could review royal ordinances. The chamber was also granted the right to interrogate ministers and engage in publicized, uninhibited debate (Gregorian, 1969: 303-305). In practice, however, legislative initiative lay with the cabinet whose ministers were accountable only to the royal court. The king possessed sweeping emergency powers, and the authority to raise taxes was never vested in the parliament. For much of the period, then, the constitution was a thin facade behind which the country was ruled by a royal oligarchy—composed after 1933 of King Zahir Shah, his uncles and cousins.

An upper house, fully appointed by the monarch, offered the most direct check on the elected lower chamber. But aside from a brief liberal interlude beginning in 1949,[16] legislators rarely balked at government proposals (Dupree, 1965: 7-9). The docility of legislators was expressive of an understanding between the central government and provincial elites. In exchange for non-interference in regional and sectarian affairs, especially in the religious courts, local influentials gladly deferred to royal discretion in national institutions. Tribal chiefs and village heads cooperated in sending pliant legislators to the capital with the assurance that these representatives would not be asked to compromise local interests. When a departure from the constitution or a national consensus was required, the royal family convened not the parliament but a constituent assembly (Loya Jirgah) composed of ethnic, tribal, and religious leaders.

In the absence of popular clamor or an opposition pressing for change, Zahir Shah's invitation in 1964 to government progressives to fashion a democratic constitution was unanticipated. The decision, in effect to broaden the ruling elite, reflected both the discord within the royal family and the king's preference for a non-repressive route to social and economic progress. However, parliamentary elections with a minimal government role, as occurred in 1965 and 1969, would certainly load the new lower house, the Wolesi Jirgah (House of the People) with a membership of independent, parochial-minded legislators. The constitution's framers gambled, nonetheless, that the responsibilities of participation in national policy-making would in time generate mutual stakes and foster unity.

Eight years of legislative politics brought neither the expected issues to override sectarian concerns nor the incentives for parliamentary cohesion. Most legislators instead grasped the opportunity to help themselves and their more influential constituents to administrative favors and scarce resources (Weinbaum, 1974). They found little time or inclination to bother with a law-making role. The Wolesi Jirgah had difficulty attracting a quorum, and in session the chamber is unorganized and unled—a state of affairs often blamed on the regime's reluctance to implement a political parties law (Weinbaum, 1972). The fear of government encroachment on their prerogatives induced legislators to snipe at government programs and intimidate uncooperative ministers. The parliament's immobility and the frailty of executive leadership prompted even the progressives to doubt the viability of Afghanistan's constitutional system. The end came in a July 1973 military coup that toppled the Durrani monarchy. A republic proclaimed by former Prime Minister Mohammad Daoud abrogated the 1964 Constitution and the troublesome parliament.

CONDITIONS OF LEGISLATIVE CHANGE

An exercise in legislative classification that stops at description falls short of its analytic potential. The variegated parliamentary experience in the three countries also contains the working materials for an investigation of the bases of legislative change. While explanations of institutional transformation are likely to be multi-variable—not easily subject to discriminate analysis—the Iranian, Turkish, and Afghan cases suggest the primacy of several factors. They also give reason to ask whether the conditions that precipitate change are necessarily the same as those that help determine its direction. We are further prompted to question if the origins of change differ when legislatures are transformed abruptly or more gradually, or whether predisposing factors may be established long before a parliamentary metamorphosis is detectable. With these considerations in mind, several propositions appear warranted about legislative change in the three countries.

Historical evidence points to executive actors as the prime movers in legislative change. *A transformed legislature commonly follows an abrupt expansion or contraction—whether involuntarily or by design—in executive powers.* Reza Shah's consolidation of his rule beginning in 1923 soon modified the Majlis. The vacuum of executive authority left by his departure in 1941 invited an even more radical parliamentary change. The Majlis was twice more transformed by the reassertion of royal influence after the 1953 coup and by the Shah's unconditional rule after 1963. In Turkey, Mustafa Kemal's drive to give social and economic reforms his personal stamp subdued an unruly National Assembly in 1923. His direct order silenced the remaining parliamentary critics two years later. The postwar decision of Ismet Inonu to allow electoral challenge to the government's party set the stage for a parliament reflective of the country's social and political realities. The National Assembly failed, however, to experience a transformation until a military coup in 1960 fractured executive power and temporarily installed a coordinate legislature. Intervention by the armed services in 1971 ended a period of legislative subordination to Prime Minister Suleyman Demirel, though the military imposed a new set of constraints on the legislators. The Afghan monarch, Zahir Shah, personally abolished the country's submissive parliament in 1964. The Wolesi Jirgah's subsequent combativeness with the executive was a direct consequence of the king's desire to share responsibility for the nation's development.

Judging from our cases, no Type III legislature seems probable without a conscious and determined exercise of executive will. Conversely, the loosening or delegation of executive power usually precedes the disappearance of a submissive parliament. Party system changes are often associated with these transformations. The Iran Novin party was born in 1963 along with the modified Majlis, and Kemal's formation of his People's party in 1923 furnished the instrument for the National Assembly's conversion. Marked parliamentary change failed to materialize in Turkey despite the lifting of legal barriers to party competition in 1946. Adnan Menderes' Democratic party merely replaced the People's party as the country's dominant and repressive force in 1950. Yet a monopolistic party's apparent utility to a submissive legislature does not prove its indispensability. As we have observed, Type III Majlises were managed between 1923 and 1941, and again from 1953 to 1957, with a combination of electoral manipulation, intimidation, and respect for class privilege. Afghanistan's royal oligarchy similarly found no need for even a single party during the 1931-64 period of submissive parliaments.

Aside perhaps from Type III legislatures, *a radical modification in the configuration of parliamentary parties or factions usually signals fundamental legislative change.* To be sure, party system mutations are sometimes reflections of change elsewhere in the political system. Thus, the sudden proliferation of Majlis parties after 1941, and an outcropping of ethnic, tribal, ideological, and personal groupings in Afghanistan's lower chamber after 1965, followed relaxed executive controls. In both cases, however, the very multiplicity of emergent parliamentary factions probably ruled out any but a Type IV, indeterminate legislature. "Party" as an independent variable in legislative transformations is further illustrated by the transition of the Majlis after 1911 from its Type V status following the breakdown of factional bipolarity. In Turkey, the conversion from Type I to Type II parliaments is directly attributable to the results of the 1965 elections. The successes of Demirel's Justice party ended an often reciprocal parliamentary-executive relationship necessitated by unstable People's party-led governments. But the Assembly's subordinate status seemed less tenable when partisan cabinet rule was replaced in 1971 by the artificial majorities of nonpartisan governments. The absence of logical coalition partners following the 1973 elections extended a period of transition. It also made more probable the Assembly's return to coordinate status.

Revisions of constitutional and statutory rules often formalize a parliament's de facto powers or prescribed a new legislative role. Thus a withdrawal of ministerial appointments from the National Assembly in Turkey's 1924 constitution ratified Kemal's accomplished end to the meddlesome behavior of deputies. Amendments to the Iranian constitution in 1963 merely ratified the Shah's reforms and the eviction of landlords from the Majlis.

Historical examples also document, however, that *the revision of formal rules can independently chart the direction of legislative change.* The initial provisions for class representation in the 1906-07 Iranian constitution, besides reflecting the revolutionary alliance, invited the kind of interest interplay peculiar to a Type V legislature. Afghanistan's 1964 constitution offers more manifest examples. The document and accompanying electoral laws envisioned a lower house in a close partnership with the government. The prime minister, although designated by the king, would presumably speak for the dominant group in the Wolesi Jirgah and serve at its pleasure. Plans for a coordinate legislature were perhaps unrealistic in view of the nation's social cleavages and institutional jealousies. Even so, the decision to delay the legalization of political parties removed any possibility that the requirements of electoral aggregation might further parliamentary or national integration. Moreover, without a party of its own, the government was badly handicapped in efforts to organize followers in the lower house. The constitutional framers' provision for a two-thirds majority to carry a non-confidence vote during the first two parliamentary terms—intended to increase government stability in the formative period—also diminished responsibility and increased executive-legislative tensions. Finally, the Wolesi Jirgah's unreasonable quorum rule, requiring a two-thirds attendance, had frequently allowed any sizable minority to halt legislative business. Taken together, these formal rules sealed the parliament's fate as a Type IV legislature.

The attempts of Turkey's constitutional draftsmen to attenuate executive power proved to be a mixed blessing. The framers underestimated voters' loyalties to the two major parties, especially their attraction to populist appeals. In every election after 1961, the Justice party was returned with an absolute majority in both houses. Both the Justice and People's parties continued to draw votes from a broad cross-section of the electorate, thereby undercutting the natural constituencies of the several new parties. Furthermore, the primaries did not so much democratize nominations as strengthen provincial leaders and spark bitter personal intraparty feuding among aspiring candidates. This factionalism helped to spawn splinter parties which by the late 1960s had cut into the parliamentary backing for both major parties. In a critical oversight, the consti- tution created no mechanism for coordination of the several autonomous political sectors. Party government found the scope of its leadership diminished by those institutions insulated from popular control. Worse still, some of these protected sectors, notably the universities and the media, cast direct challenges to the government on ideological grounds. In sum, the formal rules laid out in 1961, on the other hand, failed to sustain the projected Type I legislature and, on the other, undermined conditions for a stable Type II parliament.

Among Middle East countries, Turkey and Iran stand out for the longevity of their parliamentary experience and its idealistic asso- ciations. The Majlis' historic obstinacy in the face of imperalist demands reserves for it a sentimental link to Iranian nationalism. The early parliaments of Turkey symbolized a deliverance from autocracy for the constitutional movements. Even during the Kemalist period, the National Assembly was regularly proclaimed as the embodiment of the people's will (Berkes, 1964: 444). The parliament's continued prominence in the Turkish press betokens the public's lofty, if also unreal, image of the Assembly's role. Few emotional attachments exist to the parliament in contemporary Afghanistan. Still, wide familiarity with the equalitarian and consensus bases of tribal jirgahs (councils) rendered practices of the Wolesi Jirgah less alien.

The ideals of representative government have obviously not restricted the range of parliamentary change in Iran, Turkey, or Afghanistan. In some nations, public expectations apparently establish limits on legislative transformations beyond which fundamental system values are judged violated. The predominance of submissive parliaments in all three countries studied indicates few normative constraints. More likely, *supportive societal norms contribute to the survival of legislative systems—regardless of their status.* The continuity of parliaments in Iran, Turkey, and Afghanistan is striking for the region. Only Lebanon with a 45-year legislative history, seven of which were under suspension, compares favorably with the parliaments of Turkey, Afghanistan, and Iran. The Pahlavi monarchy passed up opportunities to rid itself of the Majlis in 1925 and 1953, and Dr. Mosaddiq's actions to dissolve both houses probably hastened his fall. The Shah's insistence that every executive decree issued during the suspension of parliament in 1961-63 stipulate later review by legislators suggests a reticence to do violence to the constitution. Turkey's parliamentary interregnum in 1960-61 was remarkably brief. Authoritarian and elitist elements in the military argued in 1960 and again in 1971 for the indefinite dissolution of the National Assembly, but the certainty of public resistance no doubt strengthened the chiefs of staff resolve to repress these demands. In some contrast, the legislature's resiliency in Afghanistan could be accounted for by those interests that profited from the status quo rather than a consensus on an ideal.

Our historical overviews give reason to believe that *failing support for a legislature among its attentive publics can help to precipitate change.* At the same time, *parliaments performing weakly integrative functions seem least affected when their public acceptance declines.* Disillusionment with the Afghan parliament had spread across the political spectrum by the late 1960s. Legislators were chastised in the independent press and other public forums for their preoccupations with client and personal errands and their long absences from the capital. Yet the willingness of the king and the Afghan military to tolerate the Wolesi Jirgah was best explained in terms of the relatively modest demands for interest aggregation directed at national institutions. In Iran, the protracted cynicism toward the Iranian Majlis among the middle classes has also had little bearing on the legislative development. Admittedly, the allegations of election fraud in 1960 and 1961 did force the parliament's dismissal. However, the scarcely improved image of the Iranian legislator in the post-1963 period has not set back the regime's efforts to further institutionalize the submissive system.

A link between public approval and parliamentary change is more manifest in Turkey. The ouster of Menderes was preceded by increased censure of political institutions from many quarters. But it was more likely the faltering economy than resentment of the prime minister's iron rule over the parliament that finally brought down the system. Public dissatisfaction with jerry-built government coalitions beginning in 1961 is given much credit for the clear-cut victory of the Justice party in the 1965 elections. Many voters accepted Demirel's argument that Turkey could only prosper under the decisive leadership offered by a majority party. Criticism of parliamentary government rose sharply during 1970 and 1971 with the near incapacity of both houses to act on pressing legislation. The military's memorandum of March 1971 thus found a not unsympathetic public.

Any conclusion that parliaments in the three countries are entirely passive in shaping their character and fate is not borne out by the case evidence. Legislatures of every stripe, even the most submissive, have deliberately or unintentionally modified their environment. As described above, the substance and style of parliamentary behavior can be instrumental in generating varying levels of confidence among critical publics. Moreover, legislative life has no doubt influenced the survival, and thus the system configuration, of political parties and factions. Parliaments have also tailored formal rules to suit their institutional needs. All the same, our historical accounts indicate that legislatures in the three countries have been preponderantly dependent, reactive institutions. By and large, changes in their status, especially modifications in their decisional and integrative capacities, were the result of events elsewhere in the political system and largely beyond their control. Any general theory of legislative development will have to accept this finding as a point of departure.

Suggestive models of transformation are an obvious way to close out an examination of legislative change. The parliamentary histories of Iran, Turkey, and Afghanistan document the probable major components of such models. The primacy of executive actors and institutions is stressed throughout the essay. We are also alerted to several conditions under which political parties, formal rules, and normative and temporal supports may serve as critical variables. What the case materials fail to provide are defensible propositions about the interactions among these variables. Thus, we are unprepared to specify sets of conditions that impel change from one class of legislature to another, or within a legislative type. More refined analysis is also required before we can hope to identify critical points at which change becomes inevitable. With a larger number of transformational "events" extracted from a broader survey of legislatures, and more operationalized variables, we may be ready to identify well-trodden pathways of legislative change. At that time we could also be in a position to ask whether a legislature may be in or out of phase with stages of political development.

NOTES

1. An analysis of four American state legislatures in Wahlke et al. (1962) continues to serve as the examplar of comparative, empirical studies. The leading thematic overview, with particular attention to legislative processes in the British Commonwealth and Western Europe is Wheare (1967). The Inter-Parliamentary Union (1966) has compiled a comprehensive (55-country) inventory of formal legislative structures and practices.

2. For example, Almond and Powell (1966) view legislative institutions in this single sense. The authors admit that in the British Parliament and the U.S. Congress, rule making often takes a back seat to rule modification and rule legitimization. But little effort is made to explore these or other alternate legislative roles in a comparative vein.

3. Among the more successful applications of "role" analysis are Hoskin (1972) and Kim (1972). Also see Jewell (1970: 475-500) for a synoptic discussion of the uses and limits of role analysis in cross-national research.

4. One suggestive effort is found in Meller (1966: 308-319), whose classification of four legislatures turns on assessments of their mode of representation, hierarchical structure, and functional performance.

5. One prefatory note is in order. In bicameral systems our focus in almost entirely on the lower chamber. This preference needs no elaborate justification. In most cases the two houses are sufficiently distinctive to warrant independent analysis. The formal powers of the lower house are typically broader in scope. Not infrequently, the upper chamber is limited to powers of amendment and delay. Its membership may also be appointed in whole or in part, or indirectly elected. The lower house, with its ordinarily popular and direct electorate, thus promises a more interesting vantage point from which to observe the play of national forces on the legislature.

6. For a useful survey of this literature, see Packenham (1970: 521-582).

7. Judgments about decisional and integrative performances are gleaned from sources listed in the Reference section.

8. A very similar understanding of "decisional" functions is found in Agor (1970: 228-272).

9. The constitution had authorized an upper house, half of its members to be appointed by the king. But legislators balked at creating a chamber they suspected would side with the monarch against the Majlis and the constitution.

10. In the sharper competition, the number of landlords elected dropped somewhat from the Thirteenth Majlis. Even so, the unity of their interests maintained the landlords as the chamber's most formidable bloc (Nezami, 1968: 264-265).

11. Avery writes: "A Prime Minister . . . was chosen when enough interests all happened to coincide in thinking a certain personality would prove either the most amenable or the least obstructive to their particular ambition. Of course, once the personality in question received the vote of such an accidental majority as then came into being, claims were pressed upon him of a variety that made satisfaction of them all out of the question" (Avery, 1965: 371).

12. A constituent assembly in 1957 had amended the constitution to set the terms of both houses at four years instead of two.

13. Government officials constituted 69% of those elected in 1963 (Shaji'i, 1965: 267). Nearly 80% of the members entered the Majlis for the first time (Nezami, 1968: 221). Landlords were an estimated 12% of the membership, although nearly all the better-known spokesmen of their class were gone. Working class and peasant members were officially placed at an inflated 17% (Echo of Iran, 1965).

14. The Senate group consists of those members affiliated with the Iran Novin party. Most of the 30 elected senators (another 30 are appointed by the Shah) are not party activists but are obliged to accept Iran Novin or Mardom party designations or lose their seats in the largely managed vote. In general, members of the upper house, who include former ministers, diplomats, generals, and successful professionals, are less regimented by the parties. Senators reputed to be policy experts are permitted to criticize openly bureaucratic mismanagement and, on occasion, may win government acceptance of minor amendments raised during the Senate's deliberations.

15. The Shah has repeatedly disavowed a one-party solution for Iran; his public pronouncements have in fact occasionally hinted that a loyal opposition might alternate in power. Yet the Iran Novin party's claims on the resources and prestige of the government put it in a position to monopolize most elective offices. To obviate this, the party leaders are instructed to negotiate in advance of each election a quota of Majlis and Senate seats to be set aside for the opposition. In 1963, some 60 regime-approved candidates were authorized either to affiliate with a revived Mardom party or to declare themselves as independents. Four years later, 32 seats in the 206-member Majlis were reserved for the Mardom party and five for the ultra-nationalist Pan-Iranist party. The majority party stood aside in 1971 while the Mardom party elected 39 of its candidates and a new Iranians party was allowed one member in an enlarged 268-seat chamber.

16. Between 40 and 50 reform-minded legislators won election to the Afghan parliament in 1949 following a relaxation of government controls over the selection process. While these members failed to enact progressive legislation, they took advantage of their parliamentary offices to attack administrative inefficiency and corruption. The liberalization also spawned several incipient political parties and a critical press, much of it irresponsible. The passing of government leadership in 1952 to Mohammad Daoud, the king's first cousin, brought a return to the prohibitions on expression and the imprisonment of the most outspoken would-be modernizers.

REFERENCES

AGOR, W. H. (1970) "The decisional role of the Senate in the Chilean political system," pp. 228-272 in A. Kornberg and L. D. Musolf (eds.) Legislatures in Developmental Perspective. Durham, N.C.: Duke Univ. Press.

ALI, M. (1933) Progressive Afghanistan. Lahore: Punjab Electric Press.

ALMOND, G. A. and G. B. POWELL (1966) Comparative Politics: A Developmental Approach. Boston: Little, Brown.

AVERY, P. (1965) Modern Iran. London: Ernest Benn.

AZRAEL, J. R. (1966) "The legislative process in the U.S.S.R.," pp. 83-100 in E. Frank (ed.) Lawmakers in a Changing World. Englewood Cliffs, N.J.: Prentice-Hall.

BAERWALD, H. H. (1970) "The Diet and the Japan-Korea treaty." Asian Survey 10 (November): 954-959.

BEER, S. H. (1966) "The British legislature and the problem of mobilizing consent," pp. 30-48 in E. Frank (ed.) Lawmakers in a Changing World. Englewood Cliffs, N.J.: Prentice-Hall.

――― and A. B. ULAM (1962) Patterns of Government. New York: Random House.

BERKES, N. (1964) The Development of Secularism in Turkey. Montreal: McGill Univ. Press.

BILL, J. A. (1971) "The politics of legislative monarchy: the Iranian Majlis," pp. 360-369 in H. Hirsch and M. D. Hancock (eds.) Comparative Legislative Systems. New York: Free Press.

BINDER, L. (1962) Iran: Political Development in a Changing Society. Berkeley: Univ. of California Press.

BRACHER, K. D. (1964) "Problems of parliamentary democracy in Europe," pp. 245-264 in S. R. Braubard (ed.) A New Europe? Boston: Beacon Press.

CROW, R. E. (1970) "The legislative role of parliament in the Lebanese political system," pp. 273-302 in A. Kornberg and L. D. Musolf (eds.) Legislatures in Developmental Perspective. Durham, N.C.: Duke Univ. Press.

DEKMEGIAN, R. H. (1971) Egypt Under Nasir. Albany: State Univ. of New York Press.

DUPREE, L. (1965) Constitutional Development and Cultural Change, Part II: Pre-1964 Afghan Constitutional Development. American Univ. Field Reports 9 (May): 1-14.

Echo of Iran (1965) For Your Information, No. 501 (November). Tehran: Echo Publishers.

EHRMANN, H. W. (1968) France. Boston: Little, Brown.

FEIN, L. J. (1967) Israel. Boston: Little, Brown.

FREY, F. W. (1965) The Turkish Political Elite. Cambridge, Mass.: MIT Press.

GERMINO, D. and S. PASSIGLI (1968) The Government and Politics of Contemporary Italy. New York: Harper & Row.

GILL, F. G. (1964) "Chile: society in transition," pp. 416-417 in M. C. Needler (ed.) Political Systems of Latin America. Princeton: Van Nostrand.

GOODMAN, A. E. (1975) "Correlates of legislative constituency service in South Vietnam," pp. 181-205 in G. R. Boynton and C. L. Kim (eds.) Legislative Systems in Developing Countries.

GREGORIAN, G. (1969) The Emergence of Modern Afghanistan. Stanford: Stanford Univ. Press.

GROSSHOLTZ, J. (1970) "Integrative factors in the Malaysian and Philippine legislatures." Comparative Politics 3 (October): 93-113.

HART, H. C. (1971) "Parliament and nation-building: England and India," pp. 125-139 in G. Loewenberg (ed.) Modern Parliaments: Change or Decline? Chicago: Aldine-Atherton.

HOPKINS, R. F. (1975) "The Kenyan legislature: political functions and citizen perceptions," pp. 207-231 in G. R. Boynton and C. L. Kim (eds.) Legislative Systems in Developing Countries.

HOSKIN, G. (1975) "Dimensions of conflict in the Colombian national legislature," pp. 143-178 in G. R. Boynton and C. L. Kim (eds.) Legislative Systems in Developing Countries.

――― (1971) "Dimensions of representation in the Colombian national legislature," in W. Agor (ed.) Latin American Legislature Systems: A Comparative Reader. New York: Praeger.

HUDSON, M. (1968) The Precarious Republic. New York: Random House.

HUNTINGTON, S. P. (1968) Political Order in Changing Societies. New Haven, Conn.: Yale Univ. Press.

——— (1965) "Congressional responses to the 20th century," pp. 5-31 in D. B. Truman (ed.) The Congress and America's Future. Englewood Cliffs, N.J.: Prentice-Hall.

Inter-Parliamentary Union (1966) Parliament. London: Cassell.

JEWELL, M. E. (1970) "Attitudinal determinants of legislative behavior: the utility of role analysis," in A. Kornberg and L. D. Musolf (eds.) Legislatures in Developmental Perspective. Durham, N.C.: Duke Univ. Press.

KARPAT, K. H. (1968) "Introduction to political and social thought in Turkey," pp. 297-305 in K. Karpat (ed.) Political and Social Thought in the Contemporary Middle East. New York: Praeger.

——— (1959) Turkey's Politics. Princeton: Princeton Univ. Press.

KIM, C. L. (1973) "Consensus on legislative roles among Japanese prefectural assemblymen," pp. 398-420 in A. Kornberg (ed.) Legislatures in Comparative Perspective. New York: David McKay.

KIM, Y. C. (1975) "The committee system in the Japanese Diet," pp. 69-85 in G. R. Boynton and C. L. Kim (eds.) Legislative Systems in Developing Countries.

KINROSS, L. (1965) Ataturk. New York: William Morrow.

KORNBERG, A. (1967) Canadian Legislative Behavior. New York: Holt, Rinehart & Winston.

LEWIS, G. (1955) Turkey. London: Ernest Benn.

LOEWENBERG, G. (1972) "Comparative legislative research," in S. C. Patterson and J. C. Wahlke (eds.) Comparative Legislative Behavior. New York: John Wiley.

——— (1961) "Parliamentarianism in Western Germany: the functioning of the Bundestag." Amer. Pol. Sci. Rev. 55 (March): 87-102.

McNELLY, T. (1963) Contemporary Government of Japan. Boston: Houghton Mifflin.

MELLER, N. (1966) "Identification and classification of legislatures." Philippine J. of Public Administration 10 (October): 308-319.

MERKL, P. (1966) "Party government in the Bonn republic," pp. 65-82 in E. Frank (ed.) Lawmakers in a Changing World. Englewood Cliffs, N.J.: Prentice-Hall.

MEZEY, M. L. (1975) "Legislative development and political parties: the case of Thailand," pp. 107-141 in G. R. Boynton and C. L. Kim (eds.) Legislative Systems in Developing Countries.

NEZAMI, M. A. (1966) "Persian legislative elites." Ph.D. dissertation. Chicago: University of Chicago.

PACKENHAM, R. A. (1970) "Legislatures and political development," pp. 521-582 in A. Kornberg and L. D. Musolf (eds.) Legislatures in Developmental Perspective. Durham, N.C.: Duke Univ. Press.

PAHLAVI, M.R.S. (1967) The White Revolution. Tehran: Imperial Pahlavi Library.

PROCTOR, J. H. (1957-58) "The legislative activity of the Egyptian National Assembly of 1957-58." Parliamentary Affairs 11: 23-37.

RAALTE, E. V. (1959) The Parliament of the Kingdom of the Netherlands. London: Hansard Society.

SHAJI'I, Z. (1965) The Representatives of the National Consultative Assembly During the Twenty-One Legislative Periods. Tehran: Social Science Research Institute. In Persian.

SISSON, J. R. (1973) "Comparative legislative institutionalization: a theoretical exploration," in A. Kornberg (ed.) Legislatures in Comparative Perspective. New York: David McKay.

STAUFFER, R. B. (1970) "The role of Congress in the Philippine political system," pp. 334-465 in A. Kornberg and L. D. Musolf (eds.) Legislatures in Developmental Perspective. Durham, N.C.: Duke Univ. Press.

THOMPSON, D. (1964) Democracy in France Since 1870. New York: Oxford Univ. Press.

TRUMAN, D. B. (1965) "Introduction: the problem and its setting," pp. 1-2 in D. B. Truman (ed.) The Congress and America's Future. Englewood Cliffs, N.J.: Prentice-Hall.

WAHL, N. (1966) "The French parliament: from lastword to afterthought," pp. 49-64 in E. Frank (ed.) Lawmakers in a Changing World. Englewood Cliffs, N.J.: Prentice-Hall.

WAHLKE, J., H. EULAU, and W. BUCHANAN (1962) The Legislative System. New York: John Wiley.

WEIKER, W. F. (1963) The Turkish Revolution, 1960-1961. Washington, D.C.: Brookings Institution.

WEINBAUM, M. G. (1974) "The legislator as intermediary: integration of the center and periphery in Afghanistan," in A. Eldridge (ed.) Legislatures in Plural Societies. Beverly Hills: Sage Pubns.

––– (1974) "Iran finds a party system." Middle East Journal.

––– (1972) "Afghanistan: nonparty parliamentary democracy." The J. of Developing Areas 7 (October): 57-74.

WHEARE, K. (1967) Legislatures. London: Oxford Univ. Press.

ZONIS, M. (1971) The Political Elite of Iran. Princeton: Princeton Univ. Press.

MARVIN G. WEINBAUM is Associate Professor of Political Science at the University of Illinois at Urbana. He has contributed articles on American and Middle Eastern political institutions and to various books and journals, including Middle East Journal and Journal of Developing Areas. He is the co-author of Metropolitan Decision Processes (1969) and Presidential Election: A Simulation with Readings (1969).

Chapter 3

THE COMMITTEE SYSTEM IN THE JAPANESE DIET: RECRUITMENT, ORIENTATION, AND BEHAVIOR

Y O U N G   C.   K I M

George Washington University

Anyone reviewing the existing literature on the Committees of the Japanese Diet is bound to be struck by its legalistic character. One searches in vain for a study comparable to the systematic analyses of the American legislative committee system. It was this very absence of theoretically and empirically grounded work on the Japanese committee system, compounded by the limited research resources available, which led the author to undertake this exploratory study. Although this research report presents some data on the Japanese Diet committees[1] in general, the focus of the paper here is on those Diet members who hold membership in either of two committees of the House of Representatives: the Committee on Foreign Affairs and the Committee on Agriculture, Forestry, and Fisheries.

This report will center for discussion on three broad questions:

(1) What factors shape recruitment or selection of Diet committee members?

(2) What is the role orientation held by the Dietman regarding his own work and toward significant role-partners?

(3) What is the actual behavior of the Diet member?

AUTHOR'S NOTE: Gratitude is expressed to Professor Hugh LeBlanc of George Washington University for his critical reading of this manuscript.

Data here came primarily from two sources: (a) minutes of proceedings of the Diet and of the Committees, and other official documents and materials available at the Secretariat of each house of the Diet; and (b) interviews[2] the author conducted with Dietmen, staff members of the research offices of the Committees, and with members of the Diet Secretariat.

SELECTION

The primary interest here is to identify the criteria, both formal and informal, that are applied by the selectors and the motivations underlying the initial preferences of Dietmen in matters of committee assignment.

LEGAL PROVISIONS AND PRECEDENTS

Diet Law specifies some actions which determine committee membership structure. Article 42 states that members of a standing committee be appointed at the beginning of a session and that they hold membership until their term of office expires.

According to the Rules of the House of Representatives, all appointment of members of committees shall be by nomination by the Speaker.[3] However, this provision has been interpreted to mean—and the precedent has been firmly established—that the Speaker will "nominate" respective slates of nominees forwarded to him by parliamentary groups. Further, Diet Law specifies that committee membership be allocated to each parliamentary group in proportion to the number of seats that group commands.[4] This principle in turn has led to a precedent that the determination of quotas be made by the Committee on House Management.

Depending on the legal size of the committee the Liberal Democratic Party's (LDP) share of membership ranges from 13 to 31, while the major opposition group, the Japan Socialist Party (JSP), has from three to nine seats. The Komeito's share is two to five and the Democratic Socialist Party (DSP) has two to three, with the Communist Party (JCP) obtaining one or two seats. In each committee the LDP controls 60% of the membership, with the strength of LDP generally three to four times that of the leading opposition party. The range of committee size as reflected in these quotas must be kept in mind when considering the selection process.

TURNOVER RATES IN COMMITTEE MEMBERSHIP

Contrary to these legal provisions there is considerable turnover in actual practice. This must also be borne in mind in examining the selection process. Changes in the 40-man membership of the Committee on Agriculture, Forestry, and Fisheries over a four-year period (July 1967-May 1971) yielded the following information: about a quarter of the members remained rather the same. Nine out of 40 members had served on the committee for four years (three out of 9 had served without interruption while 6 had served almost continually but had been off at one time or another for a short period). Eight members had held their committee post continuously for three years, 13 served continuously about two years, and 16 for a year and a half. For both LDP and JSP about half of the membership turnover occurred at annual regular sessions of the Diet, with a somewhat higher turnover rate (about 75%) at the extraordinary session following a general election, which may occur anytime within four years.

With regard to the Committee on Foreign Affairs with its 30 members, about one-third of the turnover there occurs at the regular annual session. At an extraordinary session about half the committee's membership is new and extra sessions of the Diet usually find two or three members changing committees. Yet about one third of members of this committee have served more or less continuously for three years.

PARTY LEADERSHIP'S SELECTION OF COMMITTEE MEMBERS:
THE CRITERIA

With regard to each parliamentary group, decisions on committee assignment are made by a small number of ranking party members, usually by that inner circle responsible for the strategy and tactics of their respective parties in the Diet proceedings.

Both the LDP and JSP initially elicit from their Dietmen their preferences for committee assignment. Economy-related committees such as Agriculture, Forestry, and Fisheries and the Committee on Industry are flooded with would-be candidates, while such committees as Foreign Affairs are shunned. The party leadership applies several criteria in their determination of committee membership. Preference is given to "influential" Dietmen and those who have successfully competed in a number of elections. Constituency characteristics are considered a legitimate factor by the party leadership in selecting committee members. Those Dietmen with perceived ties to major interest groups are accommodated. For example, a Dietman whose major base of support is a labor union would be likely to be granted a seat on the Committee on Social and Labor Affairs. The need for maintaining a balance between veteran and newly-elected Dietmen on a committee is taken into account. Leadership is concerned with the degree of fraternization that develops between committee members, on the one hand, and, on the other hand, government ministry personnel and other interest-group members whose activities fall within the purview of the committee. For this reason, only reluctantly is a member allowed to serve on the same committee for more than a few years. Since attendance records of veteran members are poor, new members are desired, particularly by the LDP, for purposes of meeting a quorum and ensuring the required majority at the time a vote is taken. The desirability of retaining a few veteran members to effectively look after party interests somewhat offsets this senior/freshman consideration. In this connection, ability and performance become relevant. Especially in the case of the JSP, demonstrated past performance on a committee is taken into account.

Conspicuously absent from the criteria specifically cited by respondents was mention of the strength of the Dietman's party or its factions. No spontaneous reference was made to a concern or desire which selectors might have about the increase or preservation of the strength of their respective party or factional groups in relation to other competing groups. It may be argued that to the extent that selectors consider the electoral possibilities of aspirants, this factor is present implicitly and is self-evident. An additional explanation, if not entirely an alternative one, is that such considerations do not operate since the selectors do not really consider committee activities as having a significant effect on the future parliamentary strength of their parties or factions.

DIETMAN'S MOTIVATIONS

From the perspective of the aspirant, a major factor in determining his preferences is the potential contribution of committee membership to his future electoral fortunes. There is intense interest in a strategic place which would provide the member with an opportunity to be helpful to various groups crucial to his election. Thus, the

Dietman owing his election to the support of the Japan Teachers Union desires a seat in the Committee on Education. A Dietman with a rural constituency including important agricultural interests seeks membership in the Committee on Agriculture, Forestry, and Fisheries.

The fact that assignment to the Committee on Foreign Affairs and the Committee on Judicial Affairs is generally avoided is indicative of the operation of this electoral calculation. It is freely conceded that only veteran Dietmen who have little fear of electoral defeat could afford to apply considerations other than electoral to their preferences.

Even apart from electoral considerations—although these cannot be completely excluded—economy-related committees such as Agriculture, Forestry, and Fisheries, Commerce and Industry, Construction, Transportation, and Communications are generally preferred over other committees. Membership here affords the opportunity to be useful to various groups by successfully performing the errand-boy function, and therefore enhances personal satisfaction. Members also have the opportunity to enjoy various perquisites in their interaction with various interest groups and the general public.

Dietmen are conscious of status differentials implied by membership in different committees and seek assignment to a prestigious committee. This would perhaps accord the member ego gratification through an excellent opportunity for interaction with colleagues, government ministry personnel, and the public. Indeed, membership in House Management or Budget is generally accepted as an indication that a Dietman has "arrived." The Committee on House Management is in fact composed of veteran Dietmen with long party careers, well versed in parliamentary procedure and with ability and experience in inter-party negotiations. Privileges associated with membership on this committee are not negligible, but there is great personal satisfaction to be derived from management of the affairs of the House, from participation in decision-making activities relating to Diet Law, rules, and regulations of the House, from service in an advisory capacity to the Speaker of the House.

Likewise, membership in the Committee on Budget is attractive and very much coveted. Dietmen consider it to be an honor. A seat on the committee evokes considerable deference. Its members are in a relatively strong position to attempt to influence formulation of the budget on behalf of their clientele. The committee is represented by what some interviewees termed "elite" members of the parliamentary groups.

A seat in this committee is apparently sought because it is ego-satisfying, reaffirming the sense of one's importance. Several Dietmen drew attention to the fact that "the entire cabinet headed by the Prime Minister—not just one minister—is present during committee proceedings." Dietmen, especially of the opposition parties, may be sensitive to the opportunity to demonstrate their brilliance and knowledge by firing searching questions on the full range of issues in such august company and in the full glare of media instruments.

For some Dietmen, their intellectual interests in substantive areas reflecting their specialized training and/or experience are major factors shaping their preferences for committee assignment. For this reason assignment to the Committee on Foreign Affairs has been sought by some. Dietmen are aware of the lack of electoral advantage associated with this committee but—to the delight of the party leadership—some continue to desire a seat either because they do not perceive, or are not particularly concerned with, their prospects of electoral defeat. The pull of their intellectual interests, perhaps coupled with gentle prodding by colleagues, is strong enough to overcome whatever degree of reluctance they may have. But some members of this committee have paid dearly for their choice at the next election, according to the interpretation of knowledgeable observers.

CHAIRMAN AND DIRECTORS

The Diet Law stipulates that in each House the chairman of a standing committee be elected from among the members of the committee.[5] However, the Rules of the House of Representatives state that the House may entrust the Speaker with the selection of committee chairmen, and this in fact has become the practice.

With the exception of the period covering the sixteenth to twenty-eighth sessions of the Diet, chairmanship of all standing committees has been monopolized by the ruling party. This is indicative of LDP's sensitivity to potential abuse of the committee's legal powers by an opposition party chairman. It is the chairman who is empowered to "arrange the business of the committee and maintain order." The chairman's role is not negligible in matters relating to the maintenance of order and the rendering of reports of committee proceedings to the House. What is more critical is that to effectively block deliberation of a bill a committee chairman need only absent himself without designating another to serve during his absence.

The Rules of the House provide that from among its members one or more directors (riji) of the committee are to be elected by mutual vote. In actuality the Committee on House Management determines the number of directors and the quotas to be assigned to each party group. The House Management committee chairman appoints as directors those nominees suggested by the parties' parliamentary groups. Eight directors are appointed for the committees on both Foreign Affairs and Agriculture, Forestry, and Fisheries, with five from the LDP and one each from the JSP, Komeito, and the DSP. The JCP is not allotted a directorship but one of its committeemen may participate in the director's meetings as an observer.

The committee chairmanship rotates about once a year. Incumbent chairmen are expected to resign after a year so as to allow others to assume the responsibility.[6] Among directors there is greater continuity. Although some replacements occur regularly, especially at the time of the annual shift in chairmanship, on the whole their tenure is longer.

Directors are usually selected after a period of service on that committee and often remain as members after resigning the directorship. The directors, together with the chairman, in fact run the committee. Meeting formally or informally, they confer on management of the committee and negotiate a number of inter-party matters, both substantive and procedural, prior to the formal meeting of the committee.

ORIENTATIONS AND BEHAVIOR

PROFILE OF LEGISLATIVE ACTIVITIES

When the Diet is in session, the committees usually meet two to three times a week with regular meetings lasting from two to three hours. A close examination of the minutes of proceedings and other documents relating to the business of these two committees over a four-year period (July 1967-May 1971) sheds light on the nature and quantity of the work of these committees.

Table 1 indicates the number of committee meetings held during three legislative sessions and the quantity of work processed by the two committees.

TABLE 1
ACTIVITIES OF COMMITTEES IN JAPANESE DIET

Diet Session	Length of Session	Number of Committee Meetings	Referred to Committee	Number of Bills and Treaties Passed	Shelved or Withdrawn	Postponed to Next Session
Committee on Foreign Affairs						
58th regular	160 days	25	19	19	0	0
61st regular	222 days	34	17	13	4	0
63d extraordinary	120 days	16	23	23	0	0
Committee on Agriculture, Forestry and Fisheries						
58th regular	160 days	28	16	8	5	3
61st regular	222 days	55	14	11	3	0
63d extraordinary	120 days	31	13	9	1	3

What emerges from the examination of the minutes of the proceedings is that the overwhelming proportion of committee meetings is taken up by questioning and debate by members of opposition party groups. The proceedings indicate that the activity of LDP Dietmen in the committees, indexed in terms of participation in committee proceedings, is very low. During the 59th and 60th extra sessions, for example, no LDP members participated in substantive discussion in the Committee on Foreign Affairs. During the 61st and 63rd sessions, during which the committee met 34 and 16 times respectively, only a few members did so. The Committee on Agriculture, Forestry, and Fisheries met 55 and 31 times respectively during the 61st and 63rd sessions, but LDP members participated in substantive discussion only ten and six times.

Also noteworthy is the fact that in the case of the Committee on Foreign Affairs, time devoted to deliberation of treaties or bills was far outweighed by time spent in questions and answers on current developments in international affairs.

One measure of the vitality of the committee system is to see the extent to which the committee's legal competence in the initiation of bills as enumerated in Diet Law is invoked in actual practice. The committee is empowered to submit in the name of its chairman a bill "in matters within the sphere of its work," but the incidence of this is extremely low in relation to the bills submitted by the Cabinet. Perhaps this is not surprising. What is noteworthy, however, is that even these "chairman-submitted bills" would not come about unless the government party cooperated. At any rate, such bills would not be passed by the committee without the consent of the government party. The incidence of amendments to the government's bills is equally small. In the words of committee staff members, amendments are "virtually non-existent" in the case of the Committee on Foreign Affairs and are "rare and ever decreasing" in the case of the Committee on Agriculture, Forestry, and Fisheries. The fact of perennial dominance of the LDP, coupled with party discipline, effectively constrains a potential invocation of the legal powers by a committee. The number of bills shelved at these committees during the 58th and 61st sessions was unusually large and was due to exceptionally intense inter-party conflict which permeated these particular sessions.

ORIENTATIONS[7] AND BEHAVIOR

Dietmen subscribe, verbally at least, to the normative conception that law-making should basically and properly be done by the legislature. At the minimum, they feel that they ought to be able to participate meaningfully in law-making activity by voting to amend or reject government bills. They are aware that this is not the case in actual practice and deplore the fact. Their abstract orientation may be termed "initiator," and their specific orientation "ratifier." They also subscribe to the view that committees should constitute the core of the Diet's activity, and in this respect they perceive no discrepancy between their normative conception and actual practice.

On the orientations that committee members have, none is more basic and significant in shaping their actual behavior as committee members than their mutually antagonistic partisan approach to the outcome of a given bill. Committeemen of the government party consider as their primary duty passage of a government bill, while those of opposition parties feel equally intensely that delay if not defeat of a bill is their responsibility. This feeling is not confined to controversial bills involving partisan principles but is often applicable to other bills with little regard to the substantive merits of the bill. This is despite the fact that Dietmen in general hold nonpartisan orientation in abstraction. Much depends on the general political climate reflecting the degree of antagonism prevailing between the government party and other opposition parties.

The basic attitude of the LDP committeemen is to "let the opposition fellow grumble for a time and we will ram through the bill with our majority." Normally, there is little expectation that committee deliberations will make any real difference on the substance of the bills. Tolerance of opposition rumblings, or going through the motions, is deemed essential so as to forestall the charge of tyranny on the part of the majority. While the bill is under committee consideration, committeemen of the LDP group refrain from taking up committee time so as to give opposition members maximum time. Another reason suggested by LDP committeemen for their low level of participation is that they have been kept informed on the contents of the bills and their views have already been made known at LDP policy subcommittee meetings on the subject. Intra-party disputes are resolved before the bills are submitted to the Diet.

On the other hand, members of the opposition parties, painfully aware of their minority status and suffering from a sense of futility, see little incentive for genuine substantive discussion of the merits or demerits of the government's legislative proposals. They feel that they ought to embarrass and discredit the government in the eyes of the mass media and to improve the image of their parties (and—the observer could add parenthetically—their personal image as well).

Delaying the deliberations on all government bills often becomes an end in itself for opposition committee members. This is in large measure related to their desire to obtain concessions from the government on selected bills. Toward the end of the session, the government is often confronted with a situation in which it must in some fashion placate opposition parties or be prepared to see their bills go down in defeat. This is true despite the fact that there are legal parliamentary procedures the government could invoke to hasten Diet deliberations on the bills. Government party Dietmen, however, feel constrained from making full use of these legal powers.

The basic sense of conflict between committeemen of opposition parties and the government party varies somewhat with the committees and the nature of the issue concerned. Conflict is sometimes moderated by the desire of all members of a committee to pass a bill. For example, the Committees on Education or on Social and Labor Affairs show a higher level of partisan conflict than economy-related committees. As for committeemen's abstract orientation toward their own parties, members generally feel that they ought to be able to act freely in the committees (nonparty-man orientation). At the same time, they are aware of the implications of party politics and hence are resigned to the high degree of control exerted on them by the party. At the level of specific orientation, then, they hold a party-man orientation. They sense incongruity between this "party-man" approach and deliberation of bills from the perspective of "the people." (An illustration often suggested by the committeemen themselves is the case of pollution.) At the time of voting, conformity to party position is expected of committee members and is adhered to, but committeemen, especially those of the LDP, feel that they do have considerable freedom and flexibility during the deliberation phase. Party positions on important bills are determined by party caucus in the House. This is sometimes preceded by deliberations in the appropriate extra parliamentary party organs. Committeemen are of course aware of the general party line on a given issue as they attend policy committees of their respective parties and learn party positions through ranking Dietmen of their parties. However, they feel they can, and they say they in fact do, act freely within this broad guideline.

Individual committeemen depend little on their parties for any preparation or "homework" necessary to committee work. The party office makes available the relevant research or policy papers, but mostly committeemen themselves conduct their own research with occasional support from their personal secretaries. The research office, with staff functions for each committee, is not used extensively. Individual committeemen of opposition parties avail themselves of this reference service more frequently than do their LDP counterparts.

The committeeman's orientation vis-a-vis government ministries constitutes a most critical sector. Dietmen in general are conscious of the legally exalted and perceived superior status of the Diet relative to the Administration as written into the postwar constitution.[8] Since they "represent" or act to promote the interests of constituents, or more broadly of the people, they feel that deference on the part of administrators is deserved.

Intercession on behalf of their clientele generally results in satisfaction. As Dietmen perceive it, administrative officials are "weak" or vulnerable to Dietmen and they should show due respect to the representatives (abstract superior-status orientation). The explanation provided by Dietmen for the pliant and accommodating attitude of administration officials is that these officials, after all, want to ensure favorable legislative action on their agencies' budgets as well as on bills they submit to the Diet. As the Dietmen see it, there should be and are elements of reciprocity and interdependency (specific coequal-status orientation). For their part they feel that successful performance of their job on behalf of their clientele requires sympathetic and understanding administrators. Dietmen of opposition parties are not entirely immune to the need for good will and for the cooperation of administrative officials. This fact also serves to moderate the intensity of their anti-government attack. At any rate, the satisfactory performance of a Dietman holding a particular committee seat is not limited to his activity inside the committee room during the legislation session. The Dietman sees a committee seat as a vantage point from which to deal with a particular administrative agency prior to, during, and subsequent to a legislative session.

In general committeemen tend to exaggerate—from the perspective of an analyst—their own importance and are persuaded that they indeed "allow these bills to pass for these administrative officials." Inasmuch as the Dietmen are legally empowered to present their own bills (provided certain requirements are met) as well as to amend, oppose, or reject a government bill, such pride is not wholly without justification. However, the fact of the matter is that the legal competence to reject or amend government measures is only rarely demonstrated. An important point here is that the basic sense of antagonism between the governing party and the opposition parties is moderated by the need for cooperation between the two. This is compounded in some cases by the sense of affinity and camaraderie some Dietmen show toward their administrative counterparts owing to their common career background.

Cooperation or courtesy between committees and ministry is indicated by the practice wherein ministry personnel make a point of calling on committeemen to divulge the questions the latter could raise at a committee meeting. Committeemen usually, although not always, oblige.

Committeemen are aware that they are expected to examine the bills referred to them. However, they do not seem to feel that they have a part to play as constructive critic. They are interested in either passing bills or delaying if not blocking the passage of bills. It is striking that no respondent made explicit reference to the critic function of the legislature or committee.

From the perspective of committeemen, another salient object of orientation is individuals and groups with some claim to, or ties with, their constituencies. The prevailing role orientation is that they ought to safeguard or promote the interest of their electoral district—with "electoral district" defined vaguely in terms of residents or someone with ties with the district (district and facilitator orientations). The committeeman does not perceive a sharp distinction between "public interest of the constituency" and the interests of those individuals and groups recognized as having an important bearing on his electoral fortune. In his daily activity a Dietman may not always consciously weigh the potential contribution of individuals or groups seeking his assistance or apply it to his forthcoming election. However, either implicitly or explicitly, his allocation of attention and effort among competing pleas is influenced by such a calculation. Dietmen accept this and they do not appear to hold any contradictory orientation.

Analytic distinction between pressure group and areal orientations is not generally perceived and does not appear meaningful to committeemen. As they view it, individuals and groups making "demands" or "claims" upon them are but soliciting and beseeching their assistance. Dietmen are conscious of some degree of influence which they can exercise on behalf of those seeking intercession prior to committee sessions. At the same time, they are prepared to accept the view that legislators are "weak and vulnerable" vis-a-vis these clientele groups.[9]

Readily conceding that their activity at committee meetings reflects their sensitivity to clientele's interests, they also profess to be aware of the inconsistency of their activity with their "political conscience" (which is theoretically important) but they declare that they are not particularly bothered by it (specific delegate orientation). This would be especially true of Dietmen serving on economy-related committees where occasions for such conflict are less frequent than on other committees. If the intrinsic inter-party differences are small and the general state of inter-party antagonism is low, more opportunities will present themselves for committeemen to act in consonance with their non-partisan orientation. Committeemen have developed a frequently invoked device called an ancillary resolution (futai ketsugi) by which dissenting members, usually of an opposition party, can formally record their affirmative vote on a bill in the interest of, say, a clientele group, at the same time recording their reservations and dissenting views in the interest of party principle. This practice serves to alleviate the tensions arising from any conflicting orientations.

The author's interviews elicited some data which indicated a sense of efficacy on the part of committee members. All respondents declare their committee work to be important, although they find hard to articulate readily how or to whom it is important. Based on probing questions the following observations are warranted:

(1) The Dietman feels that the influence he exerts on the government's policy formulation by virtue of being a committee member is insignificant.

(2) Dietmen feel they can, and do, influence the government during the implementation phase. During committee deliberation of a bill, ministers and other ranking members of the Administration may be compelled to accept a committeeman's interpretation of a particular provision of the bill and to pledge to take certain actions related to the bill. They consider these statements and remarks made by administrative officials to be binding on the government.

(3) Though aware of the limitations of their own influence, opposition party members are sustained by the thought that without the activities of opposition parties in committees there would be no reason for the legislature's existence.

(4) Both government and opposition party members feel rather vaguely that, by their presence and activities, they are playing an important part in the political process.

Whatever degree of satisfaction committeemen may feel, its source is not primarily the sense of successfully discharging the legally specified function of "examining government bills" and related acts, implying participation in law-making. Rather, satisfaction stems from the belief that (a) the position of the Dietman is an honor and the work prestigious, evoking appropriate deference from the people; (b) the committeeman is participating in the supreme task of statecraft and, especially for LDP members, his aspiration for a ministerial post will be realized in due course.

IMPLICATIONS

Since decisions by parties are accepted as binding by their respective members in committees, the degree of influence which committeemen qua committeemen exert on the substance of legislation is very much limited. This is compounded by the actual high turnover rates in the committee membership. In the sphere of legislation, then, committee function is one of legitimation. The function of the committee gives the substance of legislation drafted elsewhere a formal and legal approval on behalf of the House.

If high turnover rates in committee membership are not conducive to specialization affecting the capacity of committees to influence legislative output, then they are in accord with the realities of power. Moreover, high turnover provides the opportunity for a greater number of aspirants to attain more prestigious and useful committee assignments, which is consistent with the performance of a status/ honor-conferring function of the committee system. Membership in committees, more broadly in the Diet, performs a status/honor-conferring function and also instills or reinforces an "institutional commitment" for the legislative institution.

From the perspective of the government party, committee deliberation constitutes a conformity to democratic rules of the game as well as a style of decision-making by consensus. From the viewpoint of opposition parties, committee sessions provide a valuable forum for directly engaging the administration. There the government witnesses are exposed to a barrage of searching, embarrassing, and provocative questions. Although they are not always vulnerable, the forum gives opposition members the opportunity for performing the "critic function" and at the same time, enhances their status and ego-satisfaction.

NOTES

1. Most of the work of the Diet is done in committees and approval by plenary sessions usually follow. Legally speaking, the committees are empowered to examine the bills, petitions, and other matters which may come under their respective spheres of competence. They may propose a bill concerning matters under their jurisdiction, hold public hearings, request the attendance of government witnesses, demand the submission of reports and records from the government, and investigate matters relating to government.

2. Most data (including interviews) mentioned in this paper were obtained in Tokyo during June 1971, although some interview data on the Committee on Foreign Affairs were collected in the winter of 1968 as part of the author's inquiry into the process of foreign policy making in Japan.

3. Article 30. The House of Representatives has 16 standing committees for which membership ranges from 25 to 50 (Diet Law, Article 14). The committees are: Cabinet, Local Administration, Judicial Affairs, Foreign Affairs, Finance, Education, Social and Labor Affairs, Agriculture, Forestry, and Fisheries, Commerce and Industry, Transportation, Communications, Construction, Budget, Audit, House Management, and Discipline.

4. Article 46.

5. Article 25.

6. Committee chairmen enjoy approximately the same ranking as do ministers, with the appropriate perquisites.

7. It is useful to distinguish between the two kinds of role orientations: (1) orientations in abstraction, that is, the normative conception held by the position incumbent as a matter of abstract principle; and (2) orientations in specific context, those rules of behavior accepted by the actor as governing the behavior of incumbents including himself. The second category, specific orientations, is at the level of orientation and is to be distinguished from actual behavior. Situational exigencies (objectively ascertainable) intervene between specific orientations enacted or acted upon by the incumbents and the observable behavior indexed in terms other than orientational data.

8. The constitution defines the Diet to be "the highest organ of state power" and "sole law-making organ of the State."

9. An indication of the committeeman's sensitivity in this regard is that a member generally distributes a transcript of his statements at a committee meeting to various clientele groups. Dietmen claim that they make a point to return to their district to stay attuned to the needs of their constituencies.

The pleas of individuals and groups are communicated to the committees, especially to ranking members such as the chairman and directors. Anyone who has spent time with Dietmen would be impressed with the enormity of the demand that the stream of visitors—both at home and at office—makes on their time. Several Dietmen confided that they would have to, and occasionally they do, get up around 5 a.m. if they want to prepare for a committee meeting.

REFERENCES

KURODA, S. Kokkai Ho (Diet Law).

Shugiin Jimukyoku: Shugiin Iinkai Senrei Shu (Precedents of the House of Representatives).

Shugiin Norin Suisan Iinkai Giroku (Proceedings of the Committee on Agriculture, Forestry, and Fisheries).

Shugiin Gaimu Iinkai Giroku (Proceedings of the Committee on Foreign Affairs).

TSUCHIYA, S. Iinkai Seido (Committee Systems).

YOUNG C. KIM is Associate Professor of Political Science at George Washington University. He has written and edited several books on Asia, and contributed numerous articles to professional journals. His latest book (forthcoming) is *Japan and the Soviet Union: Major Determinants of Their Interactions.*

Part II

LEGISLATURES AND CONFLICT MANAGEMENT

Chapter 4

POLITICAL RISK AND LEGISLATIVE BEHAVIOR IN NON-WESTERN COUNTRIES

LESTER G. SELIGMAN

University of Illinois, Urbana

THE CONCEPT OF POLITICAL RISK

A recurrent theme in all the papers in this symposium is the minor, if not subservient, role of the legislature in policy making in non-Western countries as compared with Western democracies. The legislatures in non-Western countries neither initiate legislation nor check the' executive and the bureaucracy (Packenham, 1970: 521-82). Mezey reports that in Thailand, so powerless is the parliament that if it tried to exert greater influence the executive would dissolve it or the military would seize power (1975). What explains the subordinate role of the parliament in non-Western countries? Many of the factors that are responsible are discussed in the chapters of this volume, but a neglected one is the high risk for legislators in their recruitment and political careers (see Seligman, 1970). We shall define risk in the next paragraph, but first note here that the data is lacking for the comparative measurement of political risk. Therefore, we shall elaborate the concept and use the evidence in the symposium papers and other research on legislative behavior to illustrate and apply the concept.

AUTHOR'S NOTE: I want to thank Professor William Mitchell of the University of Oregon for his helpful comments on an earlier version of this paper.

Disraeli described advancement in a political career as a risky venture which he likened to "climbing a greasy pole." In a classic paper, Friedman and Savage (1948: 279-304) pointed out that two different kinds of behavior—gambling and insurance—are not unrelated, and differ primarily in the degree of risk they present to an individual. In an analogous way, politicians must gamble in their career decisions and try to insure themselves because every political system defines the probabilities and the uncertainties of particular outcomes of success or failure for them. The rewards of political success and the costs of political failure vary considerably among political systems. This paper attempts to differentiate the probabilities and costs of failure in non-Western systems as compared with Western systems as a factor which determines the political behavior of legislators.

The decision to seek political office relies in some degree on cognitive assessments of the probabilities of winning and losing, and its consequences. We shall define risk and uncertainty in Frank Knight's terms (Hammond, 1968: 3-5; Baumol, 1965: 550): "Risk refers to situations in which the outcome is not certain, but where the probabilities of the alternative outcomes are known, or can at least be estimated. Uncertainty is present where the unknown outcomes can not even be predicted in probabilistic terms." Therefore, risk includes two components: (1) the probabilities and/or uncertainties, and (2) loss outcomes.

If the chances of losing are great and the net costs of defeat are severe deprivations, then such a system may be marked "high" in political risk for political aspirants and incumbents. If the probabilities of losing are great but the net costs of losing are minor losses in influence—income and social status—then such a system is a low risk one for potential aspirants and incumbents (see Tables 1 and 2).

For legislators, in Western democracies, political risk is a function of competition for elective public office. An office which is equally competitive for all contestants and in all elections is equally risky for all candidates. In Western democracies such competition is the norm that justifies free elections as the method for achieving representativeness, responsiveness and accountability. In practice, such perfect and open competition does not occur frequently. Western democracies in various degrees extend opportunities for the political career more broadly than non-Western countries; but, more importantly, they protect or insure the losing candidate or the defeated incumbent. In the non-Western democracies, elections are less

TABLE 1
UNCERTAINTY IN RECRUITMENT AND THE NET COSTS OF DEFEAT

		Outcomes of Defeat		
		High Cost	Medium Cost	Low Cost
Probability of gaining office for those eligible to run	High	Non-Western one party systems		
	Medium	Non-Western democratic systems		
	Low			Western democratic systems

competitive, but the consequences of electoral defeat and other ways of losing political office are more threatening and hazardous than in Western democracies. Thus, what distinguishes non-Western legislators from Western legislators is that the former experience greater deprivations than the latter when they lose office.

The historical development of legislatures in democracies is associated with the reduction in political risk for members of the opposition and the governing elites. When party candidates could seek legislative office in opposition to the governing majority in the legislature and executive without threats to their (and their families') safety, livelihood, and public and self esteem, then a political career conducive to democracy became possible. As Hofstadter (1969: 128-131) has pointed out, the election of 1800 in the United States was significant in the history of democracies because for the first time a ruling political party was defeated and relinquished power peacefully, without becoming a subversive cabal or underground

TABLE 2
THE RESTRICTIVENESS OF POLITICAL OPPORTUNITY OR ENTRY AND THE NET COSTS OF DEFEAT

		High	Medium	Low
Restrictiveness of political opportunity or entry	High	Authoritarian developing systems		
	Medium		Democratic developing systems	
	Low			Democratic industrialized systems

army, or being punished by the governing party. The limited losses suffered by the Federalist Party after its defeat in 1800 legitimated the role of a political opposition and the governing party, and peaceful alternations in power of political parties in the legislature and/or the executive became institutionalized.

In a democratic system recruitment and career risk are especially critical for legislators because their historical contribution has been to curb excessive executive authority and actively participate in policy-making. In order for legislators to oppose or criticize executive policies in public, they must be insured against public or private losses. Legislators must be free to express choices which entail risks that they can bear, singly or collectively.

In a democracy both the governing elite as well as the opposing elite must have informed probabilities about the costs of losing power. Only if the hazards that follow defeat do not overwhelm aspiring or incumbent politicians can the incentive to pursue a political career in a democracy be sustained. Weber attributed the prominence of lawyers in political careers in Western democracies to their ability to leave their occupations for a time, run the risks of politics and return if they had to to their careers as lawyers. For this reason, Weber regarded a legal education as "the best hedge against the ever-present possibility of failure in politics" (cited in Schlesinger, 1957: 2; Eulau and Sprague, 1964).

In many non-Western countries, especially single party regimes, succession in office is not institutionalized. When a candidate for office loses or an incumbent is unseated, they may be exiled, thrown into preventive detention, or deprived of their livelihood. Most politicians, if they have private occupations, can work only in the public sector. Frequently a defeated legislator does not have a private occupation to which he can return (Singhvi, 1970: 27). Hence, a political career in non-Western democracies entails greater personal risk than in Western democratic systems. The absence of *cushions* (that is, private or public positions to which defeated politicians may retire, thereby ensuring their status and compensating for their losses), makes politics a risky career.

Other factors relevant to recruitment increase the probabilities of defeat and its consequences. The highly restricted political opportunity or entry and rigged competition for legislative positions reduces the number of contestants. Varying with the number and strength of political parties, both the number and autonomy of group sponsors of candidates are more limited than in Western democratic countries. Yet candidates can run only with sponsorship, and the proper ones. The total dependency of candidates upon sponsors deprives candidates of personal political resources. Not uncommon is the practice of the executive directly appointing members of the legislature (Schulz, 1973: 574, passim). The legislator's dependence upon such executive sponsorship heightens the insecurity of candidates for whom no honorable private or public cushions are available. The legislative candidate who faces defeat and the legislator who faces removal may face social and political degradation.

In non-Western systems the political elite is recruited from a narrow slice of society, and a great social distance separates the elites from the masses who lack the education or opportunity to participate in politics (Schulz, 1973: 574-80). Therefore, the norms of the political elites have particular significance because there is weak accountability to the voters. Hence the high risk in recruitment and the political career determines the norms of conduct of political aspirants and incumbent legislators to a greater extent than in Western democracies. Legislators act in order to protect themselves against inordinate risk. A legislator's principal defense lies in amassing a personal fortune, or the preparation of safe havens to which he may retire, inside or outside the country. Such defenses become accepted conduct which restrict recruitment to those who can prepare themselves against political risks. The narrow pool of eligible politicians becomes narrower.

RISK AND THE LEGITIMATIONS OF POLITICAL ELITES

In all political systems the legitimations of elites depend on how they are recruited to political roles or positions, and how they are removed from political positions. Entry into political positions and exit out of them are interdependent phases of a political career. Recruitment to and advancement in political office and the loss of this office with the attendant loss of status are opposite sides of the same coin. Where the norms and methods that legitimate authority are stable and secure, the mechanisms employed to gain political status employed in reverse bring about the loss of political status. In the past, kings were vested with authority at public coronations and quite consistently were removed from power at public executions. In a modern bureaucracy, appointments are made on merit as judged by performance on a competitive examination, and only equally objective judgments of incompetence can justify removal from office. When it is legitimate for a position to be secured through the patronage of influential sponsors, then only the disfavor of the sponsor warrants dismissal. Thus, it is the consistency of the criteria, methods of recruitment, and removal from public office which sustains political legitimations.

However, when the norms for acquiring political offices contradict or violate those for losing them, then political legitimations become ambiguous and lose force. Thus, the bases for loss of political status may sustain or undermine the bases for political opportunities. No one will adhere to the prescribed ways of seeking office when political positions are lost through the violation of prescribed ways. Deviant methods of recruitment and dismissal will be encouraged when the criteria of recruitment and dismissal are inconsistent. In many non-Western nations where conflicting legitimations trouble the civic order, violence is often used in removing people from office. Conflicting legitimations of recruitment and defeat or dismissal are both cause and effect of high risk in recruitment and careers.

Under conditions of high risk, the contest for political office becomes so intense that the legal norms buckle under the pressure and coercion and fraud are widely practiced. In contrast, low risk constrains the behavior of political aspirants because the winners see themselves as potential losers, and vice versa. Risk becomes controlled because it is based on exchange among winners and losers. A common interest unites winners and losers in the protection of the status of losers. The winners realize that when and if they lose, then they, too, will want their chances protected to seek office again. The maintenance of an ever-replenished pool of politicians is possible only when recruitment and career risk are kept low.

Low risk depends upon cushions for defeat during recruitment and dismissals or demotions at other points in the career. In Western Europe, important steps in democratic development took place when parties and/or groups that lacked an elite of wealth created public cushions for defeated candidates and incumbents. Political parties with leaders of modest resources had to provide the insurance against risk for their candidates and office holders. Thus, European Socialist parties provided cushions for the candidates whom they could not elect to office. Party positions were made available to aspirant politicians on the way up as well as on the way down.

The extent of political risk also influences the degree of extremism of opposition such that the greater the risk for politicians, the more revolutionary will be the goals of the opposition. The lower the risk of recruitment and incumbency, the more moderate will be the goals of the opposition (Dahl, 1966: 34; Daalder, 1966: 208). Thus, in the United States because political risk is low politicians usually have public and/or private cushions against defeat, and the opposition political parties have not sought fundamental change in the structure of American politics (Dahl, 1966: 34). Where risk is high, the opposition will espouse means and ends that differ markedly with the party in power; whereas, where risk is low the goals of the opposition will differ more on means than ends. Thus, the degree of risk is directly related to the degree of political polarization.

The history of the reduction of political risk in the recruitment of elective officials in Western democracies brought about the domestication of dissent. The history of Labor-Socialist parties shows the following. Initially, Labor or Socialist adherents and their organizations were excluded from politics. By the next step Socialist parties became legal and Labor was given the vote. Next they joined the executive coalition as minority members and then eventually became the majority party. In the process of incorporation into the governing elites the Socialist opposition lost some of its militancy. With increasing political influence came organizational hardening of Socialist parties and sluggish response to new issues. Thus, the reduction of political risk helped to institutionalise organized opposition, and reduced ideological distance between government and opposition, expanded participation, and decreased risk went hand in hand with the moderation of opposition.

The governing elite manipulates political risk as a principal technique to retain power. Governing elites use liquidation, expulsion, preventive detention, and frequent purges to ensure themselves against the loss of power. Loyalty to those in power becomes the principal criteria for selection to elite positions. The effects of high risk are cumulative, leading to the substitution of political practices that deviate from the legitimations of authority.

Low risk systems impose *fewer* barriers to political mobility and make it easier to translate social status into entry into political roles. Political opportunity in low risk systems cushions against severe loss by insuring recurring opportunities. Moreover, in low risk systems, supply and demand are in better balance because competing elites seek new candidates which tend to offset restrictiveness in political entry.

In low risk systems, public disclosure of recruitment processes and electoral behavior is vitally necessary because elites are competing for public support, and the electorate participates in the selection decisions of individuals to elective positions. Competitive selection requires support from the electorate which also tends to make elites accountable to the public.

HIGH RISK AND THE ORIENTATIONS TOWARD POLITICS AND POLITICAL ROLES

In high risk systems, the deprivation that results from the loss of political status generates political outlooks that contrast sharply with those found in low risk systems. Since political careers are hazardous vocations, politics is viewed as life or death, total power or total humiliation, and nothing in between. Politics is war-like—the winner takes all and the loser gets nothing. As Hoskins (1975) states regarding Colombia: "Government is an objective to be seized, and once won, is a bastion in which to entrench themselves, like armies of occupation, subsisting on the bureaucratic booty of the battle."

High risks give rise to exaggerated beliefs about leadership and the unique attributes necessary for political roles. It is believed that only dramatic personalities who define politics as romanticized struggles are suitable leaders. The hazardous career encourages beliefs in the role of mystical chance in achieving political success. The hazards in a political career also foster an opposite orientation, cynical opportunism, and machiavellianism. Role socialization consists in training to secure a place and in the techniques of protecting it. The right sponsors are cultivated only to be abandoned when expedient. Thus, as the conditions of risk increase, conceptions of politics and orientations toward politics become more concerned with preventing loss, rather than securing the fulfillment of objetives.

Contrast such orientations toward political careers with those of political leaders in the early days of the American republic. "To most early Republicans as well as Federalist leaders, politics was not a profession. It was rather a duty, a responsibility of gentlemen whose primary commitment was to planting, to trade, or law, or medicine, and the good life. Most hated to stand for or serve in public office. If a man was disappointed or defeated, he gracefully retired; one's career did not revolve around winning and holding office" (Goodman, 1967: 87). In what follows we shall examine the effects of political risk on the recruitment of legislators in some non-Western countries.

RECRUITMENT, RISK, AND POLITICAL TYPES

High political risk selects two predominant types of individuals who are willing to pursue a political career—the sycophants and the political adventurers. High risk favors the cautious sycophants who are flexible in pursuing safety and opportunity, fearing the severe sanctions that disfavor brings. Since vacancies are filled primarily by cooptations, they seek advancement by courting those in power. As a result, political aspirants practice a kind of "mini-maxing" behavior, trying to minimize losses rather than seeking great rewards at high risk. For these reasons a common complaint against politicians in developing countries is their diffidence and reluctance to demonstrate initiative.

Where politics is an all-or-nothing struggle, some will react with fearful conformity, others will react with devil-may-care conduct. High risk also encourages an opposite type, the political demagogue and adventurer. The latter views politics as mortal combat between good and evil (with no compromise possible), and between the oppressed, the citizen, and the governing elite. In such a context, the populist agitator arises who calls for struggles against all politicians —an appeal which reaches the sympathetic ears of those disaffected with the privileged status of political elites. Thus, the conditions of high risk and uncertainties encourages the rejected but ambitious political adventurer who seeks high stakes and risks his safety in the process. Restricted opportunity, high rewards of success, and high costs of failure encourage such political adventurers.

THE HIGH STATUS AND REWARDS OF POLITICAL ROLES

With the achievement of independence in many non-Western systems, new political institutions and political roles were created. Such roles bestowed high status, income, and privileges. "The MPs, business, military officers, and high civil servants who constitute the political elite enjoy special privileges. These include a cosmopolitan social life, untaxed fringe benefits and allowances, preferential access to loans, investment opportunities, avenues and overseas trips. The business ethic pervades this group to the extent that civil servants are often accused of being too busy with their own business to work, and MPs are characterized as opportunists" (Hopkins, 1975). In the Ivory Coast "the Assembly established for itself and for the government the highest salary scale in all of French West Africa including land grants, substantial credit on the part of European firms, the use of private automobiles, civil honors, and trips to Paris at public expense" (Zolberg, 1964: 193).

Political roles are the prime avenue to high status and to social and economic mobility. The "primacy of politics" produces many aspirants to government positions (Spiro, 1966: 152). High income positions are not available in a variety of structures as they are in industrialized societies, according to Hopkins' (1975) observations of Kenya and Styskal's (1975) of the Philippines. The high rewards of political posts makes losing them and the fear of losing them of constant concern to the office holders. High career risk is, therefore, associated with high rewards in political positions relative to positions in private occupations. The legislative position is also a major stepping stone in a political career because it is a forum for the establishment of a national reputation. "In Liberia, a legislator may go to the Supreme Court, and ambassadorship, the cabinet, or as high as the Presidency" (Liebenow, 1962: 357).

Because so many individuals seek political roles, the career of the elective officials lacks coherent structure. Roles are new and the progression of statuses is unclear. Frequent upgrading and down-grading of roles and individuals make the paths of mobility uncertain. Political roles are not structured in a pattern of orderly progression, so when an individual is shifted from one position to another, which happens quite often, it is not clear whether the direction of such mobility is up, down, or lateral.

POLITICAL OPPORTUNITY

In non-Western nations candidates for the legislatures are recruited from a privileged stratum, the educated middle class. In this respect they do not differ from the legislators of Western countries. But, a significant difference is the smaller percentage of businessmen, lawyers, and liberal professions in the ranks of legislators in non-Western nations (Schulz, 1973: 575-85). Such restrictive polit-ical opportunity is the result of restricted opportunities for edu-cation and political sponsorship.

Only a small percentage of the population, descendants of upper and middle class families, have had opportunities for higher education. The traditional social stratification based on ascription continues, despite the constitutional rights of equal political participation. Only the privileged were permitted to become educated, and where higher education was provided within the country, only sons of families of public servants and some professionals were admitted. The pool of eligible politicians is further restricted by the social stratification of tribal, religious, and linguistic groups.

A significant factor which restricts candidacy for the legislature is the restricted number of group sponsors of candidates. Mezey (1975) points out that in Thailand autonomous private associations are either not permitted or are inert. Private financial support for such associations do not exist. The small size of the middle class limits the strength of such organizations. The absence of a tradition of group activity and legal constitutional restrictions also inhibit autonomous private associations. Only government sponsored business, labor, and farm groups are permitted. The only effective sponsors are those that have some government connections, and effective candidacy for office depends upon whom they favor. Even in countries where more than one party is permitted, the government party often has disproportionate controls over the mass media, the use of public meeting places, and other political resources.

SELECTION TO LEGISLATIVE POSITIONS

Little is known about the processes of selection to legislative positions in non-Western nations. The deliberations and negotiations of party leaders when nomination decisions are made are secret. Public disclosure of the selection process would broaden the scope of conflict, invite public involvement, and threaten the oligarchical structure of politics. Moreover, the disclosure of the delicate negotiations could heighten the tensions among rival cliques and factions. Commonly, the choice of nominees for the legislature is in most instances a foregone conclusion, so few observers have been interested in investigating the subject. What we know about the selection processes we have learned from information gathered indirectly and from the shrewd inferences of perceptive observers.

The parliaments of twelve countries in Africa that were granted independence from Great Britain were studied (the study was conducted from March 1957 to October 1966; see Stultz, 1968: 479-83). Each of these states established a parliament which imitated the English model, except that a single house was created in most cases. Popular election from single member constituencies is the prevailing mode of recruitment to parliamentary office. Although the vast majority of members of these parliaments are popularly elected, in seven parliaments some 15% of the MPs owe their positions to direct executive appointment, rather than to popular election. In this way the executive bolsters his majority or brings people of special talent to the legislature and exercises his prerogative to grant legislative representation to particular groups, such as women, farmers, trade unionists, and other groups he may favor.

In single party regimes selection is used to coopt representatives from groups which are loyal to the regime or which make the regime appear broadly representative. (The recruitment strategy is variable —at times to coopt, at others to expel, elevate or demote particular elements in order to sustain support for the party and the regime.)

One party regimes control the paths to all political positions. The Egyptian constitution of 1964 specified that a single organization, "The National Union," has exclusive authority to nominate candidates for the National Assembly (Binder, 1965: 138). In the Ivory Coast, another one party state, no African can be elected without the endorsement of the PDCI (Zolberg, 1964: 193). Without such absolute control over selection, the party and regime would lose power.

Zolberg has described recruitment processes in the Ivory Coast. Some competition for nominations to the Parliament is permitted within the single party, the Parti Democratique de la Cote d'Ivoire. This ensures responsiveness to the demands of various groups in the population and widens the base of popular support for the party.

> This process of nomination within the party is not public. In theory, candidates are chosen by the general secretaries of the party, and by other major groups that participate in the coalition at the time of the election under consideration, then submitted to the Bureau Politique for final approval (Zolberg, 1964: 272).

In practice, the inner circle of the regime retains control over the entire process. The party officially encourages a certain group of eligibles, but the decisions regarding final selection are centralized in the top leadership of the party and the regime. Local party units are informed in advance of the number of places their region will have on the ticket and are then told to draw up a list of candidates for these places in order of preference. It was estimated in 1969 that between 800 and 1,000 men were competing for 100 seats in the Legislative Assembly. Since this number includes almost everyone in the Ivory Coast who might possibly hope to be a candidate, the Bureau Politique seldom needs to look elsewhere for the candidates it wants. Houphouet-Boigny, president of the Ivory Coast and leader of the PDIC, exercises great control over the nominating process. "The general secretaries of the party . . . heard his recommendations and then approved a motion to give him and the Bureau Politique full authority to draw up the slate" (Zolberg, 1964: 274).

The selection process of legislators in the Ivory Coast resembled the process in Ghana (Kraus, 1969: 35). In the last years of the Nkrumah regime, the selection of candidates for Parliament was controlled by the Convention People's Party (CPP), the ruling party. Party leaders made up the slate by bargaining among local factions, local groups, and the central authorities. The selection of parliamentary candidates was a ritual that ensured positions only to the sycophants of Nkrumah. The MPs of the CPP could no longer be said to be directly representative of the electorate. The last general election was held in 1956. Candidates thereafter were selected and approved by the central committee and then declared elected unopposed. At the height of Nkrumah's power, officials or any individuals who were regarded as unfriendly to the regime could be placed in detention, so it took a brave man to challenge the governing party by standing for election.

In the dominant party regimes, the candidates of the dominant party must compete with candidates of the other parties. To offset such competition, dominant parties build a broad coalition of interests that will ensure a majority. Thus, in India, where there is a dominant party regime, attempts are made to select candidates representative of a broad spectrum of the voter. India is a federal state; accordingly, the Congress Party is organized in the states, districts, and localities. The nominations of candidates for parliament in the Congress Party generate intense factional conflicts on the local level. Weiner (1967: 88) describes such an instance in the Kara district:

> The congress party is in theory a highly centralized organization. . . . The Congress Election Committee in New Delhi, a sub-committee of the Working Committee, has the final authority for selecting Congress

candidates not only to parliament but to all the state legislative assemblies. Recommendations for parliamentary and assembly tickets are made on the state level by the Pradesh election committee of the Pradesh Congress Committee. In practice, unless there is a major disagreement with the PCC, the Congress Central Election Committee in New Delhi accepts the PCC's recommendations.

In Kenya, the governing party is weak and does not control selection to the Parliament. Some candidates represent personal machines and patrons in particular districts. The president often sponsors candidates to coopt individuals whom he wishes to groom or test for high posts, or who will give some symbolic representation to some groups (Hopkins, 1975).

In sum, in single party states, the top leadership controls the selection of legislators. The party coopts all the officials, mindful that the officials must seem "representative," at least if the regime is to retain public support. In the dominant party regimes, elections to the Parliament permit competition among several parties. Nevertheless, the dominant party is better organized than its competitors and commands governmental resources which makes it difficult for the lesser parties to mount a serious challenge. In effect, the lesser parties become pressure groups that influence the composition of the coalition of candidates the dominant party will present.

RECRUITMENT RISK AND LEGISLATIVE BEHAVIOR

The high risk of recruitment and the political career influences legislative performance. Since political office is the principal means of gaining wealth, those with professional and technical skills depend almost exclusively on government employment. The number who seek government positions far exceeds the number of vacancies. As a result, officials who make appointments have great control over those who seek positions because applicants and officials have no alternate employment opportunities. When officials are dismissed or made redundant, they are often forced to take positions much below their former status and income.

The effect of recruitment sponsorship is suggested in C. L. Kim and Woo's study in Korea (1975). They found that sponsorship (associated with other factors) was related to both the role style and role behavior of legislators. Those legislators who were sponsored were more likely to take delegate roles than those who were not. To be sure, the type of district, the winning margin of the successful candidate, and the length of time in politics also affected role behavior. But, sponsorship was a salient factor.

Additional light is shed on sponsorship in the studies of Goodman on South Vietnam (1975) and Mezey on Thailand (1975). In both countries the legislator's primary task is to serve as a channel for distributing government partronage, licenses and other factors to his constituency. The legislator's service to his constituency is dissociated from his role in the parliament. If the legislator nurtures his constituency, he remains in office; if he fails to do that, he will be displaced. Quite arbitrarily, the government in Thailand may drop a candidate from their list and then, shorn of access to government resources, the ex-legislator faces the loss of all status.

High risk in legislative positions leads to nepotism, cliquism, corruption, and "empire building" (Nye, 1967: 418). Each of these practices protects against high recruitment and career risk. Such practices are neither unique nor of recent origins in non-Western nations. Such practices interfere with the achievement of the goals of modernization, integration, and economic development.

High risk without cushions for the legislator is characteristic of many non-Western systems. Ironically, in some Latin American countries where regimes are frequently overthrown, institutional safeguards are set up to protect ousted political victims (Scott, 1967: 126). Latin American governments recognize the right of asylum and provide a kind of life insurance that reduces the number of deaths caused by revolution. Top level corruption also serves as a cushion which enables officials to put money away in Swiss banks or foreign investments. In addition, strong kinship ties, a sense of class identification, and colleagueship among officials offer some protections against the vicissitudes of politics (Silvert, 1961: 11).

Institutionalized cushions in dominant party regimes resemble those used in democratic systems. Political positions are found for the incompetent, the trouble makers and the superannuated (Mazrui, 1968: 81-96). By expanding the number of political roles, honorific "Siberias" and sinecures are found for the demoted. The India Congress Party has provided cushions through expanding the number of political positions. New echelons of elective and appointive positions on the state and local levels have created places for those on the way down and provided new rungs lower on the political ladder for those on the way up (Weiner, 1967: 86). Thus, opportunities were created for potential elite members and cushions provided for the downwardly mobile and disaffected. These cushions also increased recruitment incentives for newer elite members by reducing the hazards of failure and the costs attendant on changes in political fortunes. Moreover, a large number of roles makes politics more accommodative to the variety of aspiration levels.

CONCLUSION

The concept of political risk has been applied to recruitment and political career and its effect on the conduct of legislators in non-Western systems. Our hypothesis has been that political risk in recruitment and in the careers of Western legislators is insurable and, therefore, sustains democracy, whereas, risk in non-Western systems is more uninsurable and contributes to oligarchy. Moreover, greater uncertainty as to outcomes prevails in non-Western systems. The concept of political risk has not been investigated empirically in non-Western or Western countries, although several studies in this symposium have alluded to the egregious insecurity and political vulnerability of non-Western legislators.

We have discussed risk as a determinant, rather than as a dependent variable. Politicians who are defeated in non-Western systems suffer more severe threats and deprivations than their counterparts in Western systems. Adequate cushions for failure are not available because of the concentration of power in the executive and bureaucracy, the halting economic progress, and conflicting political legitimations.

Great social and political distance between the political elites and the masses is characteristic in non-Western systems. Political risk contributes to that because it fosters elite corruption and indifference to public opinion. High risk prevents the development of some of the corrective processes that operate in Western democratic countries, and weakens restraints in political roles that make elites responsive and accountable. Further, high political risk stands in the way of constructive opposition, autonomous associations, and the free expression of public opinion. The role behavior that high risk encourages becomes role models for new and younger political aspirants to emulate. The conditions that give rise to high political risk are thus aggravated and self-perpetuating.

NOTE

1. When applied to a category so broad as "non-Western countries," the concept of political risk can be no more than a suggestion for further investigation. The concept of political risk, I believe, can be measured with objective data as well as perceptual data much the same as the probabilities of electoral success are measured through aggregate or survey data wherever feasible.

REFERENCES

BAUMOL, W. J. (1965) Economic Theory and Operations Analysis. 2d ed. Englewood Cliffs, N.J.: Prentice-Hall.

BINDER, L. (1965) "Political recruitment and participation in Egypt," in La Palombara and M. Weiner (eds.) Political Parties and Political Development. Princeton: Princeton Univ. Press.

DAALDER, H. (1966) "Government and opposition in the new states," Government and Opposition I (February): 208-35).

DAHL, R. [ed.] (1966) Political Oppositions in Western Democracies. New Haven: Yale Univ. Press.

EULAU, H. and J. D. SPRAGUE (1964) Lawyers and Politics. Indianapolis: Bobbs-Merrill.

FRIEDMAN, M. and L. J. SAVAGE (1948) "The utility analysis in choices involving risk." J. of Political Economy 56, 4: 279-304.

GOODMAN, A. E. (1975) "Correlates of legislative constituency service in South Vietnam," pp. 181-205 in G. R. Boynton and C. L. Kim (eds.) Legislative Systems in Developing Countries.

GOODMAN, P. (1967) "The first American party system," in W. N. Chambers and W. D. Burnham (eds.) The American Party Systems. New York: Oxford Univ. Press.

HAMMOND, J. D. (1968) Essays in the Theory of Risk and Insurance. Glenview, Ill.: Scott Foresman.

HOFSTADTER, R. (1969) The Idea of a Party System. Berkeley and Los Angeles: Univ. of California Press.

HOPKINS, R. F. (1975) "The Kenyan legislature: political functions and citizen perceptions," pp. 207-231 in G. R. Boynton and C. L. Kim (eds.) Legislative Systems in Developing Countries.

HOSKIN, G. (1975) "Dimensions of conflict in the Colombian national legislature," pp. 143-178 in G. R. Boynton and C. L. Kim (eds.) Legislative Systems in Developing Countries.

KIM, C. L. and B. WOO (1975) "Political representation in the Korean national assembly," pp. 261-286 in G. R. Boynton and C. L. Kim (eds.) Legislative Systems in Developing Countries.

KIM, C. L. (1970) "Social and political background of Korean legislators." Iowa City: University of Iowa, Laboratory for Political Research.

KRAUS, I. (1969) "On the Politics of Nationalism and Social 'Change' in Ghana." J. of Modern African Studies VII, 1.

LIEBENOW, J. G. (1962) "Liberia," in G. Carter (ed.) African One Party States. Ithaca, N.Y.: Cornell Univ. Press.

MARVICK, D. (1965) "African university students: a presumptive elite," pp. 463-97 in J. Coleman (ed.) Education and Political Development. Princeton: Princeton Univ. Press.

MAZRUI, A. (1968) "Political superannuation and the transclass man." International J. of Comparative Sociology IX, 2: 81-96.

MEZEY, M. L. (1975) "Legislative development and political parties: the case of Thailand," pp. 107-141 in G. R. Boynton and C. L. Kim (eds.) Legislative Systems in Developing Countries.

NYE, J. S. (1967) "Corruption and political development: a cost-benefit analysis." American Political Science Rev. LXI (June).

PACKENHAM, R. A. (1970) "Legislatures and political development," in A. Kornberg and L. D. Musolf (eds.) Legislatures in Developmental Perspective. Durham, N.C.: Duke Univ. Press.

ROKKAN, S. (1968) Party Systems, Party Organizations and the Politics of New Masses. Berlin: Institut für politische Wissenschaft an der Freien Universität Berlin.

SCHLESINGER, J. A. (1957) "Lawyers and American politics: a clarified view," Midwest J. of Political Science I: 26-39.

SCHULZ, A. T. (1973) "A cross-national examination of legislators VII" J. of Developing Areas (July): 571-90.

SCOTT, R. (1967) "Political elites and political modernization: the crisis of transition," in S. M. Lipset and A. Solari (eds.) Elites in Latin America. New York: Oxford Univ. Press.

SELIGMAN, L. G. (1970) Recruiting Political Elites. New York: General Learning Press.

——— (1967) "Political parties and the recruitment of political leadership," pp. 304-306 in L. J. Lewis (ed.) Political Leadership in Industrialized Societies. New York: John Wiley.

SILVERT, K. (1961) The Conflict Society. New York: Harper & Row.

SINGHVI, L. M. (1970) "Parliament in the Indian political system," in A. Kornberg and L. Musolf (eds.) Legislatures in Developmental Perspective. Durham, N.C.: Duke Univ. Press.

SPIRO, H. (1966) Africa: The Primacy of Politics. New York: Random House.

STULTZ, N. M. (1968) "Parliaments in former Black Africa." J. of Developing Areas II (July): 479-93.

STYSKAL, R. A. (1975) "Some aspects of group representation in the Philippine congress," pp. 233-259 in G. R. Boynton and C. L. Kim (eds.) Legislative Systems in Developing Countries.

WEINER, M. (1967) Party Building in a New Nation. Chicago: Univ. of Chicago Press.

——— (1966) Modernization: The Dynamics of Growth. New York: Basic Books.

ZOLBERG, A. (1964) One Party Government on the Ivory Coast. Princeton: Princeton Univ. Press.

LESTER G. SELIGMAN is Professor of Political Science at the University of Illinois at Urbana. He is the author of *Leadership in a New Nation* (1964), and co-author of *Patterns of Recruitment* (1974) and *New Deal Mosaic* (1965). He has contributed to the *International Encyclopedia of the Social Sciences* and has written numerous articles on leadership, elites, and the presidency. Currently, he is conducting research on the recruitment of political elites in the United States and other countries.

Chapter 5

LEGISLATIVE DEVELOPMENT AND POLITICAL PARTIES: THE CASE OF THAILAND

M I C H A E L   L.   M E Z E Y

University of Hawaii

The simple thesis of this discussion is that party strength and legislative strength are interdependent. The relation between the two can be approximated by the curve shown in Figure 1; that is, legislatures will be weak in systems with the very strongest and the very weakest political parties, and legislatures will be strongest in systems with political parties of only moderate strength. These are parties strong enough to support the legislative institution, but not strong enough to dominate it.

This thesis is based upon a particular understanding of the relation between parties and legislative institutions in both Western and non-Western political systems. In the Western experience, party organizations developed in close association with legislative institutions. In some cases, intra-governmental party groupings first

AUTHOR'S NOTE: This paper originally was prepared for delivery at the Shambaugh Conference on Legislatures in Developing Countries, University of Iowa, Iowa City, November 1971. The research on which this analysis is based was carried out while I was a Visiting Professor in the Faculty of Political Science, Thammasat University, Bangkok, Thailand. My stay at Thammasat was made possible by a grant from the Rockefeller Foundation's University Development Program to the University of Virginia. Also, I am grateful to the Foundation and to the University of Virginia for a further grant for the summer of 1971, during which this paper was drafted. My thanks also to the Social Science Research Institute, University of Hawaii, for typing assistance.

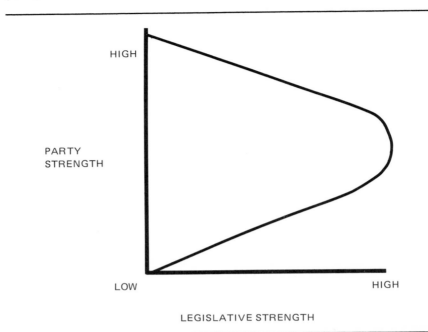

LEGISLATIVE STRENGTH

Figure 1: THE RELATIONSHIP BETWEEN PARTY STRENGTH AND LEGISLATIVE STRENGTH

formed within the legislature to facilitate common action among like-minded legislators. Alternatively, extra-governmental organizations were formed first, to mobilize the electorate in order to produce electoral and then legislative majorities.[1] The modern political party, composed of both intra- and extra-governmental organizations, was instrumental in establishing and protecting the prerogatives of the legislature against the executive.

The claim of a legislature to control the actions of an executive depends upon the assumption that the legislature represents a larger public to which governmental power is supposed to be held responsible.[2] The external party organizations facilitate the connection between this broader public and the legislature, and can marshall support for the legislature when it is required. The intra-governmental organizations require the executive to confront the legislators in groups rather than individually, making it more difficult for the executive to coopt the legislator for its own purposes. Without such parties, legislatures remain weak compared to the executive power.

It is apparent that there is a point beyond which increases in party strength are not necessarily salutary for the legislature. Party strength may increase at the expense of the legislature; that is, very strong political parties will tend to coopt the legislators and the prerogatives of their institution, and thus subordinate the legislature. It often has been suggested that in Western systems strong political parties have led to the "decline" of the legislature. A more extreme situation is the one-party state in which the legislature may be simply a benign appendage to the government. Aside from authoritarian one-party systems, this type of party domination of the legislature is probable in non-Western nations where parties commonly developed apart from and prior to legislative institutions, most likely as instruments of mass mobilization for the achievement of national independence.

INDICATORS OF LEGISLATIVE AND PARTY STRENGTH

In assessing the strength of a legislature at least two factors should be considered: its prominence in the decision-making process, and the support that it can command from the members of the political system. Sophisticated measures for these two dimensions are not available on a cross-national basis;[3] for now, certain questions can be posed, the answers to which will suggest the things that should be measured:

First, is the legislative process central to or incidental to the decision-making process of the political system? Is the legislature the place where the "action" takes place, or simply a legitimizing arena for decisions taken in other forums?

Second, can proposed legislation be freely accepted, amended, or rejected by the legislature no matter who has initiated the proposal?

Third, can the legislature exercise real and substantial control over those who make decisions in the executive branch of government?

Fourth, if other elements in the political system threaten the existence or the prerogatives of the legislature, will counter-forces be generated to oppose such steps?

Fifth, are actions of the legislature considered legitimate by the public at large as well as by the important attentive groups in the system?

The answers to these questions that would distinguish an unambiguously strong legislature from a clearly weak legislature are obvious; relatively sophisticated measurement techniques would be required to determine degrees of difference between legislatures which fall between the extreme.

For political parties, five criteria of party strength can be identified. One criterion, originally formulated by Weber (1946: 102-107) is the extent to which the party is identified with a particular leader. Weber's "aristocratic cliques" were dependent upon a central personality or family and disappeared when these individuals left the political arena. More recently, Huntington (1968: 409) has suggested that "the strength of a political party is measured . . . by its ability to survive its founder or the charismatic leader who first brings it to power." If a party disappears when its leader passes from the scene, this implies a highly personalized and, therefore, a very weak party. If leadership can be successfully transferred from one to another, this indicates a stronger party. A second criterion of party strength, suggested by Chambers (1963: 45-50), is the existence of a party structure—defined as a relatively durable, regularized, and stable connection between active leaders and followers. Such structures can be contrasted with highly transient factions which usually form prior to elections and disband shortly thereafter.

A third criterion of party strength is the complexity of the party organization; according to Huntington (1968: 410), organizational complexity refers to he linkages between the party structure and both socioeconomic organizations and voters. Strong parties have complex organizations connecting them with the rest of the participants in the political system; weak factional groupings are simply organized and only loosely related to other societal groups or to mass electorates.

A fourth criterion of party strength is the nature of the party following. Chambers (1963: 47) suggests that strong political parties exhibit a greater range, density, and stability of support than factions. To extend this criterion somewhat, the strength of a party reaches a peak when it monopolizes power in a political system to the extent that it drives other party organizations out of the political arena. By this criterion, parties that are part of a multi-party system in which no party can claim a majority following are weaker than parties in a two-party system, which are weaker than single parties operating without opposition.[4]

A fifth criterion of party strength (Chambers, 1963) is evidence that the party is performing key political functions such as nominating candidates, campaigning in the electoral arena, undertaking management of the government, providing connections among government decision-making, acting as brokers among the interests of various groups, and formulating comprehensive statements of issues, positions, and policies. Huntington (1968: 412) adds the further political function, particularly important in developing systems, of moderating and channeling the participation of newly mobilized groups in such a manner as not to disrupt the system. Although weak parties perform these functions to some extent, the strong party undertakes them in a relatively continuous, coordinated, and visible fashion.

These indicators form the framework for the following analysis of the relation between party and legislative strength in the political system of Thailand.[5]

THE LEGISLATURE IN THAILAND

THE HISTORICAL CONTEXT

An awareness of certain historical facts is essential to an understanding of the position of the legislative institution in Thailand. First, through a combination of skill and good fortune, Thailand was never colonized by a European power. This situation is a source of great and understandable national pride; however, its political consequences have not been fully appreciated. No tutorial parliamentary institutions were established by a colonial power; the educated elite never had the opportunity to play the frustrating but politically socializing game of limited self-government under European aegis. Perhaps more important than this was the fact that the Thais were deprived of their revolution. In other parts of Asia and Africa, the overthrow of colonialism was a catalytic experience in which a previously parochial people were suddenly politicized, mobilized, and confronted with demands that they become political participants. Because this did not happen in Thailand, when legislative institutions and the associated electoral machinery were established, the techniques and attitudes appropriate to the operation of such institutions were missing from all but a very small part of the elite.

Constitutional government came to Thailand quite abruptly, in June 1932, when a group of Western-educated civil servants and junior military officers ended an absolute monarchy that had existed under different dynasties since the fourteenth century. Although a few of the civilian leaders of the coup spoke the jargon of constitutional democracy, the establishment of such a governmental system was not a primary goal of those who made the coup. Rather they were discontented with the monopoly of high government positions by royal relatives and with the cutbacks in government personnel and salaries necessitated by the world depression.

The coup was not a popular uprising against the absolute monarchy; it was in no sense a revolt of the masses aimed at establishing popular control over government power. The best evidence is that the great mass of the people living in the countryside were unaware that any change in government had taken place. As Coast (1953: 5) noted: "No famines or war drove the Siamese peasants to seek the reason why; they had enough, they were content. They were completely ignorant of the world outside their provinces." (Also see Landon, 1939: 25.)

In sum, then, the circumstances surrounding the creation of constitutional government in Thailand were not of the type that spawns either strong political parties or strong parliamentary institutions. It was not the displacement of an authoritarian colonial power by a popular nationalist movement characterized by democratic aspirations. It was not the culmination of a gradual shift of power from the monarchy to elected politicians centered in a representative body. On the contrary, those who assumed power came from the bureaucracy and the military—two elements of the political system traditionally hostile to the legislature.

The primary concern of this civil-military coalition was to establish a governmental system that they, as the new custodians of the nation, would continue to control. The creation of democratic constitutional machinery was peripheral to this major goal. The leaders of the coup assumed the executive power, dividing ministries and cabinet seats among themselves in proportion to the strength of the various cliques within their coalition. The National Assembly was to be composed of supporters of the coup leaders, but all the powerful and prestigous members of the coup group were in the Cabinet.

This early precedent for government was to become institutionalized in Thailand. Throughout the post-1932 constitutional period the executive has been the presumptive holder of power and it has been assumed that the legislature would play a supporting and subordinate role. The composition of the government has been decided by the power conflicts among the various executive cliques; the results of such conflicts have been imposed upon the Assembly.

In this context, the strength of the legislature has varied inversely with the strength of the government; the strength of the government, in turn, is determined by the unity of its members. Divisions within the governing circle weaken the executive and provide an occasion for the temporary rise of legislative power. The members of the Assembly take sides in these intra-governmental conflicts, and dissident factions within the government may use these Assembly supporters to obstruct and embarrass those in power.

At such times, the prominence of the legislature is at its zenith; in the end, however, the conflict is resolved by various techniques within the executive, and not within parliament. Then those who have come to power consolidate their positions and the prominence of the legislature recedes. The vital point is that this ebb and flow of legislative power is orchestrated by forces outside the legislature; they create the conditions for the exercise of legislative power and they call a halt when the conditions change.[6]

METHODS OF EXECUTIVE CONTROL

There are multiple methods at the disposal of the executive to be used for exercising control of the legislature. Manipulation of constitutional provisions relevant to the legislature has been an often-employed instrument. As Wilson (1962a: 253-273) has noted, in Thailand the conflicts among the various military and bureaucratic cliques usually culminate in a coup d'etat and the forming of a new constitution to mark the victory and protect the position of those who have come to power. Consequently, in the 40 years since the 1932 coup, Thailand has operated under six "permanent" and two provisional constitutional schemes. A change in the legislative structure has been a part of each constitutional alteration; its purpose is to ensure that a substantial number of the members of the institution will owe their first allegiance to the group in control of the executive.

Such provisions have always involved the designation of a group of appointed legislators to share power with the elected members. The 1932 constitution, promulgated by the original coup group, provided for a unicameral legislature composed equally of members elected by the people and members appointed by the government. A ten-year transition period to a fully elected legislature was provided, but the process was never completed.

When government power temporarily changed hands at the end of

World War II, the new leaders produced a constitution calling for an upper house of the legislature to be composed of members chosen by the elected lower house. Because this particular government commanded an overwhelming majority in the lower house, the upper house predictably was packed with government supporters. The constitution further provided that the terms of the members of the upper house would overlap those of the elected members, thereby insulating the government from any prospective electoral reverse (see Vella, 1955: 387-390).

This safeguard was never needed because 18 months after this constitution was promulgated, a coup ousted its authors and established a different group in power. The constitution of 1949, which they wrote, provided for a Senate to be composed of people appointed by the King; the reason for this was that this government was in favor with the Crown and they felt that their contacts with the throne would ensure that their supporters would be appointed to the Senate. This constitution lasted three years, until 1951 when it was abrogated by another coup and replaced by a modified version of the 1932 constitution. There was to be an elected lower house and an upper house appointed by the government (as opposed to the 1932 unicameral model) and another ten-year transition period to a fully elected legislature was provided. Under this document, the existing upper house was replaced with one composed of supporters of those who had engineered the 1951 coup.

The Sarit coup of October 1958 ended this constitutional scheme and instituted an interim constitution. This "interim" lasted ten years; during this period, parties, elections, and the legislature were dispensed with. A constituent Assembly, appointed in its entirety by the government, was to draft a new constitution and perform the functions of the legislature. This was the first time since 1932 that Thailand had no legislators elected by popular vote.

The most recent constitution promulgated in June 1968, and suspended by the November 1971 coup, provided for an upper house (Senate) appointed by the King upon nomination by the government. Although ultimate legislative authority was vested in the elected House of Representatives, the upper house participated in all votes of confidence, thus ensuring the government's position. (Constitution of the Kingdom of Thailand, 1968: sections 127, 128, 137, 139, 141.)

Obviously these constitutional machinations are but the visible end product of a more decisive process for the changing of leaders—the coup d'etat. Fourteen major attempted coups can be identified between 1932 and 1971; eight of these led directly to a change in the dominant governing group (Wilson, 1962a: 283-284). The coup has been the instrument through which the armed forces have gained undisputed ascendancy over both its civilian-bureaucratic governing partners and the legislature. Command of the army, and particularly the Bangkok garrison, has been the traditional stepping-stone to political power. Once in power, the strong head of government will concurrently hold the portfolio of minister of defense; the failure to do this is an unmistakable sign of weakness (Wilson, 1962b: 253-276).

Often the actions of the legislature are cited as part of the justification for the coup. As suggested earlier, dissident elements within the governing circle may covertly instigate obstructionist activities in the legislature and then point to the government's inability to deal with the legislature as a sign of its weakness. In the period preceding the coup of 1958, General Sarit, who was to lead the coup, openly encourged parliamentary opposition to the prime minister while he was serving as defense minister. After taking power and abolishing the legislature, he noted in justification of his actions that "the garb of democracy was weighing down Thailand." His protege and minister of foreign affairs, Thanat Khoman, said in a speech to an American group that "the fundamental cause [of unstable governments in the past] for many of us, lies in the sudden transplantation of alien institutions on our soil without careful preparation and more particularly without regard to the circumstances which prevail in our homeland" (Darling, 1960: 352-356).

Alternatively, charges of corruption are leveled against "politicians" by those who make the coup. Those who led the 1947 coup, which ended a period of parliamentary prominence, indicated that they were motivated by the corruption that they felt was rampant in the country (Coast, 1953: 39). Eleven years later, Thanat Khoman justified Sarit's suspension of the legislature in the following terms (Darling, 1960: 356):

> How can representative government function if those who are elected to represent the people in the National Assembly forget the interest of the country as a whole and pursue only their selfish gains? More particularly, how can the electorate hope to choose representatives worthy of their trust if it is hardly able to distinguish between promises of an election campaign and the genuine determination to carry out a national program and to uphold political ideals?[7]

Thus it is common in Thailand to connect coups with legislative performance. In a New Year's Day editorial in January 1970, the influential Siam Rath (Jan. 1, 1970) expressed the hope "that the MPs will improve their conduct and that a coup will not take place in Thailand in 1970."

Sometimes the threat of a coup is as potent as the actual fact in encouraging the legislature to go along with the government. Prime Minister Pibul, at the height of his power in the late thirties, would ring the Assembly chamber with "protective troops" when important issues were to come up for a vote (Vella, 1955: 386). Another illustration is provided by the events following the military coup of 1947. Immediately after the coup the military leaders thought if expedient to ask a civilian, Khuang Aphaiwongse, who was popular in the Assembly and not associated with the military, to become prime minister. Clearly the military's purpose was to exploit Khuang's reputation during a period in which they wanted to consolidate their power. Khuang agreed, primarily because he was confronted with the choice of either collaborating with the military and exercising some power, or precipitating another coup that would result in no influence at all for him or his followers.

New elections were held, and Khuang and his followers achieved a large majority in the House of Representatives; his government was given a convincing vote of confidence by the Assembly. Three months later, the coup group, their power firmly established, decided to replace Khuang. He was told to resign or face overt military action. After consulting with various military leaders and determining that almost no one would support him in a showdown, he resigned without even consulting the parliament, ostensibly the source of his original mandate. The Assembly, confronted with the same realities as Khuang, then gave a vote of confidence to the military government that came to power (Coast, 1953: 41-46).

Incidents from the most recent constitutional period also can be cited. In 1970 the House of Representatives sought permission from the government to hold a general debate on the government's performance. The government refused on national security grounds. During the controversy, a government party MP close to the military leadership warned against opposition leaders who might "incite riots and disunity inside the country." He recalled that previously "revolutions or coups had taken place after general debates in the House," and that if the "present democratic form of government were changed because of disunity and disorders in the country," the opposition legislators would be responsible (Siam Rath, July 28, 1970).

In July 1970 government leaders reacted in a similar manner when confronted with legislative opposition to some unpopular tax increases. Prior to the critical first reading vote, the army in Bangkok was put on alert, ostensibly because a major Communist head-quarters had been discovered in the city and the situation, in the view of the government, was becoming increasingly dangerous. One newspaper reported a secret meeting of military leaders in which it was agreed to revoke the constitution should the tax bill fail in the House, and government leaders walked the corridors saying essentially the same thing to the legislators. In this context, the bill passed by one vote, the army alert was canceled, and tensions relaxed.

Incidents such as these indicate the atmosphere in which the Thai National Assembly has operated. Often the members are confronted with the choice of exercising marginal power while cooperating with the government, or persisting in more serious opposition and facing dissolution and a complete loss of power. The incidents just discussed here occurred at times when the legislature has exercised slightly more than minimal influence on government policy-making; its choice is to either push for more and probably confront military force, or to accept a marginal role and retreat when confronted by a firm government.

The government also has offered other inducements for legislative cooperation. Some have been negative; at various periods in Thai history legislators have been jailed and sometimes executed on charges of treasonous activity. For obvious reasons, however, the government prefers to use more subtle means. Under General Pibul's prewar government, patronage was extensively employed to encourage support for the government. At various times it has been suggested that government supporters in the Assembly have received payments above and beyond their normal salary. At the beginning of the most recent legislature, there were rumors, denied all around, that the government had allocated a certain amount of money for each of its supporters in the legislature for the payment of campaign debts. It is clear that the passage of the first budget bill to be dealt with by the new legislature was facilitated when government supporters were promised additional funds for development of their constituencies, with the MPs participating in decisions concerning their disbursal.[8]

THE LEGISLATURE IN THAILAND: AN ASSESSMENT

This brief analysis of the relation between the Thai National Assembly and its political environment forms the basis for an assessment of the strength of the legislative institution in Thailand. As suggested at the outset, the strength of the legislature can be measured on two dimensions: the prominence of the legislature in the rule-making process, and the support that the legislature can command from the public at large.

Throughout its history the legislature in Thailand usually has been incidental to a decision-making process controlled by the government of the day. The Cabinet has made the essential decisions and the legislature has been asked to ratify them; this applies to substantive issues as well as issues concerning the composition of the executive.

From time to time the legislature has been able to exercise some marginal influence on decision-making. During the first decade of constitutional government there were a few occasions on which an adverse vote in the legislature contributed to a minor shift in executive personnel (Thompson, 1941: 89-97). This happened somewhat more frequently during the so-called liberal period following the war, but only rarely since. This marginal exercise of legislative power has been in connection with executive oversight rather than law-making activities. In an earlier analysis (Mezey, 1973), it was demonstrated that the Thai legislator viewed the control of the executive as his and his institution's most significant function; few members perceived their role as one of developing solutions to the problems that confronted the nation.[9]

However, all this has occurred under the auspices of the government; through its control of the appointed members and its implicit and omnipresent threat of the coup, the government always has had the capacity to compel legislative compliance when it has chosen to do so. The only times that this did not necessarily obtain was in those periods when the government was severely divided. Then, contesting members of the government chose to play the parliamentary game in the hope of gaining advantage. Two episodes serve to illustrate the situation.

Three and a half years after the 1951 coup had severely reduced the power of the parliament, Prime Minister Pibul came back to Bangkok from a world tour. Presumably he was so impressed with the democratic procedures that he had seen in countries such as Britain and the United States that he decided to institute democratic reforms in Thailand. Shortly thereafter, a law was enacted legalizing political parties, elections were scheduled, a "Hyde Park" style forum was established to which all were invited to express their views freely, and the prime minister consented to holding regular press conferences (Berrigan, 1956; Pickerell and Moore, 1957; Wilson and Phillips, 1958).

The real reason for Pibul's sudden conversion to democracy was that some of his colleagues in the military were getting restless and he felt his position weakening. It was his hope that by posing as the champion of democracy he would establish himself as a popular leader and simultaneously provoke public and parliamentary opposition against his opponents in the government. He failed in both goals; the opposition that developed was directed more toward Pibul and his associates than toward his opponents, who in the end proved more adept at the parliamentary game than the prime minister. In the election of February 1957 the prime minister's party did win a majority of the parliamentary seats, but employed techniques which caused this election to be immortalized as "The Dirty Election of 1957." His electoral victory was quite emphemeral; seven months later he was deposed by a coup and sent into exile.

During the most recent constitutional period, there were numerous incidents which could be interpreted as indications of increased parliamentary prominence. Again these could be traced directly to divisions within the government, engendered by what appeared to be an impending struggle for succession to the leadership of the government party. One such incident occurred in connection with the consideration of the budget bill in September 1970.

The procedure for consideration of the budget provided that after the first reading a commission composed of parliamentarians and government officials would be appointed to examine the estimates, make revisions, and send the document back to the House. On this occasion, the government was dealt a severe blow when its slate of candidates for the commission was defeated in the House of Representatives and an apparent majority of the members elected were to come from non-government groups. The most significant aspect of the incident was that the alternative slate was so designed that the balance of power in the commission was held by General Prapass Charusathien, minister of interior and a man most desirous of becoming the next prime minister. He had a two-fold purpose in instigating the election of the opposition slate, even though he was a member of the government. First, he demonstrated the weakness of the government by causing an apparent show of parliamentary independence, and second, he established himself in a position to influence the distribution of government funds and in so doing dealt a blow to his opponents in other factions of the governing group.

In this case, as in Pibul's maneuvers in the 1955-57 period, the rise of parliament was a surface manifestation of divisions within the government and not necessarily an indication of a permanent increase in the authority of the legislature. On the contrary, this show of legislative strength was an essential step in the process leading to the November 1971 coup, because it was taken as a demonstration of government weakness rather than democratic vitality (Mezey, 1973).

The Thai legislature is also weak in terms of the popular support dimension. While no public opinion data exist, the lack of support for the legislature can be inferred from the equanimity with which Thais accept the innumerable coups. For the Thais in the country-side, politics is a remote thing; for them the government that they come in contact with is the bureaucracy, and no matter who is in power or what the marginal influence of the legislature might be, the bureaucracy stays the same. It is accurate to say that the last thing that those contemplating a coup consider is the domestic reaction to such an event.

Among the attentive elites, the situation is not substantially different. Because many of the most educated people in Thailand are at work in the bureaucracy, they have acquired the usual bureau-cratic disdain for the "politicians" in the legislature. Because periods of parliamentary prominence have also been periods of instability, there is a certain longing for a strong government. It is not uncommon to hear people in Bangkok talk nostaligically about the government efficiency under the absolute rule of Marshal Sarit.

Those in Thailand with the best ideas on economic development are impatient with the legislature and share the usual belief of the planners that political interference with their schemes is by defini-tion nefarious. Although these people are the Thais most familiar with Western political practices, they have given up on legislative institutions as a means of achieving the ends that they have in mind. Rather, by establishing themselves in the bureaucracy, they hope to be able to work with the generals to achieve the progress that they desire.[10]

POLITICAL PARTIES IN THAILAND

The concept of a legislature, albeit in the minimal form just described, always has been more acceptable to the nation's leaders than any type of political party. Although the leaders of the 1932 coup called themselves the People's Party, the evidence is that this was a foreign adornment. Once the legislature was established and the formation of opposition groups seemed imminent, the government banned political parties and effectively dissolved their own People's Party organization. The question of legalizing political parties came up several times during the next twelve years, but on each occasion the government opposed such proposals, maintaining that the time was not appropriate (Thompson, 1941: 69-71; Vella, 1955: 378; Wilson, 1962a: 233-234).

Parties were legalized for the first time in 1945 during the brief "liberal" period when civilians temporarily came into control of the government. Party groups remained active until the coup of 1951 when they were banned again by the military leaders. A bill to legalize parties, introduced in the Assembly in 1953, was opposed by Prime Minister Pibul on the grounds that the nation had no need for parties and that their chief effect would be to produce subversive agitation aimed at the strength and security of the state. The 1952 constitution repeated the anti-party provision of the 1932 constitution; representatives were required to perform their duty as conscience demanded and they were forbidden from being "bound by any imperative mandate (that is, party instructions) whatsoever" (Blanchard, 1957: 127-128).

In 1955, during Pibul's democratic phase, party activity was legalized and many groups emerged to contest the election of February 1957; they continued to function until October 1958, when General Sarit banned them in addition to closing the Assembly. Parties remained illegal until 1968 when the new constitution was promulgated and elections for a legislature were scheduled. As a result of the 1971 coup, parties once again are illegal. In sum, then, of the 40 years since the advent of constitutional government in Thailand, political parties have been legal for three brief periods totaling 12 years.

When they have existed, party groupings in Thailand could be divided into four categories: government parties, the Democratic Party, the left, and minor parties. A government party is a conglomerate of factions and groups tied to those who happen to hold political power. Since 1945 there have been four such parties. The first was the Constitution Front Party, created by the civilians who ruled from 1944 to 1947. The party was a coalition of three groups supporting Dr. Pridi Phanomyong, the leader of the civilians; the party disappeared after Pridi was deposed by the 1947 coup.

In 1955, as part of his democratization program, Pibul and his ally, Police General Phao Siyanon, organized the Seri Manangkasila Party. This party was coterminous with the governing circle and coopted most of the bureaucracy as well; it collapsed after Sarit sent Pibul into exile. In the year between Sarit's 1957 and 1958 coups he established the Sahaphum Party, composed of the various groups who supported his leadership. This party represented the government in the December 1957 election and then was disbanded with all the other parties after the October 1958 coup.

During the 1968-71 constitutional period, the government party was known as the Saha Pracha Thai (United Thai Peoples) Party (UTPP). Like Seri Manangkasila and Sahaphum, it was a broad coalition of the various cliques and factions represented in he government. It had a bare majority in the elected house and relied upon the occasional support of small factional parties; all of the Cabinet and almost all of the senators were members of the UTPP.

The Democratic Party has been the most persistent party in Thailand. It broke away from Pridi's Constitutional Front in 1946 and has been the major opposition party since then. Originally it was composed of royalist sympathizers, imprisoned by Pibul but amnestied after the civilians came to power in 1944. More recently it was able to attract a share of the emerging urban middle class, including some low-ranking government bureaucrats. Its greatest strength has been the very able people in its leadership ranks. The first leader of the party was Khuang Aphaiwongse, a dominant figure throughout the constitutional period until his death in 1968. His successor, M. R. Seni Pramoj, was ambassador to the United States during World War II and prime minister for a brief period after the war. Extremely articulate and respected, he is probably the only nongovernment politician with a national reputation.[11]

The Democratic Party has traditionally distinguished itself from the government party by its advocacy of democratic processes and its support for the legislative institution. Its perennial campaign themes have revolved around government corruption and military influence in civilian politics. The party is staunchly anti-Communist and has supported government foreign policy; however, it articulates a laissez-faire economic policy, contributing to its popularity in the Bangkok business community. By contrast, the government party and its members are actively involved in all sectors of the economy (Wilson, 1962a: 44-45).

The left in Thailand descends from the remnants of Pridi's

supporters. From 1968 to 1971 it was represented by a relatively small party called Naew Ruam Setthakorn (Economist United Front) Party. The party drew most of its support from the economically depressed northeast, although its leftism was extremely moderate on economic matters. It was most notable for its sole opposition to the anti-Communist line that has characterized all other Thai political parties. During the recent constitutional period, it advocated withdrawal from SEATO, opposed sending Thai troops to Vietnam, and called for better relations between Thailand and mainland China.

In addition to these three groupings, there has been a plethora of minor parties during the various periods when party activity has been legal. Some have been simply the personal cliques of local politicians whose reputation and influence did not extend beyond their local provinces; some were controlled by Cabinet members attempting to build some power outside the government organization. The strength of these parties has been highly localized and their parliamentary representation usually has been negligible.

The Thai political party system is commonly described as weak. Writing of the early party organizations that emerged after the war, Vella (1955: 388) noted that "party members were drawn largely from the small group of politically minded persons in Bangkok all of whom knew each other. No attempt was made to create a national party organization composed of members of the general population, or to enunciate clear-cut party platforms." Wilson (1962a: 68) summed up the situation in the following terms:

> These parties have little or no extraparliamentary organization. In general, each member must get elected through his own efforts in his own province. Party labels are incidental. Parties have never represented substantial social forces but only cliques and individuals within the top level of the ruling class.

Whether or not these conclusions are valid for the political parties that existed during the 1968-71 period is an empirical question; what follows is an attempt to analyze the strength of those parties, employing the five criteria of party strength outlined previously.

LEADERSHIP

Wilson's (1962a: 233) discussion of parties in Thailand emphasizes the importance of the leader to Thai political parties: "the posture of the party or group depends largely on the temperament of its leader, and its continuity and vitality rest upon his political fortunes." Wilson's analysis was essentially accurate for the parties that had existed up to the time that he wrote and clearly applied to the minor parties that existed during the late constitutional period; they continued to be the personal cadres of individual politicians. For instance, the Liberal Party, which held 17 seats in the National Assembly, was highly responsive to the wishes of General Prapass, the interior minister. The Democratic Front Party, led by its articulate Cornell-trained leader, Dr. Phaitoon Crucaew, won seven seats in the 1969 election; however, personal clashes between Dr. Phaitoon and his associates eventually caused secessions from the party and reduced its legislative representation to two. Other small parties that won no seats in the 1969 election simply disappeared.

However, it appears that leadership did become somewhat more depersonalized for the main party groups. The UTPP was the first government party without a single dominant leader. Prime Minister Thanom occupied his position because he was the most acceptable person to all of the factional leaders in his ruling group. Rather than controlling the party he moderated conflicts within it and held its component parts together. Decision-making power was dispersed among the various clique leaders in the government, to whom Thanom essentially reacted. All important government leaders held official positions within the UTPP and therefore party decisions were a collective enterprise rather than the actions of one man. While the party's supporters were still the personal followers of each of these particular leaders, the party was not strongly identified with one man as past government parties had been.

Wilson's interpretation seemed particularly apt for the Democratic Party, which had long depended on the skill and reputation of its gifted leader, Khuang Aphaiwongse. More than a year before the 1969 election Khuang died, and his deputy leader, Seni Pramoj, succeeded him. Seni has proved to be equally articulate and able as a leader and the party's fortunes did not noticeably suffer after his elevation.

The Socialist organization, since it emerged in the 1950s, had been closely identified with its leader, Thep Notuchuchit. Thep was defeated in the 1969 election; although he retained the position of party leader, his associate, Klaew Norapathi, who was elected, took on the role of spokesman for the party. This is in marked contrast to the other small parties that either disappeared after their leader was defeated or served only as vehicles for electing their leader, after which they disappeared.

Therefore, in regard to the leadership criterion, some strengthening of the major parties occurred during this latest constitutional period. Government party leadership became more collective, while the leadership of the Democratic Party and Setthakorn Party changed hands successfully.

STRUCTURE

Continuity in party structure has been difficult to maintain in Thailand because of the frequent periods of authoritarian rule during which party activity has been officially suppressed. While covert and informal associations may have continued during these periods, there is no evidence that any party maintained a formal underground structure.

The lack of a continuous structure has characterized government party activities particularly. During each period of electoral and legislative activity, the government in power has been compelled to form an organization to nominate candidates, mobilize voters, and generate legislative support. The evidence is that this task is begun anew each time; past association with government party structures is not a requirement for inclusion in a new one, and may even be a liability.

Evidence for this assertion is found from an examination of government party nominations. The last two elections prior to February 1969 were held in February and December 1957; the February 1957 election was the first time that records were kept of the party affiliation of candidates. Of the 219 UTPP candidates in the 1969 election, 88 were candidates in one of the two 1957 elections. Eighteen of these (20.5%) ran only as government candidates in those elections; the remainder ran in one or the other election as either independents or as members of another political party. Similar figures are obtained by comparing the two 1957 elections; only 24% of those on Sarit's Sahaphum slate in the December election who had run in February ran then as members of the government's Seri Manangkasila Party.

By the same measures, the Democratic Party appears to have a more continuous structure. After each period of party illegality, the Democrats have re-emerged with their leadership and following essentially unchanged. The nomination evidence contrasts sharply with the government party data. Of the Democratic candidates in 1969 who had run in one or both of the 1957 elections, 68% ran only as Democrats. In the case of the Socialist organization, all but one of the 14 nominees who ran in 1957 ran as Socialists.

The structure of the minor parties is more fluid than that of the government party. Most of these parties last for one election only; their nominees in one election run as independents or members of other parties in the next election. To confound systematic analysis, the party name may be used in the next election by a completely different group of politicians.

ORGANIZATION

If by organization one refers to the linkage between the party and private associations, Thai political parties have proved to be extremely weak on this criterion. However, this is more a manifestation of the fact that autonomous private group associations either do not exist or are inert in Thailand. Riggs (1962: 153-188) offers a number of explanations for this situation: lack of finance in private hands to support such organizations, a restricted middle class on which such organizations may draw, deeply ingrained cultural inhibitions which retard group activity, legal and constitutional restrictions on private associations, and a faulty, government-dominated communication system.

All of these factors have produced government-sponsored and controlled business, labor, and farm groups that depend upon their connections with high government officials for favors beneficial to their members. Rather than make demands on government officials, associations offer their cooperation to them in hopes of future rewards. Thus, the political party is not in a position to mobilize group support for two reasons: first, few groups exist, and second, those that do exist are dominated by the government. For the latter reason, these groups are, in a sense, coopted into the government party structure with their official patrons; for the group, their chances of success depend upon who their friends are in the government party.

For these same reasons, during the last constitutional period the Democratic Party had the support of some of the Bangkok business community, by virtue of the party's control over the local Bangkok government. Even though the municipal government had only limited authority, certain decisions that it made affected local business activity; therefore, some support from these groups was forthcoming to the Democrats. The Democratic Party's consistent opposition to the involvement of government officials in business and its support for the freedom of private enterprise won it additional adherents in this area. Outside Bangkok, independent and leftist candidates drew some support from the Chinese business community, largely because of the government's frequent propaganda campaigns against "rich aliens."

None of this, however, makes for organizational complexity; only in the government party was "group support" significant and only to the extent that a factional leader's association with a business enterprise is advantageous to him in gaining an ascendant position within the government coalition.

Another dimension of organizational complexity is the relation between the party and the voters. In this respect, Thai parties always have been very weak. While party leaders constantly talk in grandiose terms of building constituency organizations and opening party branches in far-off provinces, this rarely comes to pass, except around election time. The Democratic Party maintained offices in two provinces where they have been strong, and the leader of the small Democratic Front Party claimed to have branch offices in nine provinces. The government party spoke of opening branch offices, but nothing substantive happened. The government party could have utilized the nationwide bureaucracy for regular party work, but seemed to have no inclination to do so during the last constitutional period.

The only political party activity that penetrated to the local level revolved around the individual legislator and his friends. Data collected during 1969 and 1970 (Mezey, 1972) suggest that the legislator provided the main non-bureaucratic linkage between the people and the government. Members of the House reported that they were bombarded with requests from constituents for money and services. In meeting these requests, Democratic and minor party members were at a disadvantage because their parties had very little money. Government party members could negotiate with government leaders for funds and services with which to meet constituency demands, but such requests were not handled in any regular or dependable fashion. Usually, the legislator fended for himself in dealing with his constituents and could not depend upon a party organization to aid him.

PARTY FOLLOWING

Estimates of the following of any Thai political party must be based exclusively on election returns. Actual votes for a party are the only hard indication of party support; while many parties have sold membership cards, this has never been done on a nationwide scale and no reliable figures are maintained that can substantiate the usually inflated claims of party leaders.

The range of a party's following may be estimated by its capacity to run candidates and draw votes in all areas of the country. By this measure, the UTPP had the widest base of support in the nation; in the 1969 election it was the only party that nominated a full slate of candidates, and drew votes in all provinces of the nation. The range of the various party groups as well as the independent votes may be compared by generating gini coefficients based on the relation between the regional distribution of the party's vote and the regional distribution of total votes.[1][2] The findings are summarized in Table 1. Clearly the government party, with a gini coefficient of .06, demonstrated the widest range of support in the 1969 election. The high ginis for the minor parties as well as the Economist United Front suggest the regional nature of their efforts; it is also apparent that the Democratic Party was the only party that came close to contesting the government organization on an equal basis.

As the data in Table 1 demonstrate, votes for independent candidates are also regional in nature, but the actual number of

TABLE 1
GINI COEFFICIENTS
ELECTION OF FEBRUARY 1969

Party	GINI Coefficient[a]
United Thai Peoples Party	.06
Democratic Party	.36
(Independent votes)[b]	.51
Peoples Party	.52
Democratic Front Party	.53
Other minor parties	.58
Economist United Front	.62
Free Democratic Party	1.00

a. The GINI coefficient reflects the degree of inequality between the regional distribution of the party vote and the regional distribution of the total vote. Low coefficients indicate nationwide strength; the proportion of the party's vote from a region approaches the proportion of the total vote from that region. High coefficients indicate regional strength; the proportion of the party's vote coming from one region approaches 100%.
b. This coefficient is based on the total number of votes cast for all independent candidates by region.

independent votes—"density" in Chambers' (1963) terminology—is quite high. In both the 1969 election and the second 1957 election the total number of independent votes exceeded the votes for any other party. The results for the last three elections are displayed in Table 2. The frequency of independent voting limits the density of the support of the organized political parties and suggests the limited extent to which political parties have penetrated the Thai political system.

The data also indicate an inverse relation between the strength of the government party in particular provinces and the strength of independent candidacies. In the last three elections, the Pearson product-moment correlation between percentage of votes for government party candidates, by province, and percentage of votes for independent candidates was $-.40$ in February 1957, $-.43$ in December 1957, and $-.33$ in 1969. In each election, the magnitude of the correlation coefficient was greater than that between independents and any other party. Furthermore, the independent vote appears to be a rejection of the Democratic Party as an alternative to the government; in the three elections, the Democratic Party-independent Pearson's r's were $-.27$, $-.39$, and $-.15$.

The independent candidacies aside, the major political force in these elections have been the government organization and the Democratic Party opposition. As Table 2 indicates, Socialist and minor party followings are quite narrow and quite inconsequential to the final electoral result.

A third aspect of a party's following is stability. This term can refer to at least two factors: first, the stability of the party's gross share of the votes from election to election, and second, the continuity in its following from one election to the next—are its supporters the same people from election to election?

TABLE 2

DISTRIBUTION OF POPULAR VOTES IN THE LAST THREE GENERAL ELECTIONS IN THAILAND: FEBRUARY 1957, DECEMBER 1957, FEBRUARY 1969 (in percentages)

Group	February 1957	December 1957	February 1969
Government Party candidates	37.9	23.4	27.6
Democratic Party candidates	20.6	23.4	24.9
Independent candidates	16.8	38.6	35.1
Minor party candidates	16.6	7.8	10.2
Socialist candidates	7.1	6.8	2.2
TOTAL	100	100	100

LEGISLATURES AND CONFLICT MANAGEMENT

TABLE 3

PEARSON PRODUCT-MOMENT CORRELATION COEFFICIENTS:
PERCENTAGE OF VOTES FOR CANDIDATES OF GOVERNMENT
PARTIES, BY PROVINCE (N = 71)

	Sahaphume (December 1957)	UTPP (February 1969)
Seri Manangkasila (February 1957)	.10	.30
UTPP (February 1969)	.08	

Table 2 shows a fair stability for all parties in terms of gross share of the votes. The government party and the Democratic Party account for approximately 50% of the vote in each election; minor party and Socialist percentages have shown a mild decline while the strength of the independents has increased.

There is much less stability of following in terms of continuity between elections. The pattern of votes for government party coalitions shows little relation to one another. Table 3 shows a matrix of correlations, based on the percentage of votes polled in each province by candidates of the government party organizations participating in the last three elections. While all three coefficients are positive, the low magnitude of each clearly demonstrates the shifting nature of the government's electoral base. Government strength in a province in one election is not associated with government strength in that province in other elections. These data stand in marked contrast to the Democratic Party and Socialist correlations shown in Tables 4 and 5. These high, positive correlations imply a continuity in the following of these groups that is lacking in the shifting government coalitions. Those who vote for these parties appear to do so consistently from one election to the next.

When these data are coupled with the nomination data presented earlier, a clearer picture of the role of the parties in the electoral

TABLE 4

PEARSON PRODUCT-MOMENT CORRELATION COEFFICIENTS:
PERCENTAGE OF VOTES FOR DEMOCRATIC PARTY
CANDIDATES BY PROVINCE (N = 71)

	December 1957	February 1969
February 1957	.76	.42
February 1969	.51	

TABLE 5
PEARSON PRODUCT-MOMENT CORRELATION COEFFICIENTS:
PERCENTAGE OF VOTES FOR CANDIDATES OF SOCIALIST
PARTIES BY PROVINCE (N = 71)

	December 1957	February 1969
February 1957	.68	.76
February 1969	.64	

process in Thailand emerges. Elections for the House seem to be a highly personal enterprise in which there is a great deal of emphasis on the personality of individual candidates. Parties such as the Democrats and Socialists, which exhibit a relatively high degree of continuity in structure as evidenced by a low turnover in nominees, consequently exhibit a greater stability in voter support. Conversely, the ad hoc government coalitions, constructed primarily for contesting a particular election, are characterized by a greater turnover in personnel and consequently a greater instability in voter support. The government parties have been able to compensate for this deficiency because they have had greater resources at their command for winning votes than the more stable party groups.

PERFORMANCE OF POLITICAL FUNCTIONS

The main political function apparently performed by the government party has been to assume responsibility for governing the nation after each election. The major difference between the Thai practice and the Western experience is that in Thailand the governing function precedes the party and the election. This means that an existing governing group, confronted with an upcoming election, forms a government party whose leadership is coterminous with the current military and bureaucratic elite. After the election ritual, the group reassumes its governing function, this time clothed in party apparel. When the next election comes along, a new government party assembles, reflecting any change in elite personnel that may have occurred in the interim. Governing has not been a party enterprise in the sense that decisions are critically influenced by a party organization; as we suggested earlier, the government has been the party organization, and therefore it has been responsible to itself.

For the governing elite, the primary political function for the party is to provide and maintain legislative majorities in the Assembly. Ordinarily one would expect that the nomination process would be vital to the performance of this function; presumably, only dependable and electable people should receive the party endorsement. However, a more important consideration in deciding upon nominations is to satisfy the demands of the various factional leaders by seeing to it that sufficient numbers of their supporters are nominated. Next in importance is the popularity of the individual in the province in which he wants to run. Potential loyalty to the party as well as competence are generally secondary considerations. With criteria such as this, it is difficult, despite pronouncements of party leaders, to maintain any semblance of party discipline.

Throughout the period preceding the nominations for the 1969 elections, UTPP leaders emphasized the necessity of loyalty and discipline. Prime Minister Thanom said that "anyone not chosen to be a party candidate should help those the party considers most suitable to run for election" (Bangkok Post, Oct. 22, 1968). Deputy Party Leader Pote Sarasin gave impromptu lectures on the virtues of the American party system in which unsuccessful candidates such as Reagan and Rockefeller had supported their party's 1968 presidential nominee. Despite these efforts of party leaders, the Bangkok Post (Jan. 3, 1969) was able to report that many of the candidates seeking election as independents were "disaffected UTPP members who had failed to obtain party sponsorship." In addition, many independents undoubtedly were covert government supporters who thought that it would be difficult for them to be elected in their provinces as government-endorsed candidates.

Once the government party slate has been decided upon, getting it elected is a more difficult process. The advantage of government endorsement is obvious; government campaigns are always the best financed and best organized. Government candidates can claim responsibility for every local improvement provided in recent memory. Helpful bureaucrats (ostensibly neutral) are in every village to render assistance, and money is always available to support the repairing of a temple or to buy drinks for local campaign workers (Pickerell and Moore, 1957: 95).

The disadvantages of government party candidacy become manifest in areas where the government is not at all popular. In a centralized, bureaucratized polity such as Thailand, every villager has some grievance against a local government official. In economically depressed areas such as the northeast, or in areas where separatist sentiments are strong such as the south, these grievances are major and widespread. Opposition campaigns in these areas are based entirely on anti-government attacks, and affiliation with the government can be embarrassing, if not dangerous. In these areas, even government party candidates are tempted to attack their own leaders; six weeks before the last election, Air Marshal Dawee Chullasapya, secretary-general of the UTPP, announced that two candidates had been sacked for refusing to campaign with other UTPP candidates and joining with opposition candidates in attacks on the government party (Bangkok Post, Dec. 28, 1968).[13]

Because of the frequency of independent candidacies, it is likely that no party will win a majority of the seats in the House; in each of the last three elections the government party has elected a plurality. Thus, the first post-election task of the government party is to round up a sufficient number of independently elected legislators to provide a majority. Likely converts are the covert government supporters, unsuccessful aspirants for the government party nomination, and opportunists of every stripe. The incentives for joining the government run the gamut from patronage to direct money payments and preferred treatment for pork-barrel projects.

In the most recent election, the UTPP won 75 of the 219 seats in the House of Representatives; over the course of the next three months, 33 independents and two members of other parties were convinced to join the government party. In addition, a group of 17 independents loyal to Minister of Interior Prapass formed a parliamentary group which they called the Liberal Party, and indicated that they would support the government on most issues. In return for this pledge, the government cooperated in seeing to it that the leader of the Liberal Party was elected first vice-president of the House.

Forming the government group is less difficult than maintaining a majority once the legislative session convenes. Defections (which are facilitated by secret balloting in the House) may cause a parliamentary defeat and embarrassment to the government. During the period 1969-71 the government sought to avoid such splits by holding meetings of all government legislators (senators and assemblymen) the day before the weekly parliamentary meeting. The leaders of the Cabinet would appear at the meeting and explain the government's position on the various bills and questions expected to come up that week. The Cabinet also responded to questions from the legislators, since UTPP members were not permitted to ask questions of the government during the regular question period in the House. When differences became apparent, votes were taken;

however, the inclusion of Cabinet members, bureaucrats, and appointed senators in the balloting usually ensured the government's position. The meetings did serve to reveal sources of opposition to government proposals and the leadership found out who had to be pacified to ensure the legislative majority. In this sense, the party seemed to provide a forum within which a brokerage function was performed in order to keep the majority intact.

Evidence that this brokerage process took place within the government party was provided by the response of UTPP members of the House to the following question: "How would you describe the role of political parties in the legislature?"[14] The responses to this question are summarized in Table 6.

Members of the UTPP tended to emphasize both the development of a common position to which party members could subscribe and the control of party members' behavior in the House. One UTPP member stated that "there must be party meetings where decisions are reached"; another said that the role of the party was to "force the party members to observe the party policy." Another saw the party as a forum in which "to meet and discuss various problems" and then to "unite to vote on resolutions." In contrast, the Democratic Party members interviewed tended to emphasize opposition to and control of the government as their party's major role, in addition to policy development; very few mentioned control and discipline of party members as an explicit party function.

The omission of such responses in the case of the Democrats does not indicate less discipline in their ranks; rather it indicates that this is less of a problem in their party. This interpretation is supported by responses to another question in which the members were asked: "Under what circumstances do you think it is not necessary for a member to vote with his party." While 70% of the Democrats

TABLE 6

THAI LEGISLATORS' PERCEPTIONS OF THE ROLE OF THE PARTY IN THE LEGISLATURE[a] (in percentages)

	Oppose-Support-Control Government	Policy Development	Enforcing Discipline	Others	
Government Party members	20	53.9	30.9	27.3	N=55[b]
Democratic Party members	33.3	38.5	5.1	38.5	N=39

a. Question: "How would you describe the role of political parties in the legislature?"
b. Percentages will total to more than 100% because respondents indicated more than one role for the party.

responded "never" to this question, only 42% of the government party members responded in this manner. The remaining 58% suggested numerous situations in which they would be justified in not voting with their party.

The major political function performed by the Democratic Party has been to provide an opposition to the various government parties. The continuity of the Democrats from one election to the next and their practice of nominating candidates in almost all provinces has made them a credible opposition force compared to the transient, regional minor parties. As deficient as their campaigns may be in terms of articulating programs or organizing grass-root support, they do perform the political function of providing almost every voter with an organized party alternative to government candidates.

As noted above, members of the party in the House tend to conceive of their role as one of opposing or controlling the government. In response to another question in which the members were asked to rank various conflicts in the Assembly in order of importance, members from all parties tended to rank "Government v. Opposition" the highest; however, Democrats gave the conflict the highest average ranking—1.5 compared to 1.92 for government party MPs.

In a more general sense, the Democratic Party has performed the function of legitimizing the parliamentary process. As an institutionalized opposition independent from the government, its existence refuted any charges of repression or authoritarianism directed at the government; as a loyal opposition subscribing to the foreign policy of the nation's leaders, its existence was tolerable to the government.

Minor parties have performed only the transient function of providing particular candidates with election vehicles and certain voters with an opportunity to vote against the established regime. The Socialist organization articulates a foreign policy position very much at variance with the government's, but its following is so narrow that it presents no significant threat.

Again, it should be emphasized that a major function of political parties—that of providing a linkage between citizens and their government—is performed by Thai political parties only in the sense of organizing the election of legislators. The articulation and the communication of demands, the generation of responses to demands, the downward communication of outputs from the government to the citizens, are all functions performed by individual legislators acting alone or by the government bureaucracy, and not by any political party organization in Thailand.

The conclusion of this analysis is that the political parties in Thailand are weak, although perhaps not as uniformly fragile as previously published works have led us to believe. A salient point is that the parties that are strongest on the criteria of leadership, continuity of structure, and stability of following are parties which, given the realities of political life in Thailand, cannot significantly influence events in the political system. Conversely, the party with the most potential to influence the course of political development in Thailand—the government party—was found to be weak according to these criteria and in terms of the performance of the vital linkage functions that are usually expected from strong political parties. A weak government party persisted despite the potential for party strength implicit in its cooptation of most private groups in the system, its a priori control of the governmental apparatus, its nominal inclusion of most of the political elite, and its capability of reaching all areas of the nation.

PARTIES AND THE LEGISLATURE IN THAILAND:
A SUMMARY

The foregoing analysis demonstrates the coexistence in Thailand of a weak but occasionally influential legislative institution with a generally weak party system. It is evident that the military and the bureaucracy dominate the legislature and are usually able to manipulate outcomes to suit the purposes of the government. Decisions are arrived at by the Cabinet, and legislative approval is expected to be a formality except in those few instances when the government itself is divided. Numerous instruments are in the hands of the government to induce legislative acquiescence to Cabinet decisions, with the coup or the threat of a coup the most extreme devices. In sum, decisions generally are made by forces outside the legislature. Support for the parliamentary institution is not widespread within the country. Elites in the bureaucracy treat the legislators with disdain and the great mass of the people are unconcerned about politics; the national tradition of strong rule means that most Thais accept authoritarian government with relative equanimity.

Obviously, weak political parties are not the sole cause of this weal legislature situation; a plethora of historical and cultural explanations are readily available. However, the condition of the party system is certainly a contributing factor.[15] This connection between weak parties and weak legislatures is based on the following reasoning. First, parties have the potential to mobilize support for the legislature. Parties can act as links between constituents and their representatives in the legislature, and if they are effective they can generate the positive support so essential to a strong legislative institution. If political parties fail to perform this function, then the legislature will weaken. Increased strength is likely to accrue to the more authoritarian elements in the political system who are less dependent upon popular support for the maintenance of their positions. Rather, these elements are most secure in an apathetic situation in which they may not have the support of a mass public, but are not opposed by them. In order to create and maintain such a situation, these leaders prevent the strengthening of political parties. This has the effect of retarding the development of legislative institutions which potentially may generate opposition to the leaders; it also decreases the likelihood that parties will instigate popular opposition to the incumbent regime.

In the Thai situation, political parties clearly have failed the legislature. The prevalence of independent candidacies and the high percentage of popular votes that they account for suggest the limited extent to which the Thai party system controls and regulates political participation. The absence of constituency organizations is a further indicator of the weakness of the link between party and constituency. Legislators must confront the demands of their constituents without the aid of a party organization. Because legislators have few political resources at their disposal, a wide gap between demands and satisfactory outputs inevitably develops; this strains the very limited support initially accuring to the legislature, thereby further weakening the institution.

Consequently the Thai legislature has never been able to substantially increase its strength in comparison to the executive. The military and the bureaucracy have depended upon the general apathy of the mass public for their continued and relatively tranquil tenure in power. Their position is legitimized by their de facto control of the government; in Thai culture, those who have succeeded in gaining power are presumed to have the right to it.[16] By exploiting the symbols of nationalism and by protecting the political isolation of most of their citizens, those who rule are able to separate themselves from popular pressures.

To maintain this situation, the government has consistently prevented the strengthening of party organizations, including its own. The frequent interruptions in the legal status of political parties have increased the difficulty in institutionalizing party structures. The leaders of the government by their actions leave the distinct impression that they consider their party and the elected legislators a nuisance, and thus demonstrate to aspiring leaders that the way to political power is through the military and the bureaucracy, and not through the party. Consequently, the best people in the nation work for the government and keep themselves apart from party politics.

A well-organized government party could redound to the benefit of the government in the long run, and, prior to the 1971 coup, there were some among the leadership of the UTPP who would have liked to move the party in that direction. It is significant that it was these leaders who seemed to have lost in the coup, while those who engineered the coup were the leaders most resistant to such proposals. They had no desire to establish a strong party organization that could conceivably make claims upon them and restrict their freedom of action.

In sum, a circular process is at work in Thailand and in other countries similarly situated. Weak parties weaken the legislature which in turn reinforces the position of the military and the bureaucracy; they in turn continue to prevent the growth of strong political parties.

NOTES

1. This interpretation of party development is summarized in LaPalombara and Weiner (1966: 8-14); also, see Duverger (1963: xxiii-xxvii).

2. The classic statement of this position is found in Mill (1958: 68-70).

3. An early assessment of some of the problems of measuring legislative performance is provided by Wahlke (1962: 173-190). For a good first step toward the measurement of legislative decision-making power, see Blondel et al. (1969-70). The significance of the support dimension is brilliantly analyzed by Wahlke (1967). His analysis depends to a large extent on Easton (1965: 153-170). For an analysis of support for the Iowa State Legislature, see Boynton et al. (1968). Also see Agor (1971) for an evaluation of public support as a base for the decisional influence of the Chilean Senate.

4. This interpretation differs somewhat from Huntington (1968: 421). He maintains that there is no relation between party strength and party number; I maintain that party number is one criterion of party strength, but not the only criterion. Thus, a single party may be strong on this criterion, but weak on all others and thereby be, on balance, a relatively weak party.

5. Since this paper was drafted, two major political events have occurred in Thailand. On November 17, 1971, the government suspended the 1968 Constitution and dissolved the

legislature. Two years later, during November 1973, violent student demonstrations led to the overthrow of the regime, the exile of the prime minister and the interior minister, and the installation of a civilian government pledged to return Thailand to constitutional government. In revising this paper for publication in this volume, the only changes that were made because of the 1971 coup involved tense changes ("is" to "as"), and the insertion of some clarifying phrases that indicate an awareness of the event. No textual changes have been made as a result of the 1973 events. The analysis and conclusions have not been altered since the paper was originally drafted during summer 1971. For a detailed discussion of the background of the immediate consequences of the November 1971 coup, see Mezey (1973).

6. This interpretation is developed more fully in Mezey (1973).

7. See Darling (1962: 170-171) for a further discussion of Sarit's views on the legislature.

8. Similar observations were made in regard to the passage of the budget bill for the 1971 fiscal year. See Siam Rath (Oct. 22, 1970).

9. The major alternative function for the legislature was the symbolic reduction of demands performed by the individual legislator as he communicated with his constituents, heard their problems, supplied certain individual services, and transmitted certain complaints to the government. See Mezey (1972) for the relevant data.

10. The best analysis of the conflict between prematurely developed bureaucracies and democratic political institutions such as political parties and legislatures is offered by Riggs (1965). Also see Huntington (1968) for a similar point of view.

11. When a sample of Thai legislators was asked to name the MP who was most respected by the members, Seni received more mentions than any other legislator.

12. For the definition of a gini coeffacient and the method of calculation, see Alker (1965: 36-42). The coefficients in Table 1 and the data presented in Table 2 depend upon laborious computations ably performed by Ms. Elizabeth Hendrick.

13. For a description of the 1968-69 campaign and election, see Neher (1970: 240-257).

14. These interviews were conducted by students from Thammasat University, Bangkok, Thailand, during a period extending from August 1969 to February 1970. The original goal of the project was to interview all of the members of the House of Representatives; therefore the 129 (59%) ultimately interviewed do not compose a sample but rather an attempted enumeration. While this is not a strikingly high completion rate, the group does appear to reflect the party and regional divisions of the total membership and therefore inferences to the entire membership may be hazarded.

The interview schedule was constructed in English and then translated into Thai by Mr. Montri Chenvidyakarn of the Faculty of Political Science, Thammasat University. Mr. Montri also took responsibility for translating the responses back into English.

15. "The susceptibility of a political system to military intervention varies inversely with the strength of its political parties. . . . The decline in party strength, the fragmentation of leadership, the evaporation of mass support, the decay of organizational structure, the shift of political leaders from party to bureaucracy, and rise of personalism, all herald the moment when colonels occupy the capitol" (Huntington, 1968: 408-409).

16. "This conception is the one which must be referred to throughout this discussion of Thai politics, that is, the necessary and just unity of virtue and power. Those who have power are good and deserve power. Those who gain power are good and deserve their good fortune" (Wilson: 1962a: 74).

REFERENCES

ALKER, H. R. (1965) Mathematics and Politics. New York: Macmillan.

AGOR, W. H. (1971) "The decisional role of the Senate in the Chilean political system," pp. 3-51 in W. H. Agor (ed.) Latin American Legislatures: Their Role and Influence. New York: Praeger.

Bangkok Post. (January 3, 1969; October 22, 1968; December 28, 1968).

BERRIGAU, D. (1956) "Thailand: Pibul tries Prachathipatai." The Reporter 14, 12: 30-33.

BLANCHARD, W. (1957) Thailand: Its People, Its Society, Its Culture. New Haven, Conn.: Human Relations Area Files.

BLONDEL, J., P. GILLESPIE, V. HERMAN, P. KAATI, and R. LEONARD (1969-70) "Comparative legislative behavior." Government and Opposition 5, 1 (Winter): 67-85.

BOYNTON, G. R., S. C. PATTERSON, and R. D. HEDLUND (1968) "The structure of public support for legislative institutions." Midwest J. of Pol. Sci. 12 (May): 163-180.

CHAMBERS, W. N. (1963) Political Parties in a New Nation: The American Experience, 1776-1809. New York: Oxford Univ. Press.

COAST, J. (1953) Some Aspects of Siamese Politics. New York: Institute of Pacific Relations.

DARLING, F. C. (1962) "Modern politics in Thailand." Rev. of Politics 24, 2 (April): 163-182.

--- (1960) "Marshal Sarit and absolutist rule in Thailaud." Pacific Affairs 33, 4 (December): 347-360.

DUVERGER, M. (1963) Political Parties. New York: John Wiley.

EASTON, D. (1965) A Systems Analysis of Political Life. New York: John Wiley.

HUNTINGTON, S. P. (1968) Political Order in Changing Societies. New Haven, Conn.: Yale Univ. Press.

Kingdom of Thailand (1968) The Constitution of the Kingdom of Thailand, B.E. 2511.

LANDON, K. P. (1939) Siam in Transition. Chicago: Univ. of Chicago Press.

LaPALOMBARA, J. and M. WEINER [eds.] (1966) Political Parties and Political Development. Princeton: Princeton Univ. Press.

MEZEY, M. L. (1973) "The 1971 coup in Thailand: understanding why the legislature fails." Asian Survey 13, 3 (March).

--- (1972) "The functions of a minimal legislature: role perceptions of Thai legislators." Western Political Q. 25, 4 (December).

MILL, J. S. (1958) Considerations on Representative Government. New York: Liberal Arts Press. (Originally published in 1958.)

NEHER, C. D. (1970) "Constitutionalism and elections in Thailand." Pacific Affairs 43, 3: 240-257.

PICKERELL, A. and D. MOORE (1957) "Elections in Thailand." Far Eastern Survey 26, 6 (June): 92-96.

RIGGS, F. W. (1966) Thailand: The Modernization of a Bureaucratic Polity. Honolulu: East-West Center Press.

--- (1965) "Bureaucrats and political development: a paradoxical view," pp. 120-168 in J. LaPalombara (ed.) Bureaucracy and Political Development. Princeton: Princeton Univ. Press.

--- (1963) Census and Notes on Clientele Groups in Thai Politics and Administration. Bloomington: Indiana University Department of Government.

--- (1962) "Interest and clientele groups," pp. 153-188 in J. L. Sutton (ed.) Problems of Politics and Administration in Thailand. Bloomington: Indiana Univ. Press.

Siam Rath. (January 1, 1970; July 28, 1970; October 22, 1970.)

THOMPSON, V. (1941) Thialand: The New Siam. New York: Institute of Pacific Relations.

VELLA, W. F. (1955) The Impact of the West on the Government of Thailand. Berkeley: Univ. of California Press.

WAHLKE, J. C. (1967) Public Policy and Representative Government: The Role of the Represented. Iowa City: Laboratory for Political Research.

--- (1962) "Behavioral analysis of representative bodies," pp. 173-190 in A. Ranney (ed.) Essays on the Behavioral Study of Politics. Urbana: Univ. of Illinois Press.

WEBER, M. (1946) "Politics as a vocation," pp. 77-128 in H. Gerth and C. W. Mills (eds.) From Max Weber: Essays in Sociology. New York: Oxford Univ. Press.

WILSON, D. A. (1962a) Politics in Thailand. Ithaca: Cornell Univ. Press.
——— (1962b) "The military in Thai politics," pp. 253-276 in J. J. Johnson (ed.) The Role of the Military in Underdeveloped Countries. Princeton: Princeton Univ. Press.
WILSON, D. A. and H. PHILLIPS (1958) "Elections and parties in Thailand." Far Eastern Survey 27, 8 (August): 113-119.

MICHAEL L. MEZEY is Assistant Professor of Political Science at the University of Hawaii. He has taught at the University of Virginia and at Thammasat University, Bangkok, Thailand, where he was a visiting professor of political science. He is the editor of the *Comparative Legislative Studies Newsletter,* and the author of numerous articles on American political behavior and comparative legislative behavior. Currently, he is engaged in research on comparative legislatures.

Chapter 6

DIMENSIONS OF CONFLICT IN THE
COLOMBIAN NATIONAL LEGISLATURE

G A R Y   H O S K I N

State University of New York at Buffalo

Institutionally speaking, legislatures can be viewed as a set of interrelated expectations and behavior of a group of individuals who engage in specified activities that are determined by the functions discharged by the legislature in the political system and supported by the prevailing system of power. As a result, comparative studies of legislative behavior necessarily must not concentrate solely upon the behavior of individual legislators or the legislature as an autonomous institution without first determining the functions discharged by the legislature in the larger political system, assuming the desirability of comparative standards that are not ethnocentric and culture-bound. As Wahlke and associates (1962: 10) put it:

> If one is interested in the structure and functions of an institution, it would seem proper to ascertain and analyze those forms of behavior which are central and constitutive to the institution as such before attempting to describe or explain individual actions or individual deviations from some unspecified model of behavior.

AUTHOR'S NOTE: I want to express my appreciation to the Los Andes Political Science Department in Bogotá and the Rockefeller Foundation for their kind support of the Colombian legislative behavior project, of which this chapter forms a part. Thanks are extended to the following individuals for their comments and assistance in preparing this research: Fernando Cepeda Ulloa, Francisco Leal, Harvey Kline, Dora Rothlisberger, John Sinclair, and Gerald Swanson.

In searching for criteria of comparability that are valid from one context to another, it is hazardous to postulate, de ante mano, universal functions supposedly discharged by all legislatures and then relate behavior to those functions, for while such functions may well be present in any legislative context, the "significant"[1] functions performed by any legislature are determined structurally by the prevailing power relationships in the society and the location of the legislature therein. Although legislative behavior at any one point in time reflects, in a certain sense, the historical evolution of the legislature in terms of the functions it discharges in a political system, assessment of the position of the legislature in a society's power structure can be clarified considerably by tracing the genesis and development of the institution from an historical perspective. Only through the isolation and analysis of the functions performed by a legislature vis-à-vis the political system can legislative behavior be interpreted fruitfully from a cross-national perspective.

After formulating a series of propositions about legislative functions through careful historical analysis, the task of explaining legislative behavior at any cross-section of time becomes less problematical; yet how the various facets of behavior associated with the legislature are to be organized within a coherent framework for comparative purposes still confronts the analyst. Role theory offers one encompassing perspective from which to compare legislatures. From an institutional perspective, a legislature is conceptualized as an interrelated system of roles that orients the activities of those individuals forming a part of the legislative system, broadly conceived to include not only legislators but all individuals who interact regularly with legislators in the pursuit of their legislative tasks. Role theory offers a framework that enables the analyst to relate individual behavior with the institutional setting in which it occurs. As Katz and Kahn (1966: 197) note:

> The concept of role is proposed as the major means for linking the individual and organizational levels of research and theory; it is at once the building block of social systems and the summation of the requirements with which such systems confront their members as individuals. Each person in an organization is linked to some set of other members by virtue of the functional requirements of the system which are heavily implemented through the expectations those members have of him.

While a set of more or less stable role expectations that orient the behavior of its members is a prerequisite to institutional survival and success, this implies neither a high degree of membership consensus about institutional norms nor adherence to an unequivocal set of rules that guide behavior. In their very nature, institutional norms and roles specify, at best, only a range of expected or acceptable behavior. Roles represent ideal frameworks for behavior, and actual role transactions constitute a compromise between ideal prescriptions and a flexible role-making process. In Buckley's (1967: 148-149) words:

> Institutions may provide a normative framework prescribing roles to be played, thus assuring the required division of labor and minimizing the costs of exploratory role-setting behavior. The actual role transactions that occur, however, generate a more or less coherent and stable working compromise between ideal prescriptions and a flexible role-making process—between the structured demands of others and the requirements of one's own purposes and sentiments.

Although a conventional view of role behavior postulates complementarity of expectations within role sets (Parsons, 1951), the realities of institutional behavior suggest that social relations often are characterized by instability and conflict. In contrast to the assumptions accompanying the complementarity postulate, Buckley (1967: 129) underscores the conflict surrounding role expectations as a primary source of institutional change: "The internal source of dynamics from the ongoing process is the continuous generation of various degrees of tension, 'stress' or 'strain,' within and between the interacting components; such tension is now being recognized as an inherent and essential characteristic of such systems."

Assuming, then, the importance of examining conflict surrounding institutional norms and behavior as a prime source of change, what are the principal foci of such cleavage within an institution such as a legislature? Generally speaking, three major sources of institutional conflict can be specified. First, within the wider context of the legislative system, a major source of tension may arise from differing expectations on the part of (1) legislators and (2) actors representing diverse constituencies who interact with legislators. This type of cleavage may take one of two forms, inter- or intra-positional conflict (Wahlke et al., 1962:10). In regard to the former, legislators may, for example, perceive the location of the legislature in the political system in a manner quite distinct from high executive officials. Differing role expectations among legislators regarding their behavior with "counter-positions," constitutes intra-positional conflict. This occurs, to take one case, when there is little agreement among legislators themselves vis-á-vis their relationships with the executive branch of government.

A second major source of legislative conflict stems from the extent of consensus among legislators regarding what Wahlke and associates (1962: 11-12) label the core-role sector of the legislature. Such disagreements may arise from divergent orientations on the part of legislators regarding their purposive roles, representational roles, and the extent to which they adhere to written prescriptions and the informal rules of the game. In each of these cases, role strain is derived from differing expectations among legislators in relation to interactions within the legislature itself.

Finally, it should be stressed that not all legislative conflict stems from ambiguities surrounding role expectations. Within the framework of acceptable role behavior, tension may be embedded in differing perceptions held by legislators regarding what kind of policies the legislature should enact. While this possible source of legislative conflict obviously is affected to a considerable extent by the degree of normative consensus regarding the proper relationships between legislators and their diverse clienteles, as well as the extent of agreement pertaining to core-role sectors, conflict arising from differing orientations of legislators that fall within the range of accepted institutional behavior should be distinguished analytically.

The legislature, in summary, is viewed as an open system, with emphasis upon the structural interrelationships within the institution and transactions between the legislature and its environment. Such systems are "distinguished precisely by the fact that, rather than minimize organization, or preserve a given fixed structure, they typically create, elaborate, or change structure as a prerequisite to remaining viable, as ongoing systems" (Buckley, 1967: 5). The constant adaptation of an open system such as a legislature to its environment is related closely to the sources of tension that surround role behavior, along with divergent legislative perceptions and behavior that are legitimized by institutional norms. The emphasis upon boundary interaction between the legislature and its environment brings to the foreground the impact of the wider political system in molding legislative behavior. By establishing the functions discharged by the legislature in the political system, boundary exchanges between the legislature and its environment inevitably must be considered, which should expedite explanation of why legislators behave as they do.

The present inquiry focuses upon sources of conflict within the Colombian National Congress. The data are drawn mainly from extended interviews with 220 Colombian congressmen, representing 70% of the universe of 106 senators and 204 representatives. While the study design called for interviewing each member who regularly attended the 1968 session, around 30% refused to cooperate for diverse reasons. Sixty-five percent of those interviewed were representatives and 35% senators; 84.5% were serving as principals and 15.5% as alternates.[2] The interviews, with both open and closed items, averaged around two hours in length, with one lasting less than an hour and 25 more than three hours. During the field stage of the research, the principal investigators were associated with the Universidad de Los Andes in Bogotá, and the bulk of the student interviewers likewise were affiliated with Los Andes. The framework for the larger study encompassed two theoretical approaches: the first a sociological-historical model for interpreting legislative behavior from 1930 through 1968 (Leal, 1973), and the second a role model for explaining the cross-sectional data generated from the interviews—a model which was influenced notably by the study of state legislators executed by Wahlke and associates (1962).

After discussing the principal functions seemingly discharged by the legislature in the Colombian political system, as determined by the structure of power characteristic of the society, the paper concentrates upon three areas of legislative conflict. The first area of inquiry is concerned with the reported views of legislators as to the principal conflicts that confronted the 1968 session. Second, we shall examine the principal dimensions of conflict among legislators in respect to their preferences for political groups and political leaders. The conflict poles are isolated through multidimensional scale analysis. Third, the interrelationships between a set of attitudinal syndromes expressed by congressmen are examined, with emphasis upon the degree of constraint among such attitudes and their variation according to political party affiliation. In the conclusion of the paper, these sources of cleavage are summarized and some generalizations are extrapolated. Discussion of the specific areas of conflict within the Colombian Congress reflects a combination of the three sources of institutional cleavage mentioned previously, with emphasis upon tensions arising from interaction between political groups.[3] While such conflicts permeate the Congress, their generation and resolution often can be traced to political party behavior, the dynamics of which are not necessarily congruent with norms and roles associated with the legislature itself.

In general terms, the argument suggests that a fairly high degree of consensus prevails in the Colombian Congress regarding the major conflicts confronting the legislature, in part a consequence of democratic norms that legitimate legislative activity, in part a result of shared perceptions of the role the legislature plays in the political system. The locus of political conflict, historically as well as presently, pivots around three dimensions, control of the government, ideological differences, and regional cleavages. Contrary to some studies of Colombian politics (Payne, 1968), ideological differences are present in the Congress, although not always expressed along political party lines—in part because of the overarching commitment of traditional party leaders to the defense of the political system, as reflected by the present coalition agreement between the Liberal and Conservative parties.

THE COLOMBIAN CONGRESS:
ITS ENVIRONMENT AND FUNCTIONS

THE STRUCTURE OF POWER

Legislative behavior is molded in large part by the functions the legislature discharges in the political system, as determined by the structure of power that prevails in the society. The Colombian Congress is no exception in this regard. Since the early days of the Republic, Colombian society has been marked by rigid patterns of class stratification and the concentration of power at the apex of the social structure. But it was not until after the consolidation of an "oligarchical hegemony" during the latter part of the nineteenth century—an offshoot of economic relations arising from agricultural production, mostly coffee, for an international market—that the political system became fairly integrated.[4] Challenges to the oligarchical patterns of domination that emerged late in the last century have been thwarted consistently throughout the twentieth century owing to the capacity of dominant groups to mobilize their resources at crucial junctures in the country's development when serious threats have materialized (Fals Borda, 1969; García, 1971). The one exception was in the latter stages of the period known as *la violencia,* in the late 1940s and 1950s, when political control temporarily eluded the grasp of upper-echelon political leaders and civil strife became widespread.[5] The perpetuation of oligarchical patterns of control is reflected in the party system by a series of political coalitions formed between the two traditional parties, Conservative and Liberal, whenever pronounced threats to the system have emerged.

The political response of traditional groups, designed to perpetuate their power in the face of challenge, has been a pattern of politics referred to as the politics of compromise. The cornerstone of such a strategy has involved coopting dissident groups into the power structure, provided they adhere to accepted rules of the game. As a result, the power structure resembles a "living museum" of traditional and new groups existing side by side, with no single element being eliminated from the power complex, assuming the rules are respected (Anderson, 1967: 104). This situation, obviously, is conducive to the preservation of the status quo, as the power of traditional groups is magnified beyond what their power base in the society might warrant, and the power of opposition groups is curtailed as a result of their cooptation and consent to follow established rules of the game. The politics of compromise involves largely an elite game that is embedded in the structure of domination, resting—elections notwithstanding—upon a restricted participatory base in both the economic and political systems.

COLOMBIAN POLITICAL PARTIES

Before turning directly to the Congress, we shall discuss briefly Colombian political parties, for they have discharged crucial roles in the political system in terms of representing an extension of the structure of domination in the political arena, as well as constituting an overarching structural determinant of legislative behavior. During most of the present century, political parties have been free to operate within an environment of electoral competition and have been situated structurally at the center of the political system, in the sense that parties, in one way or another, have constituted the locus of political activity. Since the latter part of the nineteenth century, Colombia's two traditional parties have contributed significantly to the formation and maintenance of the oligarchical structure of power, monopolizing political activity throughout this period, with the exception of the interlude in the 1950s when the military, under Gustavo Rojas Pinilla's leadership, governed the country.

Organizationally speaking, the Liberal and Conservative parties fall somewhere between Duverger's (1963) models of cadre and mass parties. Decision-making patterns resemble cadre-style organizations, for leadership tends to be highly concentrated in the hands of a closed circle of professional politicians. Moreover, the traditional parties are not well-differentiated organizations, with highly structured organizations running from the *barrio* to the national level. Instead, base organizations tend to be intermittent, with considerable activity during electoral periods, after which they disappear or become inactive. In this sense, the core of organizational activity is located mainly in the Congress, resting upon regionally based *políticos* tied to a national faction or party leader. While ideological differences between the parties have historical roots and appear in varying degrees of intensity from time to time, the commitment of the leadership of both parties to the prevailing structure of power thwarts the expression of such differences in periods of political crisis, seemingly ever present in the Colombian case.

In contrast to what might be expected of cadre organizations, Colombian parties resemble the mass model in terms of mobilizing the population for political activity, as a consequence of the hereditary party affilications of the population at all levels of the society. Both parties have been eminently successful in socializing the population for political action, to such an extent that most Colombians are labeled either Liberal or Conservative virtually from birth. The semi-ascriptive basis of partisan recruitment stems not so much from organizational activity or from social class differences as from a mysticism generated by each party, facilitated by extended networks of personal relationships that permeate economic and social relations of the society. The traditional parties constitute a series of clienteles, running from the local to the national level, that are based upon networks of personal relationships. Because both parties contain *policlasista* memberships that cut across the social structure, the party system has served as a means of integrating the population and, at the same time, offering support for existing power arrangements.

After the overthrow of the military regime headed by Rojas Pinilla in 1957, control of the government was returned to the traditional parties under terms of the National Front—Frente Nacional—a bipartisan pact designed to curb traditional party rivalries through *alternaći*on in the presidency and *paridad* between the two parties in all legislative and administrative posts. Since the Frente was instituted in 1958, the Liberal and Conservative parties have cooperated closely in governing the country. Open electoral competition between parties will be restored at all levels of the political system for the 1974 presidential elections, but the sharing of certain bureaucratic posts will continue. Although the National Front has achieved considerable success in realizing one of its major goals —reduction of traditional party hatreds emanating from the struggle for governmental control—it has contributed to the undermining of the two-party hegemony, in large part because of the inability of traditional parties to adapt to changing societal circumstances, either in terms of organization or policy.

By far the most significant alteration in the party system during the National Front period involves the formation and growth of a political movement headed by former military leader Rojas Pinilla, the Alianza Nacional Popular (ANAPO). Initially spanning both party labels, ANAPO constituted itself as a third party in the spring of 1971. Because leaders of the two traditional parties were instrumental in the overthrow of Rojas' military government, it is not surprising that ANAPO directs its rhetoric and activities against the traditional party establishment. ANAPO differs from the traditional parties in that it has a formidable populist base and a well-developed organizational apparatus, particularly in the urban areas of the country. At the same time, ANAPO resembles the traditional parties because of its highly personalistic leadership, a network of clienteles held together by personal relationships, and pronounced commitments to the existing political system. ANAPO's notable electoral successes stem precisely from the National Front agreement in that ANAPO has capitalized on the popular discontent with Frente governments.

LEGISLATIVE FUNCTIONS

Turning now specifically to the Colombian Congress, it becomes apparent that the functions it discharges in the political system have been shaped significantly not only by Western democratic theory and the role of the legislature therein but also by structural characteristics of the Colombian society, particularly the power structure and the party system. While most Colombian congressmen justify their activity largely in accordance with normative postulates associated with democratic theory, facile acceptance of such explanations leads to erroneous conclusions, for legislative activity in Colombia deviates significantly from the formal model. The argument is not that the Colombian Congress performs no salient functions in the political system or that functions generally postulated for legislatures are not performed, only that the development process in Colombia has fixed the parameters of legislative behavior in a fairly restricted manner.

The legislature has played a prominent role in the formulation of policy congruent with the predominant power relationships of the society. Before the "crisis of oligarchical hegemony" in the late 1920s, Congress was composed of predominantly upper and upper-middle class gentlemen, who worked closely with the executive branch of government and enjoyed considerable power within the political system. No major status differentials existed between upper-echelon political leaders in all three branches of government. At that time, however, the government tended to be extremely limited in the scope of its activities, when compared with the present, and the locus of political power stemmed primarily from the private sector of the economy. As a consequence of the crisis of oligarchical hegemony, Congress assumed a significant role in the restructuring of power relationships in the society through the cooptation of new groups into the political system in accordance with the politics of compromise (Leal, 1973). Within the legislative context, new groups were recognized as legitimate political actors, the areas covered by their interests were delimited, and mechanisms for institutional conflict between political groups were developed. As noted above, such activity had the effect of preserving the status quo in terms of power relationships, even though accompanied by considerable political conflict.

As a result of the increasing heterogenity of interests represented in Congress and the conflict resulting from that, political power has been transferred increasingly to the executive branch of government—to a degree that surpasses what seemingly is a universal trend (Bracher, 1964: 363). The 1968 constitutional reforms represent a culmination in the shift of power from Congress to the executive, for congressional power and initiative were drastically curtailed, particularly in budgetary and fiscal matters. In terms of both recruitment patterns and policy orientations, the executive branch remains a more faithful spokesman for the traditional power structure than the legislature. As one congressman puts it (Sedano, 1971: 23):

> With the populist movements that have arisen in the country, people such as myself who identify with the popular classes have become congressmen. It is important to the governing class that the popular classes not be

elected to parliament and if they are elected, their actions are not taken into consideration. In this manner, the oligarchy, through many means at its disposal, sees to it that parliament does not function, because if it does work well it is a weapon against the elite or governing class of the country.

The function of law-making has been usurped to a great extent by the presidency, leaving Congress with the task of legitimizing those actions. This does not imply, however, that Congress is a rubber stamp for the president, because sustained congressional opposition to the president can be formidable and effective (Dix, 1968: 172). Such opposition generally crystallizes not around institutional struggles for power between the executive and legislative branches of government but from conflicts between the president and political parties and factions (Payne, 1968: 249). As discussed below, the activity of parties or factions in the legislature can be viewed partly in terms of tactics designed to maximize the power of a party or faction, often for reasons of patronage associated with control of government. If the president advocates policies not perceived to be congruent with the goals of particular parties or factions, then formidable opposition may ensue. Whenever parties or groups involved command considerable political strength in Congress, the president usually compromises with the leader of the faction or party in question.

The Colombian Congress traditionally has served the function of providing a forum for the expression, and to a lesser extent the resolution, of conflict in the political system. Generally speaking, societal conflict has pivoted around the instability and insufficiency of the economic system, the fragility of governmental structures, and the decentralization of power in various regions of the country. These conflicts have been expressed within the Congress primarily in three respects, varying in intensity from one epoch to another yet remaining salient to the present—regional differences, ideological disputes, and the struggle for governmental hegemony. Political conflict revolving around control of the government has been the most forceful source of dissension, producing intense cleavage that frequently has been resolved through compromise between leaders of the traditional parties. As Dix (1968: 180) observes, "The parties have treated government as an objective to be seized and, once won, as a bastion in which to intrench themselves like armies of occupation, subsisting on the bureaucratic booty of battle." While ideological conflicts and their expression in Congress have been curtailed by the struggle for governmental control, such differences have assumed major proportions at times. The National Front has inhibited the expression of such conflict, but with the return of open party competition at the national level in the 1974 presidential elections, ideological battles will probably become more forceful. Finally, the intensity of regional conflict has subsided somewhat as the country has become more integrated and developed, yet regional differences remain forceful in legislative politics, often over-shadowing conflicts arising from party affiliation or ideological differences (Hoskin, 1971).

In summary, the Colombian Congress does not constitute a strategic institutional locus of decision-making in the political system, in large part because of the predominance of power in the executive branch of government. This is not to say, however, that Congress discharges no significant functions in the political system. As noted above, Congress has performed a key role in the integration of new groups into the political arena, along with delimiting and legitimating the activity of those groups. Not only has the legislature assisted in the absorption of new groups but likewise it has served as a key political institution in the territorial and political integration of the country, providing a forum where regional politicians interact and relate to political party and governmental activity. The impor-tance of the legislature as a forum for the institutionalization of political party relationships should not be minimized, even though the legislature as an institution only intermittently figures in the exercise of political power. Moreover, congressional approval of executive actions cloaks them in an aura of legitimacy, although the gap between theory and practice in the legislative arena places Congress in an increasingly vulnerable position regarding criticism of the institution.

With such a circumscribed role portrayed for the Colombian legislature in the political system, the obvious question arises, why study legislative behavior? The argument suggests that Congress is embedded in a structure of power that curtails its legitimized activities but, at the same time, the traditional power structure and the political structures that reflect it are becoming increasingly susceptible to mounting pressures for change. Because of the forthcoming return of open interparty competition and the rather weak political bases of most groups not presently represented in Congress, those parties and factions currently in Congress, particu-larly ANAPO and a possible regrouping of the more change-oriented políticos from the traditional parties, probably will constitute the nucleus of an opposition that will become considerably more forceful in the nation's politics. In summary, conflict expressed within Congress assumes significance, for the sources of political change in the near future are found here, although this does not necessarily imply that Congress as such will be at the center of the stage.

PRESENTATION OF THE FINDINGS

LEGISLATIVE CONFLICT AS PERCEIVED BY CONGRESSMEN

Colombian congressmen were presented a card with a list of conflicts and asked to identify the five most significant ones, in order of importance, that they observed during the 1968 session. The results are summarized in Table 1 which, in addition to showing the percentage of responses for each conflict in terms of the order it was mentioned (columns 1-5), indicates the percentage of those interviewed who mentioned each conflict (column 6), and the percentage represented by each conflict alternative in terms of the total number of conflicts mentioned (column 7). Generally speaking, four areas of institutional tension predominate: (1) conflicts associated with political party or faction behavior, (2) congressional-executive relations, (3) relationships between *técnicos* and *políticos*, and (4) national-regional cleavages. At least 50% of those interviewed mentioned each of these conflicts; combined they represent 79% of the total conflicts mentioned. These four general areas of legislative conflict very much overshadow those associated with economic group activity, left-right differences, generational gaps, and dissension arising from legislative experience.

The data shown in Table 1 confirm the generalization offered in the previous section of the paper that the Colombian Congress has discharged a significant political function by serving as an institutional arena for the expression and, to a lesser extent, resolution of conflict pertaining to political parties. Congressmen were asked to evaluate three conflicts concerning parties: those stemming from inter-party, inter-faction, and intra-faction relations. Viewed as a whole, these three sources of conflicts represent 36% of all conflicts expressed by the congressmen. Consequently, Congress occupies a strategic position in the political system for understanding political party behavior.

TABLE 1
LEGISLATORS' PERCEPTIONS OF CONFLICTS OBSERVED IN CONGRESS (in percentages)

Conflicts	First	Second	Third	Fourth	Fifth	Percent of Members Mentioning[a]	Percent of All Activities Mentioned
Congressional-Executive	45	19	22	7	1	92	20
Within political factions	18	16	16	11	9	67	14
Between political factions	11	24	9	10	8	59	12
Técnicos-Políticos	2	9	12	19	20	58	12
Nation-Region	1	9	14	12	18	50	11
Between parties	20	10	4	7	5	45	10
Economic groups and the Executive	0	4	9	8	16	33	7
Economic groups and Congress	1	6	6	7	8	26	6
Generational	.5	1	4	6	7	16	3
Left-Right	1	1	2	7	4	15	3
Legislative experience	.5	.5	2	5	5	11	2
TOTALS	100	99.5	100	99	101		100
(n)	(219)[b]	(216)	(211)	(202)	(184)		(1032)

a. The sum of these percentages exceeds 100% because most congressmen expressed more than one conflict.
b. The number of responses is less than 220, because one person refused to cooperate and several members mentioned less than five conflicts.

Inter-party conflict constitutes the least important source of political party cleavage of the three mentioned, in part a reflection of the bipartisan cooperation in Congress resulting from the National Front agreement. The Liberal-Conservative coalition partners have worked together closely in Congress, although some notable exceptions arose that had to be resolved by compromises between top leaders of the two parties. The Independent faction of the Conservative Party, followers of the late Laureano Gómez, began as the Conservative group in the coalition, but they withdrew from the government and went into the opposition after their poor electoral showing in 1960. The Union faction, headed by ex-President Mariano Ospina Pérez, replaced them and has continued to serve in the government since then. Inter-party competition as such has stemmed mainly from opposition to the Frente coalition on the part of the Independent Conservatives and ANAPO. While ANAPO claims to be vehemently against the National Front, numerous examples exist in Congress that demonstrate ANAPO's timidity in this respect. Perhaps the most pronouuced oppostion to the government coalition came from the Movimiento Revolucionario Liberal (MRL) before rejoining the Liberal Party in 1967 when its leader, López Michelson, became governor of Córdoba.

As a result of the divisions within the traditional parties, conflicts between political groups or factions often became more significant than inter-party conflict, as suggested in Table 1. This has become even more so since the data were gathered, as a consequence of the Liberal Party split in the spring of 1971, with one faction following Carlos Lleras Restrepo and Alfonso López Michelsen and the second adhering to Julio César Turbay's leadership. However, in anticipation of the 1974 elections, both factions once again joined forces in October 1972. Despite recurring discussion of party unification, the Conservative Party division persists. Building a winning coalition in Congress involves the cooperation of various factions of Liberals, Conservatives, and Anapistas. The dynamics of legislative conflict tend to revolve around political factions as they jockey for position in crucial votes and often try to utilize their congressional strength to obtain concessions from the president. The congressional delegation of a faction or party is responsible, in many cases, for the formulation of party or faction policy, sometimes overshadowing the national party directorate in terms of power. This is less pronounced in ANAPO, a more highly centralized organization than the other parties and factions.

The third conflict associated with political party activity arises from dissension internal to political factions or, in other words, the problem of group discipline. Party and faction discipline in Colombia fluctuates widely between the polar extremes of unity and disunity, depending upon the issue and its perceived importance to the faction or party in relation to other factions or parties and the president. This vacillation can be explained by structural characteristics of parties and factions in the sense that they constitute diverse groups of people held together, in large part, by the rewards associated with party or faction membership. Thus on crucial issues, such as the Constitutional Reform of 1968, congressional voting follows strict party and faction lines. On most issues, however, congressmen are not pressured to vote along party or faction lines, which allows them to vote in accordance with their personal predilections. The high degree of factional unity on key issues should not, however, disguise the importance of intra-factional warfare in the Congress.

Turning to another area of legislative conflict, congressmen agree highly that differences between the legislative and executive branches of government figure prominently in the Colombian Congress; 92% of those interviewed listed this source of cleavage as important. As noted earlier, there has been a formidable transfer of power from Congress to the executive since the 1930s as a result, in part, of the politics of compromise. This shift in the locus of power reached a high point with congressional consent to the 1968 constitutional reform, which severely limited congressional powers. Congressmen are highly cognizant of this power disparity; 86% agreed that Congress has lost considerable power over the past 30 years. Most believe that Congress should try to recuperate lost powers, but this is highly unlikely. In addition to the constitutional powers lodged in the presidency, the chief executive can use governmental resources at his disposal for influencing Congress, generally with a high degree of success. During the National Front period, the executive branch generally has encountered little difficulty in pushing legislation through Congress, particularly if no disagreement exists between the coalition partners. But if congressional opposition to a president's legislative program is pronounced, this may lead to its abandonment, as occurred with Carlos Lleras' bill to create a forced-savings program for purposes of national development.

Tension between technocrats and politicians represents a third major area of conflict expressed in Congress. This source of political dissension is fairly universal in the sense that as governments discharge ever-growing roles in economic development and assume greater responsibilities for the welfare of their citizens, increased emphasis is placed upon governmental planning to maximize the utilization of limited resources. As a consequence, técnicos are relied upon to a greater extent, assuming tasks and occupying posts formerly falling within the domain of traditional politicians. This confrontation between técnicos and políticos assumed major proportions during the government of Carlos Lleras (1966-70), for he tended to be disdainful of traditional politicians—not, however, to the exclusion of other groups—and turned to young, expertise-laden technicians to man his government. In the process, Lleras bypassed traditional politicians in the selection of candidates for governmental posts. To take only one example, the National Planning Commission virtually became isolated from congressional pressure, leaving the formulation and execution of development projects to the técnicos. After Lleras left office in 1970, his successor, Misael Pastrana Borrero, abandoned rigid adherence to the technocrat model of government and returned many prerogatives to the traditional politicians.

Lastly, congressmen reported that national-regional differences registered high on their lists of conflicts during the 1968 session (Hoskin, 1971). This is not surprising in light of the historical legacies associated with regionalism in Colombia, a country marked by pronounced geographical, cultural, and economic differences from one region to another. But unlike that found in most Latin American countries, Colombian regionalism is more complex, in part because it has not involved solely conflict between the capital city and the remainder of the country; besides Bogotá, large metropolitan areas dominate each major region. Consequently, political conflict often has centered around regional differences, with Congress figuring prominently in the expression and resolution of regional conflicts. Before the constitutional changes in 1968, congressional activity focused in large part upon the distribution of governmental resources, *partidas regionales,* to the departments. Moreover, while the major political parties have organizations and electoral support in each department, their strength varies considerably from one area of the country to another. Presidential elections, likewise, reflect the importance of regionalism in Colombian politics.

CONFLICT DIMENSIONS AS DERIVED FROM MULTIDIMENSIONAL
SCALE ANALYSIS OF PREFERENCE-ORDER DATA

After discussing congressmen's overt responses as to what conflicts were prominent in the 1968 session, we turn now to an indirect approach to the identification of legislative conflict: spatial analysis. Interviewees were asked to rank-order nine political factions and nine political leaders in accordance with those groups or leaders closest to their own political predilections. The preference orders were obtained by a card-sort technique, in which respondents were given two sets of randomly ordered cards, one for the nine factions and another for the nine leaders (Milbrath et al., 1970). The underlying assumption was that each congressman would rank each stimuli according to some unspecified criteria that subsequently could be identified. It should be emphasized that, according to this technique, respondents may not have been conscious of viewing legislative conflict in terms derived from analysis of their preferences for factions and leaders. This contributes to the validity of the technique in the sense that interviewees are less likely to disguise their attitudes, in comparison to a direct question about a substantive matter, if they are unaware of the analysis possibilities related to their responses.

At least for the author, the theoretical underpinnings of spatial analysis stem from Downs' (1957) landmark study, An Economic Theory of Democracy, in which he builds a formal model of political party competition based upon party positioning and voter choice, once certain assumptions are made concerning the rationality of party leaders and behavior choices of the electorate. While Downs postulated that voters can be aligned along a single ideological dimension and that parties position themselves along this dimension to maximize their vote, subsequent criticism of this assumption of unidimensionality has paved the way for a theoretical extension of the model into multidimensional space (Converse, 1966; Campbell et al., 1966; MacRae, 1970). This criticism, along with other methodological contributions (Coombs, 1964; Kruskal, 1964; Shephard, 1966), has enabled social scientists to operationalize the use of spatial analysis for explaining preference-order data in an r-dimensional space.

Extension of the analysis of the original preference-order data to multidimensional space is operationalized in this study by a computer program, TORSCA, written by Young (1968). Briefly, the program takes N-orders of n-stimuli and "finds a spatial configuration and set of vectors of given dimensionality such that the given ranks from the preference data can be represented as the ordering in which the stimuli project on to the vectors" (Green, 1968: 34). Unlike factor analysis, this scaling program assumes that the data are monotonic rather than linear, although the derived spatial configurations can be interpreted in metric terms (Shephard, 1966: 299-300). That is, the projection of the original preference-order data into spaces of higher dimensionality produces distances between the points in the spatial configuration that can be interpreted in the same manner as in any physical context. The program tells the computer to search heuristically within a specified range of dimensions until the best fit is achieved. The "stress-level," as the statistic is called, reveals when a space of a given dimensionality yields satisfactory solution in reconstructing the original relationship of n-points (stress levels of .05 are considered good). The derived spatial configurations, showing the original stimuli projected onto vectors or dimensions, leaves the analyst with the task of identifying those dimensions.

Generally speaking, the original preference-order data are converted into a distance matrix, which is projected into multidimensional space. By looking at the resulting stress-levels for each specified number of dimensions, the analyst can determine how many dimensions are needed to explain the rationale that respondents utilized in expressing their preferences for the stimuli, in this case either party factions or leaders. If a satisfactory solution is achieved—an acceptable stress level results—the researcher then identifies the dimensions. While the methodological aspects of the analysis tend to become tedious, further discussion can be skipped here, for the resulting configurations are not difficult to comprehend. (For a more detailed explanation of the method, see Hoskin and Swanson, 1973.)

Figure 1 reveals a derived spatial configuration for the interviewees' rank-orders of party factions, with an acceptable stress level for two dimensions.[6] The horizontal axis is a left-right ideological dimension, with the negative pole of the axis representing the left side of the political spectrum and the positive pole the right. The second dimension, the vertical axis, expresses congressmen's perceptions of the degree of support or identification with the government on the part of various factions.[7] The stress level for the two-dimensional solution (.059) indicates that the bulk of the variance in explaining why congressmen ordered the factions the way they did

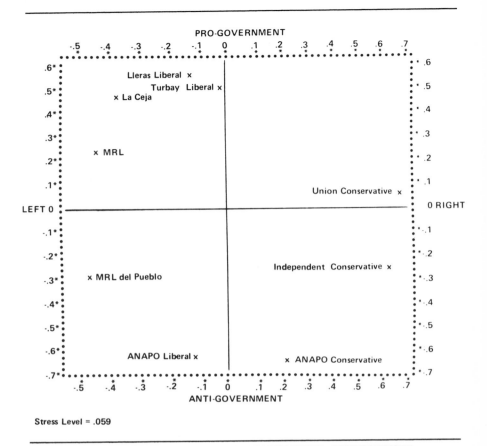

Figure 1: TWO-DIMENSIONAL SPATIAL CONFIGURATION: CONGRESSMEN VIEWING POLITICAL FACTIONS

can be interpreted largely in terms of their perceptions of factions along the lines of ideology and government support. Both dimensions appear equally salient for respondents, in terms of the length of the axes generated (1.185 for governmental support and 1.130 for ideology), which constitutes a measure of the relative centrality of a dimension for respondents. Converse (1966: 201) argues that insofar as one respondent may differ from another, "with respect to relative involvement in one dimension of party difference (x), by comparison with some other dimension (y), then the x dimension should seem extended, and the y dimension foreshortened, in his view of party space."

The two-dimensional solution portrayed in Figure 1 conforms fairly closely to political realities in Colombia; that is, the factions are located on the two dimensions in a manner that approximates political discourse and analysis by knowledgeable observers. Turning first to the vertical axis (government support), all Liberal groups fall on the support side, with the exception of the MRL del Pueblo, a very small splinter group in the MRL that is opposed to the National Front, largely for ideological reasons. The Union Conservative faction, likewise, is located on the support side of the axis, reflecting its participation in the government coalition with the Liberal Party although its degree of governmental support is not pronounced, stemming in part from the domination of the presidency by the then Liberal President Carlos Lleras. The position of the Independent Conservatives suggests that they are not terribly opposed to the government coalition, and probably would have served in the coalition since 1960 had they been the major faction of the Conservative Party. The most vehement opposition to the National Front comes from both wings of ANAPO, which reflects the realities of interparty competition in Colombia. To say that ANAPO's opposition to the National Front has constituted one of the overarching determinants of intergroup behavior during recent years is not in any way an exaggeration. The growing political power of ANAPO has provided a strong stimulus for coalescent behavior on the part of the National Front partners.

The distribution of the factions on the horizontal axis (ideological dimension) also does not deviate much from expectations. The MRL del Pueblo, MRL, and La Ceja are seen as the most leftist, followed closely by the remaining Liberal factions. The Union and Independent factions of the Conservative Party firmly anchor the right side of the political spectrum. In terms of ANAPO's rhetoric and, to a lesser extent its behavior, one might have anticipated that both wings of the group would fall much further to the left. This departure from expectations may have resulted from differing interpretations of what ANAPO represents; that is, Liberal and Conservative respondents may have considered ANAPO as a rightist or centrist group, while Anapistas placed themselves on the extreme left. As a result, ANAPO would end up near the center of the dimension, as is the case. As pointed out earlier in the paper, ANAPO is a heterogeneous political movement in terms of ideology and programs which lends itself to diverse interpretations. Finally, note the greater length of the right side of the ideological axis in comparison to the left, once again an accurate characterization of Colombian party factions in ideological terms.

The distribution of political factions on the two conflict dimensions clearly demonstrates that three distinct faction clusters—
parties—prevail, as expressed by the distance relationships. These are
the Liberals, Conservatives, and Anapistas. Despite the cooperation
between the Liberal Party and the Union faction in the National
Front governments since 1960, which supposedly reduced traditional
party hatreds between the two, the Unionistas remain closer to the
Independientes on the support dimension than to the Liberal
factions. On the ideological axis, the Liberal groups are located to
the left and both wings of the Conservative Party to the right.
Despite the ambiguity surrounding its ideological positioning,
ANAPO remains separated by considerable distance from either the
Liberal or Conservative factions, in terms of the governmental
support axis and for reasons of deep personal animosities between
upper-level leaders of ANAPO and of the traditional parties. In
summary, the distribution of the various Liberal, Conservative, and
ANAPO factions on these two dimensions is such that the conflict
bases for interparty competition are deeply embedded in the
country's major political groups.

In addition to ranking party factions, congressmen were requested
to give their preferences for nine political leaders, most of them
associated with one of the factions included in the previous data set.
Figure 2 shows the results of a multidimensional scale analysis of the
nine políticos. Similar to the analysis of faction preferences, an
acceptable solution is found in two dimensions, one representing
ideology and the second governmental support. Both dimensions are
about equal in terms of the length of the axes generated, but the axes
are longer in the resulting configuration for leaders than in the case
of the factions. While this may imply that political leaders constitute
a more forceful point of reference than factions for Colombian
congressmen, the most outstanding generalization that can be drawn
from comparing the two configurations is their high degree of
similarity, in terms of positioning both leaders and factions on the
two dimensions. Liberal leaders (Lleras Camargo, Lleras Restrepo,
Turbay Ayala, Agudelo Villa, López Michelsen) fall within the same
general areas of the configurations as Liberal factions, the positioning
of Conservative leaders (Ospina Pérez, Gómez Hurtado, Guillermo
Valencia) and factions follows suit, and Rojas Pinilla is located fairly
close to both wings of ANAPO.

Some differences between the two spatial configurations emerge,
however. López Michelsen, for example, is placed slightly in the

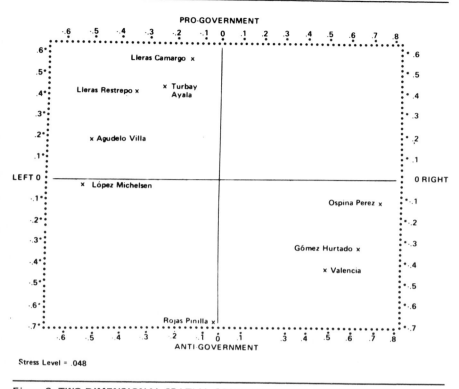

PRO-GOVERNMENT

Lleras Camargo x

x Turbay
Ayala

Lleras Restrepo x

x Agudelo Villa

LEFT 0   0 RIGHT

x López Michelsen

Ospina Perez x

Gómez Hurtado x

x Valencia

Rojas Pinilla x

ANTI-GOVERNMENT

Stress Level = .048

Figure 2: TWO-DIMENSIONAL SPATIAL CONFIGURATION: CONGRESSMEN VIEWING POLITICAL LEADERS

non-supportive quadrant, while the MRL is located firmly on the support side. The same difference, though less pronounced, holds for Agudelo Villa and his faction, La Ceja. Likewise, the Union Conservative faction is positioned in the support quadrant, while its leader, Ospina Pérez, falls in the opposition. Considering that the respondents ordering the stimuli are congressmen who know personally the political leaders, it is not surprising that some slight differences emerge in their evaluations of factions and leaders. Finally, the location of Alberto Lleras Camargo on the extreme end of the support pole lends credence to the validity of the configuration, for he was one of the principal architects of the National Front.

In summary, the multidimensional analyses of the preference-order data have permitted the specification of underlying bases for legislative conflict associated with political party activity, which forms one of the most significant determinants of legislative behavior. The empirical revelation that ideology and government support constitute two principal dimensions for interpreting congressmen's evaluations of factions and leaders conforms with the discussion in the last section of the paper, in which it was argued that legislative conflict traditionally has revolved around these two overarching cleavages, along with regional differences.[8] Moreover, the spatial configurations not only facilitated the identification of the principal conflict dimensions but placed political factions and leaders along those dimensions in accordance with an ordered metric.

IDEOLOGICAL CONSTRAINT AMONG COLOMBIAN CONGRESSMEN

After having established the importance of ideology as a major source of political conflict in the Colombian Congress, the task remains of analyzing the structure and content of that ideology. This is necessary because, as one author puts it, "the use of such basic dimensions of judgment as the liberal-conservative continuum betokes a contextual grasp of politics that permits a wide range of more specific idea-elements to be organized into more tightly constrained wholes" (Converse, 1964: 227). But before looking at various facets of ideology expressed by Colombian congressmen, a brief note about the disputed role of ideology in the Colombian context.

While most students of Colombian politics agree that there were ideological cleavages in the essentially intra-elite politics of the nineteenth century, as well as during the years from 1930 to 1958, such a consensus does not prevail regarding the National Front period. Colombian writers such as Fals Borda (1969), García (1971), and Leal (1973) generally emphasize the ideological similarities of political party elites in terms of class homogeneity and interests rather than any pronounced differences. Dix (1968: 253) observes that ideological differences between the parties have not been erased as a result of the National Front but the gap between the traditional parties has narrowed and points of similarity emphasized. In sharp contrast, Payne (1968: 249) writes that

> the observer who seeks to find a Left and a Right in the Colombian Congress is doomed to error if he makes a superficial study and is likely to go insane if he makes a careful examination. The search for a progressive or reactionary segment in the Colombian Congress is about as pointless as attempting to divide birds along the same lines.

The position maintained here is that the National Front has blurred ideological differences between the traditional parties, although not eliminated them, and that the return of interparty competition in the 1974 presidential elections will accentuate ideological differences, particularly in light of the growing capacity of ANAPO to mobilize large segments of the population in terms of social class appeals. Thus while the National Front may have reduced ideological differences between Liberals and Conservatives, at the same time it has contributed significantly to the revitalization of ideological cleavages in the society. The data presented in this section of the paper offer empirical justification for such a generalization.

For the purposes of this paper, the concept ideology will be operationalized in terms similar to what Converse (1964: 207) labels a belief system: "a configuration of ideas and attitudes in which the elements are bound together by some form of constraint or functional interdependence." Such constraints, if they are present, need not be logical in nature: they may stem from either psychological or social characteristics of individuals and the society. In analyzing data from the United States, Converse argues that different belief systems need not hang together, and that the degree of constraint varies directly with the location of respondents in the social hierarchy—that is, the higher the social position, the greater the likelihood of constraint among belief systems. Thus in the context of this study, the relatively privileged social status of Colombian congressmen should facilitate the expression of constraint among diverse belief systems.

Ten distinct belief syndromes are presented in Table 2, based upon a series of Lickert items that were included in the questionnaire administered to Colombian congressmen. The individual items were pretested on students, upper-level business executives, a sample of middle- and upper-class Bogotá residents, and former congressmen. As a result, several items were discarded or rewritten and new ones added in accordance with criteria for Thurstone and Lickert scaling. After the interviews had been completed, the final set of 48 items was reduced by 11 when they failed to meet standards for Guttman scaling. Thus each belief system listed in Table 2 consists of a set of attitudinal items that are interrelated both theoretically and empirically.[9]

Looking at the individual attitudinal syndromes shown in Table 2, the scale labeled political ideology consists of six items related to political institutions and non-economic governmental policy, essen-

TABLE 2
MATRIX OF CORRELATIONS AMONG ATTITUDINAL DISPOSITIONS OF COLOMBIAN CONGRESSMEN

	Economic Ideology	Political Ideology	Orientation toward the U.S.	Religiosity	Nation-Region	Executive Orientation	Economic Assn. Orientation	Upper-Class Orientation	Middle-Class Orientation	Lower-Class Orientation
Economic Ideology	1.00									
Political Ideology	.44	1.00								
Orientation toward the United States	.29	.39	1.00							
Religiosity	−.18	−.19	−.02	1.00						
Nation-Region	.19	.36	.28	.21	1.00					
Executive Orientation	−.02	.15	−.15	.07	.20	1.00				
Economic Association Orientation	−.15	−.04	−.17	.14	.01	.22	1.00			
Upper-Class Orientation	−.31	−.17	−.40	.23	.02	.20	.31	1.00		
Middle-Class Orientation	.18	.15	.21	−.14	.07	−.15	−.12	−.15	1.00	
Lower-Class Orientation	.22	.24	.33	−.21	.05	−.27	−.11	−.21	.22	1.00

tially a scale tapping political liberalism; the five items dealing with economic ideology focus upon economic development and governmental policy in economic matters; and the orientation to the United States (four items) taps congressional attitudes toward *gringolandia.* The six-item religiosity scale is concerned principally with the political role of the Church. Orientation toward the executive (six items) and orientation toward economic associations (four items) tap congressmen's attitudes toward two major reference groups in the political system. Whether congressmen are oriented toward the nation or regions is reflected in the nation-regions scale (four items). Lastly, respondents' orientations toward social classes are measured in three separate sets of questions, of three items each, related to orientations toward the upper, middle, and lower classes. When the correlation matrix is factor analyzed, the scales load heavily on three underlying dimensions: the first factor favors social class orientation, the second reflects ideology, and the third relates to religiosity and nation-region orientation. Table 3 summarizes the loadings of the scales on the three factors.[10]

The correlation matrix presented in Table 2 indicates a high degree of constraint among congressmen's diverse attitudinal syndromes; lack of inter-scale constraint is the exception rather than the rule. As might be expected from the earlier-mentioned factor loadings, the scales pertaining to economic ideology, political ideology, and orientation toward the United States are highly interrelated; those congressmen who are leftist in terms of political and economic ideology tend to express anti-United States feelings. These three scales correlate negatively with religiosity; that is, congressmen with leftist leanings do not score high on religiosity, although the matrix suggests that anti-United States feelings can result, in part, from

TABLE 3
FACTOR LOADINGS OF THE ATTITUDINAL SCALES

	Factor 1	Factor 2	Factor 3
Economic ideology	−.254	.652	−.167
Political ideology	−.059	.839	−.034
United States orientation	−.558	.479	.308
Religiosity	.158	−.239	.843
Nation-Region	.071	.571	.606
Executive orientation	.718	.380	−.009
Economic associations	.563	.026	.075
Upper class	.611	−.239	.184
Middle class	−.414	.208	−.037
Lower class	−.546	.258	−.086

conservative political belief systems as well. Likewise, left-leaning legislators are oriented more toward the nation than toward regions. Those with more radical economic and political ideologies tend to be oriented negatively toward the executive branch of government as well as toward economic associations. The pronounced correlation between economic ideology, political ideology, and United States orientation on the one hand, and social class orientations on the other is not at all unanticipated, considering the structure and significance of social class relationships in the political system. The more radical congressmen quite obviously display negative attitudes toward the upper class and positive orientations toward the middle and lower classes.

The religiosity and nation-region scales load highly on the same factor, which is testimony to the close association between regional orientations and religiosity, in part a manifestation of uneven development patterns in the country. Those congressmen who score high on the religiosity scale are favorably oriented toward the upper class and negatively oriented toward the middle and lower classes. While nation-region predispositions do not correlate highly with social class orientations, those nationally oriented congressmen are quite favorable toward the executive branch of government—which probably signifies that regionally oriented congressmen are more staunch supporters of Congress, which would be congruent with one of Congress' traditional functions, namely the manifestation of regional differences.

Earlier in this chapter the generalization was offered to the effect that the executive branch of government constitutes a more faithful representative of oligarchical interests than Congress, as a result of the politics of compromise and the increasing heterogenity of interests in Congress. The high correlation between a favorable orientation toward the executive and supportive attitudes toward economic associations constitutes some justification, for economic associations in Colombia are closely interwoven into the structure of oligarchical power. Moreover, favorable orientations toward both the executive and economic associations correlate positively with upper-class orientations and negatively with middle- and lower-class orientations. The high loadings on Factor 1, shown in Table 3, of the scales pertaining to orientations toward the executive, economic associations, and social class reveal the interrelatedness of social class and structural components of the political system.

To generalize, the matrix of correlations between diverse belief systems of congressmen clearly reveals a high degree of constraint from one belief system to another, along with some pronounced attitudinal manifestations of prominent structural characteristics of the Colombian political system, particularly those stemming from social class relationships. If a congressman forms a part of the oligarchical structure of power, or defends it, chances are he will display favorable attitudes toward both the executive and economic associations, manifest conservative economic and political beliefs, and will be negatively disposed toward middle and lower classes.

In some cases, the belief systems presented in Tables 2 and 3 vary in terms of the political party affiliations of congressmen. Table 4 shows the relationship between party affiliation of congressmen and their scores on the scales related to economic ideology, political ideology, orientation toward the United States, religiosity, and orientation toward the executive branch. Neither the nation-region orientation of congressmen nor their orientations toward economic associations is related highly to party affiliation. The same generally holds for social class orientations, for the small differences between the Liberals, Unionists, and Independents generally produces a low chi-square. ANAPO, however, deviates significantly from the other three party groups in that Anapistas are oriented more negatively toward the upper class and more positively toward the middle and lower classes. This is not unexpected, considering ANAPO's lower-class support and anti-establishment predilections.

Turning now to the four-fold tables, some pronounced differences emerge between parties in terms of economic ideology, as revealed in Table 4A. Liberal congressmen are the most radical, followed by Anapistas, then Unionistas, and lastly the Independientes. The only departure from what might be expected is that Liberals tend to be more to the left on this scale than ANAPO members, which is testimony to the presence of some rather conservative Anapistas in Congress. Put differently, the composition of ANAPO, is such that blockages are present that inhibit the consistent implementation of a populist ideology and program. In terms of political ideology, shown in Table 4B, the rank order of the parties shifts somewhat in comparison with economic ideology; going from the most radical, the order is Liberal, ANAPO, Independent, and Union. Anapistas tend to be even more conservative on political ideology than economic ideology, and the Union Conservatives more to the right than the Independents. Liberal congressmen appear significantly more radical on this scale than cogressmen from other groups. The

TABLE 4

RELATIONSHIP BETWEEN CONGRESSMEN'S POLITICAL PARTY AFFILIATION AND BELIEF SYSTEMS (in percentages)

Belief System	Liberal	Union Conservative	ANAPO	Independent Conservative	
A. Economic Ideology					
Low	17.5	44.2	30	54.5	(67)
Medium	43.7	32.6	45	36.4	(89)
High	38.8	23.3	25	9.1	(63)
TOTAL	100	100	100	100	
N =	(103)	(43)	(40)	(33)	(219)
	Chi-square = 24.567		Significance Level .001		
B. Political Ideology					
Low	16.5	58.1	47.5	45.5	(76)
Medium	35.0	27.9	32.5	42.4	(75)
High	48.5	14.0	20.0	12.1	(68)
TOTAL	100	100	100	100	
N =	(103)	(43)	(40)	(33)	(219)
	Chi-square = 40.40		Significance Level .001		
C. Orientation toward the United States					
Positive	21.4	39.5	15	27.3	(54)
Neutral	48.5	51.2	20	51.5	(97)
Negative	30.1	9.3	65	21.2	(68)
TOTAL	100	100	100	100	
N =	(103)	(43)	(40)	(33)	(219)
	Chi-square = 34.97		Significance Level .001		
D. Religiosity					
Low	49.5	4.7	35.0	12.1	(71)
Medium	37.9	30.2	47.5	15.2	(76)
High	12.6	65.1	17.5	72.7	(72)
TOTAL	100	100	100	100	
N =	(103)	(43)	(40)	(33)	(219)
	Chi-square = 75.12		Significance Level .001		
E. Executive Orientation					
Low	21.2	11.6	62.5	54.5	(76)
Medium	31.1	30.2	27.5	33.3	(67)
High	47.7	58.1	10.0	12.1	(76)
TOTAL	100	99.9	100	99.9	
N =	(103)	(43)	(40)	(33)	(219)
	Chi-square = 41.3		Significance Level .001		

distinctiveness of ANAPO vis-á-vis other groups is revealed clearly in Table 4C, which shows the relationship between party affiliation and orientation toward the United States.

Congressmen from different political parties manifest varied attitudes in regard to the religiosity scale (see Table 4D). The Independent and Union legislators not only are more religiously oriented than Liberal and ANAPO members but remarkably so. The Liberals score the lowest on the religiosity scale, followed by Anapistas. These religious cleavages are deeply embedded in the traditional political parties and quite obviously have not disappeared. With the introduction of a Liberal-sponsored bill now in Congress to alter provision of the Concordat with the papacy, these attitudinal cleavages may well provide the basis for prolonged and heated debates. Although few Anapistas fall in the high cell of the religiosity scale, they are considerably more ambivalent on this scale than members of the other three parties.

Finally, Table 4E cross-tabulates party affiliation with orientation toward the executive. The Liberals and Union Conservatives are oriented positively toward the executive, while Anapistas and Independents assume a more negative stance toward the executive. This reflects the National Front coalition in which, to repeat, the Liberals and Unionists have formed the government, with ANAPO and the Independents in the opposition. In view of the distribution of congressmen on this dimension, in all probability attitudes toward the eecutive would shift considerably if a non-coalition government were in power.

CONCLUSIONS

This paper has focused upon dimensions of conflict within the Colombian Congress, particularly those associated with ideological differences. Before treating these aspects of legislative behavior, the functions discharged by the Congress in the political system were discussed, by means of historical analysis, in order that legislative conflict might be interpreted meaningfully not only within the Colombian context but for purposes of comparison with other legislatures as well. The argument in brief suggests that the role of Congress in the political system, especially its institutional autonomy, is determined to a great extent by the structure of power prevailing in the society. With the crisis of "oligarchical hegemony" in the late 1920s, Congress assumed a significant role, through the politics of compromise, in the alterations that occurred in terms of power relationships. Accompanying this strategy, the locus of political power shifted increasingly to the executive branch of government. This trend reached a climax with the passage of the 1968 constitutional reforms which the National Front government successfully pushed through a docile Congress. Within this context of executive prerogatives and power dominance, Congress became principally a forum for criticizing the executive, for structuring political party and faction behavior, and for the expression of regional cleavages.

The generally subservient role Congress has played during the National Front period in relation to the executive and the coalition parties has not meant that all congressmen have accepted such a restricted role for Congress or that expressions of political cleavage have disappeared, even though Congress cannot be characterized as highly representative of societal conflicts. Congressmen report that four major areas of conflict predominated in the 1968 session: conflicts related to political party and faction behavior, conflicts between Congress and the executive, conflicts between técnicos and políticos, and regional differences. Each of these areas of conflict is embedded deeply not only in Congress but likewise in the political parties. The conflict between technicians and politicians is something of an exception, for it assumed importance as a source of political tension fairly recently during the government of Carlos Lleras Restrepo, who relied heavily upon técnicos to staff administrative and political posts, often infringing upon traditional prerogatives of politicians in selecting governmental officials. In part, the técnico-político cleavage can be subsumed under the more general category of conflict between Congress and the executive.

Because Congress traditionally has constituted an institutional framework for structuring political party relationships in a political system where parties are highly institutionalized, the salience of party conflict in the legislative arena is not unexpected. Two overarching dimensions of conflict underpin party relations in Congress, as determined by multidimensional scale analysis of congressmen's preference-orders for political factions and leaders. The first conflict pole relates to party struggles aimed at gaining control of government. Ideological cleavage constitutes the second major conflict revolving around party differences. Barring the suspension of Congress and the existing party system, these two conflict dimensions will remain as salient bases of party cleavage, for they are anchored firmly in the attitudes and, to a lesser extent, the behavior of politicians. The distribution of both party factions and leaders along these two poles of conflict reflects the wide differences separating representatives of the three major party constellations —Liberal, Conservative, and ANAPO. Despite the National Front coalition between the Liberal and Conservative parties, the basis for conflict between the two parties remains formidable.

While the National Front agreement undeniably has involved the muting of ideological differences between the two traditional parties in the formation and execution of governmental policy, the data presented in this paper suggest that such historical differences still are manifested in the attitudes of Colombian congressmen. Because of the ideological differences between legislators, the question arises as to why the coalition has not been plagued with highly disruptive interparty rivalries. The answer rests, in large part, with the commitment of both traditional parties, at least the upper-echelon leaders of both, to the existing power structure and the desire for its perpetuation, which has been facilitated by the coalition agreement in the sense that both parties have shared control of the government and the bureaucratic rewards associated with it. The coalition has throttled the expression of interparty competition along one of the principal conflict dimensions, the struggle for governmental hegemony, and in the process ideological differences have been relagated to the background. Paradoxically, the moratorium placed upon traditional party rivalries has contributed an unanticipated consequence in that ideological conflict has become more pronounced in the political system, as a consequence of the complacency of traditional parties in adapting to changing societal conditions and in the formation and execution of governmental policy capable of meeting such challenges. At the level of political rhetoric, ANAPO appears to be the principal manifestation of an ideological challenge to the traditional parties. This is not an inaccurate characterization of ANAPO in terms of its bases of political support, which stem from ideological and class appeals but, ironically, the major challenge posed by ANAPO comes not so much from ideology but from the threat to the governmental hegemony shared by the two traditional parties. The data examined in this paper show, for example, that Liberal party congressmen fall further to the left on economic and political ideology than ANAPO congressmen.

With the return of open electoral competition between political parties for the 1974 presidential elections, Congress may not be as pliable and complacent as during most of the National Front period. Assuming that the coalition arrangement is not extended—which is not to be discarded at this juncture—interparty conflict undoubtedly will heighten as each faction seeks to gain control of the government. With the absence of restraint associated with the National Front, the underlying ideological differences between Liberals and Conservatives once again will come to the foreground, with assurances that ANAPO will follow suit. If the present governmental and political structures are not suspended, Congress may become a more significant institutional locus of power in Colombian politics and, even if this is not the case, the dynamics of political conflict will revolve around these cleavages and political groups discussed in this study.

NOTES

1. Designation of some legislative functions as "significant" does not imply any preordained determination of what constitutes significant functions, only that such functions are an outgrowth of a particular context in which a legislature is embedded. In some legislatures, those functions generally associated with democratic theory may represent significant legislative functions, while in other settings these may well not be important determinants of legislative behavior.

2. Each party list for Congress contains two types of candidates, principals and alternates. If a candidate elected at the polls—necessarily a principal—decides not to discharge his legislative duties, he is replaced by an alternate until the principal decides to resume his post. This practice is fairly common in Colombia, often because principals become members of the government, which requires their withdrawal from Congress. Colombian congressmen are elected from departmental constituencies every four years under a system of proportional representation. The lists usually are formulated at the departmental level by party leaders who control their respective regional directorates, and who generally form a part of the diverse clienteles represented in a national party or faction. If regional party bosses do not form a part of a national faction, they often are coopted into a party or faction for reasons of the benefits associated with such relationships.

3. In contrast to the present study, Hoskin (1971) focuses specifically upon institutional conflict in the Colombian Congress arising from divergent conceptions of purposive and representational roles.

4. For a discussion of the concept "oligarchical hegemony" within the Latin American context, see Graciarena (1967). The author utilizes oligarchy in conjunction with the concept of elite, each anchoring one end of a leadership continuum. As a result of the "crisis of oligarchical hegemony" in the 1920s, patterns of leadership have shifted away from the oligarchical pole toward the elite side, as a result of the newly emerging groups and their cooptation into the power structure.

5. According to the standard reference work on la violencia (Guzmán, 1968: 346), around 180,000 people were killed in the interparty feud from 1949 to 1958.

6. The two-dimensional solution was selected rather than one of higher dimensionality or a one-dimensional solution for several reasons. Because the minimal number of

dimensions possible should be utilized in scaling data, assuming the stress level is acceptable, the three- and four-dimensional solutions produced by the TORSCA program were rejected. Not only are these solutions difficult to decipher but they add little in the way of distinguishing between the stimuli. Likewise, a one-dimensional solution is unacceptable because the TORSCA stress level is too high and the one-dimensional ranking of the stimuli does not conform closely to Colombian political realities, as Liberal and Conservative stimuli alternate positions irrationally, and the solution violates methodological requirements of scaling (Converse, 1966: 188). The two-dimensional space is appropriate, therefore, because respondents resorted to more than a single criterion in ranking the factions and leaders, and the solutions of higher dimensionality appear redundant.

7. See Hoskin and Swanson (1973) for confirmation of the validity of the two-conflict dimensions emerging from multidimensional scale analysis of Colombian political party leaders, using additional data generated by the questionnaire. Respondents were rank-ordered on both data sets, then Spearman rank-order correlations were computed. Because of the high degree of similarity of the distribution of both factions and leaders on the two dimensions for both studies of congressmen and political party leaders, I felt no compulsion to undertake the laborious task of confirmation for this study.

8. The third dimension that emerges from the multidimensional analysis may well be related to regionalism, but this provides some difficulties in interpretation, for it probably is impossible to isolate this dimension solely with this data set. It presupposes an ability to rank both factions and leaders in terms of their regional orientations, which is complicated because of the national appeals of parties and leaders. In the near future, I plan to utilize the derived spatial configurations and project individual legislators, ranked in accordance to their scores on a nation-region scale, back onto the dimensions.

9. The interval assumption about the Lickert responses, along with the use of a product-moment correlation matrix, need not have been made in analyzing the relationships between attitudinal syndromes, but appeared justified for the purpose of this chapter, which pretends only to examine the relationships in very general terms. The number of respondents reflected in the correlation matrix is 219.

10. A Statistical Package for the Social Sciences (SPSS) program was utilized for the factor analysis, consisting of a principal component solution with orthogonal, varimax rotation. The three factors, each with eigenvalues of over 1.0, account for 53.9% of the variance.

REFERENCES

ANDERSON, C. (1967) Politics and Economic Change in Latin America: The Governing of Restless Nations. Princeton: Van Nostrand.

BRACHER, K. (1964) "The crisis of modern parliaments," in R. Macridis and B. Brown (eds.) Comparative Politics: Notes and Readings. Homewood, Ill.: Dorsey Press.

BUCKLEY, W. (1967) Sociology and Modern Systems Theory. Englewood Cliffs, N.J.: Prentice-Hall.

CAMPBELL, A., P. CONVERSE, W. MILLER and D. STOKES (1966) "Spatial models of party competition," in Elections and the Political Order. New York: John Wiley.

CONVERSE, P. (1966) "The problem of party distances in models of voting change," in K. Jennings and H. Zeigler (eds.) The Electoral Process. Englewood Cliffs, N.J.: Prentice-Hall.

——— (1964) "The nature of belief systems in mass publics," in D. Apter (ed.) Ideology and Discontent. New York: Free Press.

COOMBS, C. (1964) A Theory of Data. New York: John Wiley.

DIX, R. (1968) Colombia: The Political Dimensions of Change. New Haven, Conn.: Yale Univ. Press.

DOWNS, A. (1957) An Economic Theory of Democracy. New York: Harper & Row.

DUVERGER, M. (1963) Political Parties. New York: John Wiley.

FALS BORDA, O. (1969) Subversion and Social Change in Colombia. New York: Columbia Univ. Press.

GARCIA, A. (1971) Dialéctica de la Democracia. Bogotá: Ediciones Cruz del Sur.

GRACIARENA, J. (1967) Poder y Clases Sociales en el Desarrollo de América Latina. Buenos Aires: Editorial Paidos.

GREEN, P. (1968) "Non-metric scaling methods: an exposition and overview." Wharton Q. (Spring).

GUZMAN, G. (1968) La Violencia en Colombia: Parte Descriptiva. Cali: Ediciones Progreso.

HOSKIN, G. (1971) "Dimensions of representation in the Colombian national legislature," in W. Agor (ed.) Latin American Legislative Systems: A Comparative Reader. New York: Praeger.

――― and G. SWANSON (1973) "Interparty competition in Colombia: a return to la violencia?" Amer. J. of Pol. Sci. 18 (May): 316-350.

KATZ, D. and R. KAHN (1966) The Social Psychology of Organization. New York: John Wiley.

KRUSKAL, J. (1964) "Multidimensional scaling by optimizing goodness of fit to a nonmetric hypothesis." Psychometrika 29 (March): 1-28.

LEAL BUITRAGO, F. (1973) Estudio del comportamiento legislativo en Colombia. Tomo I. Bogotá: Ediciones Tercer Mundo.

MacRAE, D. (1970) Issues and Parties in Legislative Voting. New York: Harper & Row.

MILBRATH, L., R. JOHNSON, L. KELLSTEDT and E. CATALDO (1970) "Card sorting as a technique for survey interviewing." Public Opinion Q. 34 (Summer): 202-215.

PARSONS, T. (1951) The Social System. New York: Free Press.

PAYNE, J. (1968) Patterns of Conflict in Colombia. New Haven, Conn.: Yale Univ. Press.

SEDANO, J. (1971) "Por qué no opera el parlamento?" Flash, Bogotá, 8 (September): 9-23.

SHEPHARD, R. (1966) "Metric structures in ordinal data." J. of Mathematical Psychology 3 (July): 287-315.

WAHLKE, J., H. EULAU, W. BUCHANAN and L. FERGUSON (1962) "Theory: a framework for analysis," in The Legislative System: Explorations in Legislative Behavior. New York: John Wiley.

YOUNG, F. (1968) "TORSCA, a fortran IV program for nonmetric multidimensional scaling." L. O. Thurstone Psychometric Laboratory, No. 56 (March). Mimeo.

GARY HOSKIN is an Associate Professor of Political Science at the State University of New York at Buffalo. During the academic year 1973-74, he was a visiting professor of political science at Los Andes University in Bogota, Colombia where he conducted research on Colombian political parties and the Colombian National Legislature. He has contributed to numerous books and journals, including American Journal of Political Science, Comparative Politics, and International Journal of Comparative Sociology.

Part III

LEGISLATURES AND INTEGRATIVE FUNCTION

Chapter 7

CORRELATES OF LEGISLATIVE CONSTITUENCY SERVICE IN SOUTH VIETNAM

A L L A N   E.   G O O D M A N

Clark University

> The South Vietnamese often seemed to have a strong impulse toward political suicide. They hated the Communists and wanted to be able to run their own lives. But they had great trouble trying to govern themselves. . . . When there were demonstrations or protests, the South Vietnamese were described as lacking in patriotism. When the government moved to limit protests, the leadership was called dictatorial. . . . I had moments of deep discouragement, times when I felt the South Vietnamese were their own worst enemies.
>
> Lyndon B. Johnson
The Vantage Point

HOW TO SUCCEED AS A LEGISLATURE WITHOUT ANY POWER

Viewed from whatever vantage point, South Vietnam is an almost classic example of a praetorian polity (Huntington, 1968: 192-263). Its government throughout the period under study was weak and its politics were fragmented; no effective link between the population and the government had been developed, and the base of support for the government itself was narrowly confined to a few principals in

AUTHOR'S NOTE: This paper was prepared for the Conference on Legislative Systems in Developing Countries, University of Iowa, November, 11-13, 1971. Field research was conducted during 1969-70, made possible by a generous and unfettered grant of support from the Asia Society's Southeast Asia Development Advisory Group. My colleague, Harry Cummings of the Clark University Geography Department, assisted in the data analysis presented in this article, and Emilio Casetti of the Ohio State University made important methodological suggestions.

the military officer corps and, to a lesser extent, religious organizations. The formal structure of the government, however, was and continues to be an elaborate one. There are four branches of government—each guaranteed autonomy and specified authority by the Constitution but, with the exception of the executive, unable to enjoy the fruits of either in politics.

At the local level, the government system is even more complex. Executive decrees provide for more than a dozen autonomous agencies in each province in addition to the regular "services."[1] What this meant in terms of those who served the system—some with power, and very many without—can best be illustrated by the reporting chore faced by each of the 44 province chiefs appointed directly by the President. Each of these officials is responsible for preparing more than 100 reports a month on as many programs. In addition, recently-enacted local government reforms specify for villages a measure of fiscal and administrative autonomy reminiscent of the era when such governments could proudly boast that "the laws of the Emperor stopped at the village gate." The major difference, of course, between that period and the current one is that the "emperor" has a great deal more power than his Nguyen dynasty counterpart.

The governing elite of the Second Republic, as well as those who have supported it, have continually stressed the need to decentralize power as a means of improving governmental effectiveness and the ability of the government in the countryside to compete with the Viet Cong apparat. The significance of the progress achieved for either goal has not been a matter of great controversy because, fundamentally, there was no power to decentralize. However elaborate institutional draftsmen were during the period, the stark fact remained that the GVN was distinctly praetorian in character: as one political leader who had a chance to observe both the GVN and the VC at close hand remarked: "The present regime presents an image of a centralized government filled with power, but cowardly, incapable, confused and closed, under an administration of decrees and *arretés,* and in reality an administration of money." Throughout its tenure, the Thieu government—as was true for its predecessors—has had enough power to rule, but not enough to govern.

How could more power have been created? Proponents of reform or change within the Vietnamese political system offered two suggestions. Initially, reform and change-oriented proposals involved a demand for transformation of the government from a military-dominated one to one run by a coalition of civilian leaders. These proposals came with increasing frequency during the period of the juntas (1963-67) and then declined. More recent proponents of change have demanded that the Thieu government broaden the base of its support by providing a role for alienated religious or secular political forces in national decision-making. Neither approach, however, is likely to create more political power for the government by linking it to the population. After the fall of Diem, Vietnam was governed by three civilian prime ministers, but the nature of their governments—and their ability to govern—differed little from the present regime's. They, like Thieu, sought to remain in office by keeping every other political force relatively weak, encouraging their internal division. They neither shared power with other groups, nor created any. Similarly, the inclusion of alienated political and religious factions whenever it was tried neither helped to reduce the factionalism among those thus included, nor expanded the bases of regime support among the population.

The inclusion of essentially weak political groups—themselves alienated from much of the population and even those they claimed as principal supporters—no matter how precipitous or timely, is hardly likely to result in the creation of more political power for either such groups or the government. Rather, what is required is the forging of links between the government and organizations, on the one hand, and between both and the population, on the other hand. Group-to-government reconciliation is a preliminary step to creating power but not an indispensible one. The creation of more political power in a praetorian polity requires, fundamentally, the expansion of political participation, and this both regimes—whether civilian or military dominated—and political organizations in Vietnam have been reluctant to foster or unable to promote. Praetorian polities do not lack political organizations but rather ones that are capable of expanding participation. The ability to transform the demands and needs of the new participants into interests is also lacking. Creating political power thus requires both the expansion of political participation and the creation of national interests.

How could such a process be begun? I had long thought that Vietnam required the appearance on the scene of a new and dynamic type of political organization that stressed service to the people. I had failed, however, to take quite literally the lesson implied in the comments of those who suggested that political organizations in Vietnam were bankrupt (Goodman, 1971): the people no longer believed in politics or trusted political organizations. This absence of trust might well prove an obstacle that could not be surmounted by the present generation of political organizations, no matter how dynamic or progressive. What had to be sought, instead, was a process (rather than an organization) that might now be in its incipient stages and which would at some future time[2] produce both more power and an alternative to praetorianism.

Such a process was, I now believe, at the root of the development of relationships between the deputies elected (in 1967) to the Lower House of the National Assembly and their constituents. The trust so lacking between the people and the government and the people and the political organizations was instrumental in this relationship. Indeed, the amount of trust developed reflected the degree to which deputies were able to convert the needs and demands of their constituents into interests that fostered linkages between the people and that portion of the government acknowledged as legitimate. From the deputies' point of view, this was a limited trust; they could not, coming so closely on the heels of the bankrupting of political organizations by the regimes and the former's own fissiparousness, convert such a relationship into a political organization. "If anything," one deputy noted in retrospect, "this was the beginning, rather than a consummation."

That the legislature could be the source of such a development, of course, seemed unlikely. Constitutional prescriptions to the contrary, it was clear to deputies from the very start that the Thieu government had no intention of sharing the limited power resources it did have with an unruly legislature; even Ngo dinh Diem, who personally selected the members to be elected to his National Assembly, did not. Nor, soon after the first session opened and the blocs were organized, did they expect Thieu to look to the legislative groupings as a means of increasing his support within the polity. More surprising was the fact that the legislature was not dissolved. The legislature opposed the government consistently on economic measures, reflecting a jealousy and preoccupation with preserving the initiative in these matters granted it by the Constitution. Boisterously and unceremoniously, the legislature served as a voice of criticism of government actions. Government ministers were interpellated with embarrassing regularity, and the spectre of voting no confidence was a continued source of anxiety to a regime that did indeed wish to have certain cabinets thus voted out (that is, those loyal to Vice President Ky), but at a different pace than the legislature appeared willing to underwrite.

The House specialized early in local government reform. With the objective of eliminating the all-powerful appointed province chief in favor of a popularly elected one constantly in mind, the House pushed for a spectrum of changes that would have markedly altered the control over the provinces that the center could exert. Institutional preoccupation with corruption was also consistent, if bizarre—as many members of the House were "caught in the act" by ever more attentive security police, or charged with corruption by an increasingly cynical press, as the legislature itself discovered in the executive. The major difference between the criticism of the legislature and that made by it was that the latter was much more detailed. The resources of the House Bureau, coupled to the privilege of debate, produced vivid descriptions of corrupt practices at the province level. Of the six serious campaigns launched by deputies for the removal of corrupt province chiefs, three were successful, and one stimulated the province chief to stop, fire his accomplices, and, in comparison to what he formerly was, become a paragon of administrative virtue and efficiency.

Groups of deputies applied varying degrees of pressure, much of it successful, to government agencies to have students, peasants, and religious leaders released from detention under a series of contradictory military laws and emergency executive decrees. Due process, after local government reform, was an important legislative priority. Decrees that could not be changed by direct legislative action were frequently the subject of deputy-initiated Supreme Court cases, and, to nearly everyone's surprise, were more often than not declared unconstitutional. The Anti-Corruption Committee of the House first revealed the inequities and injustices perpetrated under the Phoenix program, contributing to a mood in this country and in Vietnam making for declining American support for and participation in a program ostensibly designed to arrest Viet Cong suspects, but which proved yet another source of harassment for the peasant and graft for the local official. In those provinces where the abridgement of civil liberties was most acute under the program, and the conditions of imprisonment most inhumane, the committee was able to effect change, while active deputies began to offer themselves as bail for suspects arrested on suspicion of Communist sympathies.

Deputies who found that local government agencies worked at cross-purposes or who regularly intervened on behalf of the population for justice in local administration contributed to making government work better at the local level. In some cases this was such an improvement that province chiefs found they could work on practical matters with some of the most opposition-oriented militant Buddhists; in fact, both parties often found it to mutual advantage. Moreover, the experience of working within the House itself functioned as a training process for both budding politicians (though their numbers were few) and administrators. The latter often reported that this experience had made them want to return to jobs of lesser national visibility in order to make the system of regional and local governments work. While still too early to tell, the experience may have provided those who would otherwise have considered themselves *fonctionnaries* with a new perspective on government service, and with a new source of interest in local government affairs.

In retrospect, observation of the four years of the Lower House suggests that the functions of the legislature (when either newly created or associated with a new regime) depended upon the scope of its members' activities. No constitutional specification of functions or grant of authority could be taken as given. Nor did there exist forces—of either opposition or pro-government orientation—to which the legislature had to respond. The circumstance of each deputy's election rarely produced in the latter's mind a mandate for specific activity. In South Vietnam, as must be true in many other polities whose politics are praetorian, there existed during this period neither the framework for a legislature to function nor the power for it to develop. What did happen, consequently, depended less on demands made upon the legislature than upon the demands it created.

CONSTITUENCY SERVICE AND THE CREATION OF DEMANDS

The approach to be taken here challenges the growing body of literature on comparative legislative development that stresses the utility of role analysis (Packenham, 1970; Sigel and Pindur, 1969; Hunt, 1969). Proponents of role analysis suggest that such a focus

is valuable because it provides a means for studying the legislature as an institution: its relationship to the political system and culture; its development as an institution; its relationship to other organs of government; and its impact on its own members. It is one means for exploring theoretically interesting questions about the functions of legislative bodies and the demands made upon them in various political systems. It is a flexible technique, tested in previous research, and appropriate for comparative analysis [Jewell, 1970: 500].

Such a view presupposes elements of a political system that are often lacking in developing countries, particularly those whose politics are praetorian.

The concept of role implies, for example, that there exists "constitutions, statutes, rules of procedure, and similar 'formal enactments' [which] help determine the character of the role by dictating at least the skeletons of roles for all legislators, as well as skeletons of various official specialized subroles" (Wahlke et al., 1962). Rarely is this panoply of formal ingredients found; in South Vietnam, as in most countries where dissolution of national assemblies from one regime to another has taken place, such changes often spell the demise of the old order and with it those procedures and practices upon which roles could be based. In addition, the change from one regime to another may affect governmental institutions differently; the "formal enactments" of some may remain intact, while others are dismembered or in a state of flux. In South Vietnam, in fact, the extent to which formally specified responsibilities are unchanged from republic to republic or from regime to regime often are a good index of the distance particular institutions are from playing important roles in government. The most stable ministries in terms of personnel and statutory authority are the least influential in the decision-making process. Past legislatures, in contrast to the ministries, suffered from both distance and instability. Always far from the center of power, they were so wholly a creature of the executive that they never developed a continuity of practices and procedures that provided their successors with a clue to appropriate behaviors.

Role conceptions also depend upon clusters of prior experiences ranging from involvement in political organizations to contemplation of what being a legislator might mean. But opportunities for such experiences—and hence for role conceptions to develop—are precisely what are lacking in Vietnam. Despite the more than 60 political organizations that existed in 1967 when the congress was elected, 27% of the deputies ran with no prior political experience. Those deputies who had experience and often deep involvement in a political organization frequently used the opportunity to be elected to the House as a means of either bolting from the party or consciously reducing its ability to influence behavior. In many cases, however, the party or organization itself was simply too weak to exert much influence over the deputy's activity either in the House or in the constituency. Finally, the whole of a deputy's prior experience may prove inconsistent with his behavior once in office, reflecting a fundamental lack of integration between conceptions of representative roles and representative action (Kim and Woo, 1975).

In the absence of those elements normally thought to contribute to the development of legislators' roles, the use of and focus upon such a conceptual framework as role analysis would be inappropriate. Role is grounded in the notion of response to demands—albeit complex and often conflicting ones: "The role of a legislator consists of the rights, duties, and obligations that are expected of anyone holding that position" (Jewell, 1970: 462). None of the legislators interviewed, however, felt that they had come to office with a clear notion of any of these elements. The position of the executive was so predominant, moreover, that no deputy felt he inherited a set of rights—ranging from the ability to investigate government activities to that of parliamentary immunity itself—that provided meaningful parameters for or safeguards of behavior. Finally, weak and factionated political organizations were unable to oblige deputies to respond to their interests in a particular way. Few deputies valued the support of political organizations to the extent that they would violate their own personal beliefs about particular legislation, and occasions when such a conflict might loom were so rare that even deputies familiar with Edmund Burke's counsels did not see in their situations a parallel case. And, to a certain extent, the existence of so many organizations coupled to a fluid bloc structure meant that deputies could move from one to the other without fear of sanction.

The notion of demand, inherent in the role analysis perspective, also applies to the analysis of legislative behavior itself. As Jewell observes (1970: 496; Styskal, 1969), "Whatever functions a legislature may serve, in order to evaluate its performance we need to know what demands are being made on it." The analytical task in studying legislatures in praetorian polities is just the reverse, however. What is crucial to know is what demands the legislature creates, that is, how it functions as an instrument of mobilization and participation.[3]

The concept adopted in the case of South Vietnam, under the proposition that legislative functions depend upon the scope of a member's activities, was that of constituency service.[4] Constituency service is the orphan of legislative studies. The process underlying it in most democratic polities is regarded with suspicion—either it is inherently too trivial to be significant (that is, the legislator "running errands" for his constituents), or, since at the national level all legislators appear to serve their constituents, it is argued that analysis of it would add little to explaining such phenomena as re-elections. Frequently constituency service work indexes a grey area of the legislator's behavior that too often surfaces in charges of misconduct, ranging from favoritism to corruption. Instead, studies of legislative behavior, while concerned with representational roles, have tended to focus upon the backgrounds of legislators to explain attitudes towards the constituency. Theories and analyses of legislative behavior are thus divorced from the study of activities that consume large portions of a congressman's resources and time.

Part of the reason for this analytical inattentiveness lies in the consistently negative valuation placed upon constituency service by the modern legislator. After observing the work of several U.S. congressmen and their staffs (as preparation for my own study in South Vietnam) I asked why, if a good part of their days and most of their staff were taken up with constituency-related activities, these were not considered more important in explaining legislative behavior. The reply was:

> Every member of Congress does just about as much as I do and in the same way. You cannot differentiate between us on these grounds. In fact, we spend our time and our staff's in order to be free to exercise our responsibilities to the nation without having to worry about taking care of our constituents. We feel we provide them good care and attention—and that they would have it independently of whoever was elected.

The American congressman, and his counterpart in Western Europe, are descendants of Edmund Burke. In contrast, the legislator in South Vietnam views his responsibilities to the nation in terms of his constituents. In response to previewing my findings that one-third of the Lower House did constituency service, one deputy observed:

> While you say that this is about the same number as in American state legislatures [referring to the Wahlke et al., 1962 study], this is a very sad fact to us. We have no responsibilities to the nation because the nation is controlled by the government and many of us do not support it. Even if we did, we would not be permitted to have these responsibilities because that would require us to have power over Mr. Thieu and his associates. Faced with this situation, we can only have responsibilities to our constituents. They have no government or nation, they only have needs and these we must serve.[5]

But, to the deputies who engaged in it, constituency service was a supplement to, rather than an extention of, their participation in

TABLE 1
CONSTITUENCY SERVICE AND AFFILIATION[a]

	Organizational Affiliation By Type					
	Local-Diffuse	Local-Cohesive	Regional-Diffuse	Regional-Cohesive	National-Diffuse	National-Cohesive
Service oriented	10	7	3	12	5	7
Non-service oriented	26	16	9	16	13	15

a. χ^2 of 2.3 for 5 degrees of freedom. N for service oriented is 44; non-service oriented, 95.

existing organizations. Having a particular type of political affiliation did not have a significant effect upon constituency service (see Table 1). In examining this relationship the null hypothesis—that constituency service was not associated with type of political affiliation—was not rejected by the χ^2 test.[6] The absence of such a relationship reflected the fact that most deputies avoided mixing their activities at the national level with those in the province. In their view, the province was a separate world from Saigon.

THE DETERMINANTS OF CONSTITUENCY SERVICE: QUALITATIVE HYPOTHESES AND THE LIMITS OF EMPIRICAL ANALYSIS

THE HYPOTHESES

The parameters of analysis for newly created legislatures in praetorian polities are limited as much by the absence of opportunities for legislators to have a broad range of political and socializing experiences as they are by the need for new theoretical constructs. If the functions of a legislature are determined by the scope of its members' activities, then those activities are important —and perhaps singularly so—determinants of the way legislators characterize their jobs. What this perspective suggests is the need for detailed observations of legislative behavior and then development, sui generis, of constructs for analysis. The present study, consequently, grows out of a desire to subject what was previously described in my own work on the Lower House to empirical analysis.

To put it simply, I was intrigued by what I had found. A handful of deputies (one-third of the total membership) had engaged in constituency service and their activities had markedly influenced the character of legislative work and intra-institutional politics.[7] No easy answer emerged to explain why some deputies developed a service orientation and why others eschewed the process. During the months of interviewing and compiling biographic records, only the rudiments of null hypotheses were suggested. The propensity to engage in constituency service appeared to be independent of what I had expected. Active deputies came from all backgrounds and careers, from provinces where there had been a great deal of competition for their seats and from those where there had been little, from provinces with many political organizations and few, from those which experienced the most war and the least, and from both sides of the non-Communist political spectrum. In discussing their roles, deputies did not describe their activities in demand-response terms, either in relationship to events or to the pressure of organizations. Rather they suggested roles appropriate to the level of their activity and involvement vis-a-vis the population. But when I asked if the people in their constituency had demanded such involvement, the response was almost uniformly negative.

I had, consequently, noticed certain anomalies in the interviews. First, I was amazed that among those deputies most active in opposing the government, many did constituency service work. This required a relationship of trust and cordiality with province chiefs that, I expected, would be out of place, given the intensity of the anti-government struggle. This was the view I maintained in Saigon. When I went to the provinces to observe the deputy in action or to try to assess the significance of his work after he had gone, I discovered that opposition to the Thieu government was seen, as one deputy put it, as "a national issue which must be kept separate from our local work." Another deputy observed: "We struggle for the people at two levels, and each requires a different behavior. At one level we oppose the tyranny of Thieu and we do this in Saigon. But here, we must get the government to help the people, and this means we must work with the province chief." There were, in short, two worlds of politics for the deputies; those with a service orientation had learned to operate successfully in both.

Second, constituency service work appeared to be done largely by those deputies who had retired from positions of public authority in order to run for the House. The interviews, however, revealed a variety of conceptions of authority. To some active deputies, authority meant control of governmental resources—money and personnel—and they attempted to develop ways in which the office of the deputy in the province would resemble the office they had been associated with in public life. These deputies usually had the most well-organized local offices in terms of staff and records, and had a highly regularized schedule of visits, for example, worked out for each district in the province on usually a bi-monthly basis. To other deputies the term public authority connoted a relationship that they enjoyed previously with the population. Military officers who were active in constituency service, for example, tended to have had experience in liaison between a military base near a large populated center.

Third, some active deputies engaged in constituency service as a means of bolstering the prestige of their position within the province, and particularly vis-a-vis the province chief. They had reasoned that in order to hold their own with the province chief—since no formal specification of the authority of either the province chief or the deputy had been made in the constitution—they had to demonstrate that their activities in the province could facilitate the latter's job. Most often, the chance for such a demonstration came in times of adversity. During the Tet Offensive of 1968, active deputies often worked with the province chief and other military officials in coordinating operations against Viet Cong positions so as to cause the least damage to civilian property. Post-Tet recovery assistance in some cases was coordinated by the deputy as a means to assure that the proper persons received what was due them, and to reduce thereby the diversion of supplies to black marketeers. In other emergency situations, when the province required commodity supplies from regional distribution centers that had been delayed, the province chief often asked the deputy to see what could be done at a regional headquarters.

Fourth, constituency service work was consistently separated from the political objectives of those deputies who did it. Without exception, deputies expressed uncertainty about how it would affect their chances for reelection. Many felt, in fact, that the more a deputy got involved with the people, the more they would expect him to do, to the point where they would be dissatisfied with whatever he was able to achieve. Others felt that the population was really unprepared for such behavior; some actually observed in interviews that they had been told that the people they helped were made uncomfortable by such solicitous behavior. Those deputies who frequently encountered this reaction often had to organize their effort by proxy. They had to work through the traditional leadership of the village or settlement rather than through their local offices.

Finally, I had felt that the incidence of constituency service work was related to the type of district from which the deputy was elected. Initially, in fact, I maintained that constituency problems could not be divorced from the war; the more the war had affected the population, the more likely deputies would be to seek to respond to these "ready-made" needs. But service-oriented deputies came from all types of provinces, including those which had had the most war and the most peace over the period. Similarly, I had thought that the level of competition for a seat in the House would act as an important determinant of constituency service. In the course of my field studies, however, I observed too many deputies engaging in constituency service work who were elected with large pluralities, as well as many who were elected with 1-5% margins, to feel that the expected relationship would hold. Finally, I had thought that socio-political complexity such as is associated with urbanization would be an important determinant of constituency service (Eulau, 1957; Cutright, 1963). But observations in the most rapidly growing cities and provincial towns suggested just the reverse. Urban growth appeared to stabilize constituencies (for example, DaNant and Hue) and increase the size of the election margins or made constituencies so complex that the level of political competition and a deputy's activities appeared independent (as was the case in Saigon, Can Tho, and Khanh Hoa)[8] (Gould and Schmidhauser, 1960; Nie et al., 1969).

THE ANALYSIS

Based upon publicly available information on the backgrounds of Lower House deputies (published by the House in its biographic register) and the information gathered in interviews during 1969 and 1970, a data file was prepared and coded for this analysis. The data reflect the backgrounds and prior experiences of the deputies, the character of the province from which they were elected, and their activities while in office. Two types of analyses were performed on the data. First, a series of cross-tabulations for all variables were run in order to separate those independent variables that, when paired with the dependent variable, proved to be statistically significant. The results of this phase of the analysis will be discussed below. Second, the assumptions about the determinants of constituency service work derived from the interviews were codified into statements of relationships between the dependent and independent variables and then tested by means of a step-wise multiple regression.

TABLE 2

SIGNIFICANT[a] DETERMINANTS OF CONSTITUENCY SERVICE IN SOUTH VIETNAM

A. Position Toward Government

	Anti-govt., Independent	Anti-govt., Organization	Pro-govt., Independent	Pro-govt., Organization
Service oriented	9 (20%)[b]	16 (36%)	8 (18%)	11 (25%)
Non-service oriented	8 (8)	16 (17)	34 (36)	37 (39)

B. Prior Position

	Private	Local—No Authority	National—No Authority	Local— Authority	National— Authority
Service oriented	13 (30%)	11 (25%)	2 (5%)	12 (27%)	6 (14%)
Non-service oriented	34 (36)	28 (29)	21 (22)	4 (4)	8 (8)

C. Re-election

	Re-elected	Not Re-elected
Service oriented	18 (41%)	26 (59%)
Non-service oriented	22 (23)	73 (77)

D. War: Combat Factor Scores

	Very Low	Low	Medium	High
Service oriented	12 (28%)	19 (43%)	11 (25%)	2 (5%)
Non-service oriented	10 (11)	57 (60)	20 (21)	8 (8)

E. War: Population Effects Factor Score

	Very Low	Low	Medium	High
Service oriented	13 (30%)	15 (34%)	10 (23%)	6 (14%)
Non-service oriented	14 (15)	65 (68)	12 (13)	4 (4)

F. Role Characterization (by degree of activity implied)

	Educator— Intellectual	Lawmaker	Agent	Mobilizer	Educator— Mobilizer
Service oriented	2 (5%)	12 (27%)	11 (25%)	6 (14%)	13 (30%)
Non-service oriented	3 (3)	44 (46)	44 (46)	3 (3)	1 (1)

a. That is, χ^2 significant at the .05 level.
b. Figures in parentheses are percentages that each cell is of the row total. Percentages may not add to 100 due to rounding error. N=44 for service oriented deputies and 95 for non-service oriented deputies.

The key independent variables suggested by the interviews all bore a significant relationship to the dependent variable (see Table 2). Indeed, of the entire set of cross-tabulations for the matrix of 22 variables, only six, when paired with constituency service work, had χ^2s that were significant at the .05 level or higher. These tabulations are reproduced in the cluster below. That such a large proportion of anti-government deputies engaged in constituency service work confirms the separability of position toward the government and activity at the local level. Somewhat less expected was the obviously important connection between the propensity to engage in constituency service work and the deputies' affiliation with either pro- or anti-government organizations. The interviews had tended to play down the importance of association with political organizations, and if anything, had stressed the need for anti-government deputies to remain independent from political organizations in order to have a free hand to deal with the province chief. But those organizations that were anti-government at the national level (such as the militant An Quang Buddhists or the southern-oriented Movement for the Renaissance of the South) often suggested that they worked quite well with local government officials. The militant Buddhists in particular stressed the autonomy that they enjoyed from any central direction and the latitude that this provided them in their dealings with local government officials. As one monk observed:

> Out here, there is no An Quang or Quoc Tu [the two national Buddhist organizations in conflict], only the little world of the pagodas. We consider what the national leadership has to say, and often respect their judgment on national political questions and issues, but we feel quite independent from them when it affects local issues.

Indeed, one of the striking features of my observations in more than a dozen provinces throughout South Vietnam was the extent of inter-religious cooperation and the ability of the religions to work well with government and even military officials.

Deputies who are deeply involved in their provinces and who are members of particular organizations, therefore, must be a part of this environment, making their membership in anti-government organizations and their support of them in Saigon not incompatible with taking an active role in constituency service and developing the relationships with local officials that such work ultimately required. Province chiefs, too, reported their surprise at seeing such relationships develop and finding areas of common cause between themselves and anti-government deputies, but such comments as the ones presented below are admittedly candid and rare:

> When I was appointed to this province, I had heard in Saigon about the militant Buddhists in the capital's pagoda and the strong anti-government feelings on the part of the population. I actually spent a good deal of my time at first working as though this was true, but my province was very quiet; there were no demonstrations against me or the government and I began to suspect that the view from Saigon was distorting my own vision. Things are alright here, but the fact that we can work closely with religious groups must remain invisible.

If position toward the government was not an inhibitor to deputies doing constituency service work, what impact did politics at the local level have? Deputies ought, I had reasoned, to be more likely to engage in constituency service if they had been elected with a small plurality; constituency service would consolidate the plurality or expand it so that re-election would be assured. Size of plurality (see Table 3A), however, did not serve to differentiate service-oriented deputies from the rest. Each group's pattern of distribution

TABLE 3
CONSTITUENCY SERVICE WORK AND PATTERNS OF LOCAL POLITICAL COMPLEXITY[a] (in percentages)

A. Size of Plurality

	Under 10%	11-20%	21-30%	31-40%	41-50%	Over 51%
Service oriented	9	45	27	7	9	2
Non-service oriented	16	42	20	8	3	10

B. Urbanization (Factor Score)

	Very Low	Low	Medium	High
Service oriented	14	25	25	36
Non-service oriented	8	27	36	28

C. Political Presence (Factor Score)

	Very Low	Low	Medium	High
Service oriented	5	34	20	41
Non-service oriented	8	42	17	33

a. None of these tables had χ^2's significant at the .05 level. Figures in the cells are percentages that each cell is of the row total. Percentages may not add to 100 due to rounding error. N for service oriented deputies is 44; N for non-service oriented deputies, 95.

is approximately similar, with the exception of those elected with at least a majority of the votes cast. So, also, urbanization did not prove to be an important means of differentiating between the deputies, although the trend presented in Table 3B would suggest that highly urbanized provinces[9] were more likely to have service-oriented deputies in office. Urbanization and electoral competition appeared separate from both the incidence of constituency service work and local political complexity. Indeed, only in the relationship between constituency service and political presence[10] was there a clear and differentiating pattern. As Table 3C indicates, the presence of non-Communist political groups is high for those provinces with service-oriented deputies in about the same proportion as it is low for non-service oriented deputies (and vice versa). Since the political presence construct includes both pro- and anti-government groups, the data suggest that just as constituency service work may be supplementary to party and group preoccupations at the national level, such organizations also may not be particularly salient at the local level. Patterns of local political complexity—whether considered from the vantage point of electoral competition, urbanization, political presence, or all three—thus contribute little to explaining the determinants of constituency service.

The expected relationship between the positions deputies retired from in order to run for the house and constituency service, while statistically significant within the matrix, was less clear than the hypothesis derived from the interviews would suggest. So also was the association between constituency service and re-election (Table 2C). Clearly, those deputies who did not engage in constituency service had the least chance of being re-elected, thus confirming the view advanced by election analysts that those deputies who had a blatant disregard for local problems and activities were not returned to office. The only statistically significant and nonspurious relationship with re-election was constituency service.[11]

The pattern expected between the incidence of constituency service and the war on the basis of impressions received in interviews and preliminary analyses of the impact of the war in provinces was confirmed. In Table 2D comparing constituency service work with the combat aspects of the war[12] factor scores were used to index the extent to which the war figured prominently in the characteristics of the deputies' districts. As the table makes clear, there is if anything a strong negative relationship between those provinces where combat was the highest and the incidence of constituency service. Proportionately, however, there is little difference in the distribution of both types of deputies in the higher ranges of the combat factor scores. The war does not appear—if viewed from its combat aspects—strongly related to constituency service work.[13]

The impact of the war on the population was indexed in the factor by the refugee variables (1967-69), the number of terrorist incidents that occurred in the province (1967-1968), and the reported civilian war casualties (1967). Here the negative relationship between the war—this time, indexed by its impact on the population—and constituency service is even more pronounced (Table 2E). Almost two-thirds of the service-oriented deputies came from provinces with low factor scores. Population effects also serve as a better differentiating variable than combat, as made clear by the dissimilarities in pattern between each group of deputies. While the shape of the curve for the non-service oriented deputies would be the same in the case of both variables, the relationship between these deputies and the low category is much more pronounced for the latter variable. Many more provinces than would be expected actually experienced very little of the war, and just as the war did not emerge in the interviews as a determinant of constituency service, so also it does not emerge as that in the data matrix analysed here.[14]

The independent variable that provided the clearest pattern of differentiation between service-oriented and non-service oriented deputies was that of role characterization (Table 2F). This construct was developed from the deputies' self-characterization of their activities. It is an effort to measure the scope of their activities along the dimension of constituency involvement.[15] Rather than represent a tactic of responding to demands (or avoiding them), role characterization indexes deputies' perception of their involvement in a demand-creation process. What does each of the categories mean in terms of constituency activities? The educator as intellectual or as mobilizer believes that the population must be made aware of its needs and rights, but that this cannot be achieved through existing political organizations. While the intellectual understands this, he acknowledges openly that he is not personally suited to, or temperamentally inclined toward, the degree of local involvement and association with the population that constituency service work requires. While he is most often to be found in the editorial offices of a newspaper or on the college campus, he is not a political mobilizer. He feels that he makes a contribution to politics not by what he does but by what he has the courage to stand for, and in so doing, by the inspiration provided to others for more active forms of involvement. The educator as mobilizer, in contrast, feels that a close relationship to the population is essential. The closer this relationship, the less perforce it can be related to politics or a particular organization because of the absence of popular trust in either. What he tries to mobilize instead are citizens and not cadre; he would prefer to see the population stand up for their rights rather than for a political party.

The lawmaker eschews close involvement with the population and is somewhat more identified with the House as an institution than is the educator-qua-intellectual. Lawmakers are concerned with questions of institutional reform and administrative justice, and generally their goals are limited. They feel that procedural and institutional frameworks must be built before the population can realize their rights and before the government can effectively serve their needs. Like the intellectual, the lawmaker does not feel that constituency service work is part of his job; to engage in it, given the present structure and character of the government, would be premature. An agent believes that his primary job is to defend the interests of a particular group, that this group is his constituency; he implies that there is little need to expand the bases of his support but not necessarily that cooperation with other groups should be ruled out. Indeed, the agents generally defined as paramount among the interests of their group the need to work with other groups to increase their leverage vis-a-vis the province chief. In so doing, the agent hardly responds to group pressures—which, if they are at all apparent, are generally against such cooperative undertakings; rather, he seeks to convince his group of the need to work with others.

The mobilizer, like the agent, is usually associated with a particular group, and, like the educator-qua-mobilizer, is concerned about organizing the population. Unlike the agent who deals primarily with leaderships, however, he is most concerned about the membership of the group and how it could be expanded. He is an advocate of building new organizational links to the population and of revamping goals. Unlike the educator-qua-mobilizer, he believes that only when people become cadre can they be effective citizens. Constituency service figures prominently therefore in the mobilizer's conception of his job, but as the demands of constructing an effective organization increase, he is likely to delegate more of his case work to subordinates; he is also likely to keep his visibility low in the province as he becomes associated with a particular political movement. The mobilizer, like the educator-qua-mobilizer, realizes the lack of trust most people have for politics.

In their pattern of distribution on the role characterization variable, service and non-service oriented deputies differ both within and between each category. Service-oriented deputies are more evenly spread over the range of the role characterization variable, while non-service oriented deputies are concentrated primarily in the lawmaker and agent categories (92%). As would be expected, the most populous category for the service-oriented deputy is that of educator-qua-mobilizer. But what is surprising is that the proportion of deputies in this category is so small (30%). Fifty-two percent of the service-oriented deputies expressed opinions that would place them in the lawmaker and agent categories, both of which imply a lesser degree of involvement in constituency work than either the mobilizer or the educator-qua-mobilizer categories. To these deputies their role characterization and constituency service work implies that they live essentially two lives, operating in the milieu both of local constituency involvement and of national (or at least national institutional) politics. To be sure, the involvement at both levels required of the lawmaker and the agent must have figured prominently in their re-election; as Table 4 makes clear, deputies from both categories were the most likely to be returned to office. The potential lesson to a legislator from this data is that survival may require deputies to engage both in politics (either within the House or within a political organization) *and* in constituency service, but the two must be kept separate. Indeed, the apparent absence of integration between role characterization and actual constituency service activities may be crucial to the survival of the legislator in a praetorian polity.

TABLE 4
RE-ELECTION AND ROLE CHARACTERIZATION[a]
(in percentages)

	Educator-qua-Intellectual	Lawmaker	Agent	Mobilizer	Educator-qua-Mobilizer
Re-elected (N=40)	2	36	30	5	18
Not re-elected (N=99)	4	42	41	7	6

a. χ^2 was not significant at the .05 level. Figures in cells are the percentage that each cell is of the row total. Percentages may not add to 100 due to rounding error.

AN ANALYTICAL PROGNOSIS

Can the findings and impressions reported on in this study be expressed in more precise terms? The results of the step-wise multiple regression carried out on two dependent variables, constituency service and re-election, illustrate the difficulties inherent in such analyses and the paucity of constructs that can easily be transferred from the literature on comparative legislative development to a case study. Regardless of how the variables were manipulated in terms of assumptions usually made in studies of legislative development, suggested by the data, and implied in the interviews summarized in this study, the explanatory power of the regression equations was so low that almost any set of randomly chosen independent variables could have done as well. A total of five tests were conducted, principally by reducing the regression equations to only those independent variables that either the cross-tabulation analysis, other studies,[16] or the interviews themselves suggested as important determinants of constituency service work. The average variance explained by each of the regression equations was about 20% (multiple R^2). Consequently, only the equation which produced the highest multiple R^2 is presented in Table 5. While the independent variables included in the equation are the ones expected, either from the literature or the assumptions discussed in this study, the fact that only 36% of the variance is explained suggests the analytical paucity of constructs and theories (at least as

TABLE 5
STEP-WISE MULTIPLE REGRESSION[a] RESULTS:
CONSTITUENCY SERVICE WORK AS THE DEPENDENT VARIABLE

Variables	Regression Coefficient[b]	Multiple R^2
Constant	.35427	.16
Age at election	−.05101	.16
Party affiliation	.03907	.21
	−.02335	.23
Position toward government	−.11790	.25
Impact of war—population effects	.11947	.30
	.16871	.30
Age at entry into politics	.19883	.32
Position left	.04846	.34
Prior political experience	.07473	.36

a. Based upon the Bio-medical computer programs series (BMDO2R).
b. Only those coefficients significant for each of the independent variables are shown. Significance was determined by a T-test for N-m degrees of freedom of the regression coefficient of the .05 level significance for a 1-tailed test. Total multiple R^2 for the complete equation (that is, including those independent variables which failed the T-test) was .41.

TABLE 6
STEP-WISE MULTIPLE REGRESSION RESULTS:
RE-ELECTION AS THE DEPENDENT VARIABLE

Variable	Regression Coefficient[a]	Multiple R^2
Constant	.68505	
Place of birth	.06627	.05
Age at election	.06260	.12
Party affiliation	.03224	.15
Urbanization	.07194	.19
	.10385	.21
Prior experience	.06681	.23
Career changes	.10216	.25

a. Only these coefficients significant (determined by the T-test) for each of the independent variables are shown. Total multiple R^2 for the complete equation was .31.

much as the culpability of the data itself) that can codify the growing body of literature on legislative development for the study of praetorian polities. The regression analysis of re-election fared even worse, as Table 6 indicates. Four tests of assumptions were conducted, and the highest multiple R^2 achieved still left three-quarters of the variation in the dependent variable unexplained.

If the premise of future studies should be the one advanced here—that the functions and significance of the legislature in praetorian polities depend upon the scope of its members' activities—then both the focus on determinants of constituency service work in this study and the construct of role characterization advanced need to be improved. There is a pattern to the functioning of the legislature in South Vietnam, as one deputy put it:

> The legislature can be regarded as a hand. The hand has fingers of many different sizes and yet it is a very versatile organ of the body. A legislature has many different members, and we are searching now to find out how with this diversity it can function as an effective organ of government.

Thus far, however, this pattern remains observed but unexplained.

NOTES

1. A service is the provincial branch of a GVN ministry.

2. Whether in the long or medium range would depend on the accelerating effect of the end of the war and the prospect of competing with the Communists in a postwar political struggle.

3. Demands, like representation and effective legislators themselves, are acquired characteristics of political systems.

4. The nature of constituency service in South Vietnam is described in detail in Goodman, 1973. Briefly, the process involved deputies working for their constituents on problems generated by the inefficiency and injustices of government at the province level. During 1969-70, for example, deputies sought to have constituents released from imprisonment under the Phoenix program, to combat corrupt and change ineffective administrative procedures, to facilitate the processing of emergency and regular relief assistance petitions, and to have public works projects funded on the basis of priorities set within the village rather than the province government. While deputies' modes of operation differed greatly, their activities shared a common concern to make local and provincial government responsive to public interests. Each deputy approached individual problems with detachment; the reliance upon or the image of reliance upon personal favoritism as the only way to get things done was de-emphasized. Each believed that the only rights the population had were those they learned to demand.

5. As many deputies suggested during the course of the interviews, the existence of such needs alone do not constitute demands. Indeed, one of the most common problems associated with constituency service was to get the population to realize that their needs (ranging from emergency relief to due process in military field courts) could be transformed into demands upon local and provincial governments.

6. See, however, Table 2 and the discussion of the relationship between constituency service and pro- and anti-government orientations.

7. Deputies of a service orientation tended to chair the most active committees and were frequently the floor managers of governmental reform bills; more importantly, these deputies focused the activities of the House on a set of legislative priorities that grew directly out of the problems associated with constituency service.

8. This is not to say, however, that the use of smaller units than the province might not justify renewed belief in urbanization and competition variables, but no reliable way of characterizing electoral districts smaller than a province is currently possible with the Vietnamese data (Coulter and Gordon, 1968).

9. The measure of urbanization is based upon the factor analysis described in the following pages.

10. The political presence construct, also derived from the factor analysis described in the following pages, included measures of the presence of Buddhist pagodas, Northern Catholics, and the government's civil and military services.

11. Position toward the government and re-election, while below a significant χ^2 by only a decimal, was almost identical to the pattern observed for constituency service and re-election. Those deputies who were associated with political organizations (either anti-government or pro-) had the highest rate of success in re-election, and within this group, anti-government deputies were returned with a slight edge over their pro-government cohorts.

12. The combat factor, which accounted for 26% of the total variance (all factors explained 87% of the total variance), included such indicators of the war as US battalion days of operation in the province (for 1967 and 1968), the total number of Viet Cong/North Vietnamese Army attacks (1967, 1968), the average number of US and VC battalions present (1967, 1968), and the reported number of civilian war casualties (1968 only). Extracted from a factor analysis of war variables in a matrix of 47 variables, reflecting social, economic, and political patterns in the 44 provinces and reported in Goodman (1972).

13. Indeed the war in 1967-68 was fought at such a level of intensity between the United States and the Communist military forces that the population either moved rapidly out of the affected areas (that is, as refugees or as rural-urban migrants) or the war, while intense, was geographically concentrated. The significance of this dichotomy is that if the latter were the case, little population movement would have been required in the first place, and in fact this tends to explain one of the striking features of the analysis of the provincial

data: urbanization (that is, the growth in the number of people living in Vietnamese cities of 20,000 or more from 1960-70) had no significant correlation with any of the war variables. Indeed, in the factor analysis urbanization emerges as a separate dimension altogether (explaining 9% of the variance), and if anything its correlation with the war data are the weakest of a series of very weak correlations between urbanization and the rest of the variables in the matrix.

14. Indeed, only four provinces had high combat factor scores; only three had such scores for the population effects factor. Twelve provinces scored in the medium range for the combat factor, and eight for population effects. In surveying the results of the factor analysis, it would appear that the GVN has been left out of the war. It has not, however, been left out of the analysis. The original data matrix included two variables on the GVN's participation in the war, GVN battalions present in the province and GVN battalion days of operation in the province. The former correlated with nothing in the matrix of other variables, and did not load at all on the factors. GVN battalion days of operation was nearly as distinctive; it bore a significant correlation with only a single war variable, US battalion days of operation (1967). GVN battalion days of operation, in fact, correlated much more strongly than variables indexed by the political presence construct, and was, consequently, loaded on that factor in the factor analysis.

15. In constructing such a ranking, I tried to locate each deputy on the basis of record of service, background experience, and opinions toward constituency service expressed either in public statements or in interviews as compared with reports and observations of their behavior. Role characterization thus is not a correlate of role theory.

16. The 15 articles in the Kornberg-Musolf (1970) collection provide a good sampling of work already done and current conceptual developments. A similar series of studies is expected over the next three years from James Heaphy's Comparative Legislative Development Studies Center, Graduate School of Public Affairs, State University of New York at Albany. Blondel et al. (1969-70) focuses on construct development for comparing legislative output. In contrast, the study of legislators' behavior is less advanced and focused primarily on time series analyses within single countries using established constructs. See, for example, preliminary reports of such work in progress as Agor (1969), Robins (1969), Grossholtz (1969), Kuroda (1971), Wurfel (1971), and Woo and Kim (1971).

REFERENCES

AGOR, W. H. (1969) "Senate: integrative role in Chile's political development." Paper presented at annual meeting of the American Political Science Assn., New York (September).

BLONDEL, J., P. GILLESPIE, V. HERMAN, P. KOATI and R. LEONARD (1969-70) "Legislative behaviour: some steps towards a cross-national movement." Government and Opposition 5 (Winter): 67-85.

COULTER, P. and P. GORDON (1968) "Urbanization and party competition: critique and redirection of theoretical research." Western Political Q. 21 (June): 274-88.

CUTRIGHT, P. (1963) "Urbanization and competitive party politics." J. of Politics 25 (August).

EFROYMSEN, M. A. (1960) "Multiple regression analysis," in A. Ralston and H. S. Wilf (eds.) Mathematical Methods for Digital Computers. New York.

EULAU, H. (1957) "The ecological bases of party systems: the case of Ohio." Midwest J. of Political Science 1 (August).

GOODMAN, A. E. (1973) Politics in War: The Bases of Political Community in South Vietnam. Cambridge, Mass.: Harvard Univ. Press.

––– (1972) After the War, What?: A Report to the U.S. Department of State on the Alternative Political Conditions Affecting the Participation of International Organizations in the Economic Recovery and Development of North and South Vietnam. New York: Columbia University School of International Affairs.

––– (1971) "Conflict and accommodation within a legislative elite in South Vietnam." Pacific Affairs 64 (Summer): 211-27.

GOULD, D. and J. R. SCHMIDHAUSER (1960) "Urbanization and party competition: the case of Iowa." Midwest J. of Political Science 4 (February).

GROSSHOLTZ, J. (1969) "Integrative factors in the Malaysian and Philippine legislatures." Paper presented at annual meeting of the American Political Science Assn., New York (September).

HUNT, W. H. (1969) "Legislative roles and ideological orientations of French deputies." Paper presented at annual meeting of the American Political Science Assn., New York (September).

HUNTINGTON, S. P. (1968) Political Order in Changing Societies. New Haven, Conn.: Yale Univ. Press.

JEWELL, M. E. (1970) "Attitudinal determinants of legislative behavior: the utility of role analysis," in A. Kornberg and L. Musolf (eds.) Legislatures in Developmental Perspective. Durham, N.C.: Duke Univ. Press.

KIM, C. L. and B. WOO (1975) "Political representation in the Korean national assembly," pp. 261-286 in G. R. Boynton and C. L. Kim (eds.) Legislative Systems in Developing Countries.

KORNBERG, A. and L. MUSOLF [eds.] (1970) Legislatures in Developmental Perspective. Durham, N.C.: Duke Univ. Press.

KURODA, Y. (1971) "The Japanese Diet: 1890-1963: recruitment opportunity and recruitment paths." Paper presented at annual meeting of the Assn. for Asian Studies, Washington, D.C. (March).

NIE, N. H., G. B. POWELL, Jr., and K. PREWITT (1969) "Social structure and political participation: development of relationships." Amer. Pol. Sci. Rev. 63 (June-September).

PACKENHAM, R. (1970) "Legislatures and political development," in A. Kornberg and L. Musolf (eds.) Legislatures in Developmental Perspective. Durham, N.C.: Duke Univ. Press.

ROBINS, R. R. (1969) "The Indian upper house and elite integration." Paper presented at annual meeting of the American Political Science Assn., New York (September).

SIGEL, R. S. and W. PINDUR (1969) "Self-image as a guide to representational styles and behavior." Paper presented at annual meeting of the American Political Science Assn., New York (September).

STYSKAL, R. A. (1969) "Philippine legislator's reception of individuals and interest groups in the legislative process." Comparative Politics 1 (April): 405-422.

WAHLKE, J. C., H. EULAU, W. BUCHANAN, and L. C. FERGUSON (1962) The Legislative System. New York: John Wiley.

WURFEL, D. (1971) "Legislators in Singapore: social background analysis of a positional elite." Paper presented at annual meeting of the Assn. for Asian Studies, Washington, D.C. (March).

ALLAN E. GOODMAN is Chairman of the Department of Government and International Relations at Clark University. He is the author of several studies on the development and significance of the legislature in South Vietnam. During the academic year 1974-75, he is on leave at the Hoover Institute of Stanford University to write a book on Vietnam negotiations.

Chapter 8

THE KENYAN LEGISLATURE:
POLITICAL FUNCTIONS AND CITIZEN PERCEPTIONS

R A Y M O N D   F.   H O P K I N S

Swarthmore College

This essay discusses how the Kenyan legislature operates in national politics. First, it describes some of the political features that affect the performance of the National Assembly and some of the consequences (functions) of legislative activity. Next, the perceptions of citizens, both toward politics and toward parliament in particular, are described based on a sample survey of 435 Kenyans in 1971. These perceptions, I will try to show, are not only a reflection of social and economic conditions in a "developing" state, but also a reflection of the realities of Kenyan political life. In conclusion, I offer some general hypotheses about Kenyan politics and the role that the legislature plays in response to its political environment.

POLITICS AND THE NATIONAL ASSEMBLY:
EMBOURGEOISMENT AND THE ORGANIZATION OF CLEAVAGES

Although the National Assembly in Kenya embodies many of the rituals and legal forms of the Westminister pattern inherited from

AUTHOR'S NOTE: This essay is based on research supported by the International Development Research Center at Indiana University. I am grateful to George Stolnitz, the director of IDRC until September 1972, and to G. Robert Boynton, Gerhard Loewenberg, and Chong Lim Kim of the Comparative Legislative Research Center at the University of Iowa for their assistance and advice in revising this paper.

British colonial tutelage, important changes have occurred. Since independence in December 1963, the Kenyan legislature has been altered from a bicameral to a unicameral assembly, and has acquired increased formal authority as the Majimbo (regional) constitution with its federal system was abandoned for a more unitary form of government. The activities of Kenya's parliament not only have consequences for law-making and legitimation similar to most other legislatures, but also have special consequences related to particular elements in Kenyan history, contemporary political structure, and the organization and strength of current political cleavages.

THE EMBOURGEOISMENT OF KENYA

The newly organized Kenyan political system was bequeathed three important legacies at independence. First, the relatively prosperous modern economy was largely organized by the white community, approaching 60,000 in 1960. Whites held top positions as owners or managers running large farms, especially those established in the fertile highlands area that had been legally "reserved" for whites only, and dominating commercial and industrial firms, largely concentrated in Nairobi. A second legacy was the colonial administrative political structure. An ensemble of roles and a supply of skilled manpower had been assembled by the British for the purpose of running the country. This structure for governance was transferred largely intact to African leadership in the pattern of transfer described by Apter (1963). Finally, the Emergency period of the 1950s had a momentous impact. The Mau Mau movement involved almost entirely Kikuyus, a tribal group living in the economically most developed area of Kenya around Nairobi. The rebellion retarded the growth of national political organization, facilitated the rise of local political "bosses" while the key national leadership was in detention, accelerated social change among Kikuyu—and yet artificially depressed Kikuyu recruitment to modern posts. It also had a psychological impact exposing nearly every adult Kikuyu to some incident that threatened his security.

The contemporary political system in Kenya has been heavily influenced by each of these factors. Kenya has retained the basic economic structure inherited from the colonial period. Boards of directors have added African members but have seldom changed their business policies. African civil servants and politicians have begun their own businesses; have purchased singly, or in cooperative endeavors, farms from departing Europeans; have undertaken to build and rent houses and apartments; and in general have utilized capitalist opportunities to promote their own well-being and that of their immediate families.

The political forms of the colonial era have also been largely retained. The role structure of the political instruments of control used by the colonial regime—namely, provincial administration, the police, educational organization, and government financial boards— operate with much the same norms. Even superficially, African politicians wear Western suits while provincial and district commissioners frequently wear safari suits and pith helmets.

Finally, the "emergency" has had continuing effects. While the movement heightened the shared interest of Kikuyus in politics, it also led to severe deprivations for many. After independence, compensation for Kikuyu "lossess" resulted in their "over-appointment" to government posts (Okumu, 1970; Bienen, 1970). Solidarity has continued to be important. The 1969 oath-taking ceremonies that pledged Kikuyu loyalty was reminiscent of the functions of Mau Mau oathing. The insecurity of a privileged group, under attack in parliament among other places, was bolstered by clandestine Kikuyu oathing meetings at Gatundu, President Kenyatta's farm.

The political structure in Kenya is largely molded by these economic patterns and political heritage. Jomo Kenyatta, who led Kenya at independence, lacked the ability or will to build a national party that dominated regional/ethnically based local leaders. Rather he kept intact colonial bureaucratic and economic structures, even strengthening the government bureaucracy. He has increasingly relied on it as an instrument of rule. Kenyatta became a political hero during the "Emergency," spending nearly ten years in prison or detention. His historic role places him in a special category above party and tribal rivalries; while his popularity has waned, he is still revered, and almost all politicians calculate that Kenyatta will be President as long as he is physically able. The Kenyan African National Union (KANU) exists as the de facto one party in Kenya, initially attaining this position when members of the pre-independence opposition group, the Kenyan African Democratic Union (KADU) joined KANU in 1964. It re-established its dominance when the Kenya Peoples Union (KPU), a radical splinter party formed under Odinga Oginga's leadership in 1966, was legally banned in 1969, shortly before national elections for parliament were held for which only winners of the KANU primaries were eligible.

KANU, in spite of its dominance as a party, remains weak. A strong party could limit the influence of those currently in political control who make the effective choices, and this is recognized by some as a potential threat. Party structure is a loose coalition of regional and local "bosses," imposing no leadership criteria or ideology upon party adherents. Even political functions such as exhortation for national themes and the recruitment of local leadership are performed by the government bureaucracy rather than KANU. Consolidation of power within the executive and administrative branches of government provides top national leaders with a loyal and relatively unchecked instrument of control. Since 1965 Kenya's provincial administration has expanded its control over local areas, the General Service Unit, a para-military police, has been reformed and placed under the Office of the President, and intelligence activities monitoring political dissidents have been expanded (Gertzel, 1970, describes all these changes).

Concurrent with the rising power of the bureaucracy and the decline of inter-party competition has been an Africanization of high positions in the government and economy. One result has been an increase in economic and social inequality among Africans. Extremes of poverty and wealth are not unusual in economically poor states. Countries such as India, China, and Brazil have manifest extremes far in excess of the current differences in Kenya. The situation in Kenya differs, however, in at least one important respect, in that inequalities among Africans have been rising rapidly in the past few years. Salaries, wages, and benefits among all Africans employed have grown from an average of £68 to £175, an increase of 160% from 1960 to 1969. Meanwhile, employment has grown only 4% (Kenya Statistics Division, 1970: 170-1). In 1969 unemployment was estimated to be approximately 25% in Nairobi in 1970 and possibly as high as that throughout the country.[1] Kenya's economy, however, is growing. Gross domestic product, for instance, between 1964 and 1969 grew at an average annual rate of nearly 8% (Kenya Statistics Division, 1970: 32). In a broad sense, the rich seem to be getting richer and the poor poorer; at least this view is expounded by critical Kenyans, including government officials (Mohr, 1972: 10). While the economy is growing, the number of jobs is not growing. The increased income has gone primarily to a small portion of the population, for the most part a small elite residing in Nairobi. An economic basis for class conflict has been created, one which has occasionally emerged in electoral politics.

In addition, the MPs, businessmen, military officers, and high civil servants who constitute this political elite enjoy special privileges. These include a cosmopolitan social life, untaxed fringe benefits and allowances, and preferential access to loans, investment opportunities, earnings from private (second) businesses, and overseas trips.[2] Election to the legislature provides fairly automatic entry into this association of the privileged.

Since rapid expansion of economic opportunities among Africans requires substantial financing, often provided by loans and mortgages from European economic brokers, large numbers of the African elite are heavily indebted. They have become heavily dependent upon substantial economic growth, high rents and profits, and maintenance of the political and economic status quo. It is not surprising, therefore, that excited expressions of discontent, aside from its use in xenophobic speeches, is unpopular and opposed by most of the embourgeoised and rather conservative class of leaders.

POLITICAL ORGANIZATION AND THE LEGISLATIVE ELITE

Political organization is structured by three interest clusters: economic classes, communal ties, and patron-client relationships. The distribution of values that has emerged since independence has laid the foundations for political conflict over economic issues, both informally and by MPs in the legislature. Demands have been made to limit the amount of land that any one individual (or household) may own, to distribute land more equitably, and to increase monies for loans, housing, and educational opportunities for lower income groups. In 1966-69, at the time of the KANU-KPU conflict, the KPU called for greater benefits to urban and rural poor at the expense of the capitalist and salaried middle classes (European and African).

However, such political entrepreneurship has had little success building an organization based on economic appeals. Economic marginals in the more advanced areas do not usually make direct claims on the government. Rather, they frequently attempt to solve their problems by other means such as crime, squatting on unused land, defaulting on loans, and relying upon relatives whose aid is induced by extended family obligations. Moreover, government policy to address economic needs has often been only symbolically successful. The Tri-partite Agreement, drawn up in June, pledged unions, private industry, and government to a plan to expand employment by 10%. The plan was highly popular but had few positive effects.[3]

The articulation of political interests based on economic differences thus remains nascent in Kenya. This is due in part to government actions to provide economic opportunities, often largely symbolic, and to suppress organizations that agitate on economic grounds. It is also due to the relative importance of other bases for organizing political interests.

One such base consists of communal ties which are highly salient in Kenyan politics. Even among urban populations ties to tribal and clan identities remain strong and shape participation in modern social and political life. Although KPU began as a coalition of "radicals" from several tribes, it increasingly came to have a single tribal component, the Luo. Friendship patterns, access to employment or favors, and political identification all tend to follow communal rather than economic, geographic, or social lines. During the parliamentary elections of 1969, voting followed almost exclusively tribal identities in ethnically mixed urban areas and clan lines in rural constituencies (Hyden and Leys, 1971). Many jobs, both in government and in private business, are expected to be allocated by tribal connections (Ross: 1968). Allocation, however, has not been even.[4] This has led to a general resentment at the overrepresentation of Kikuyus who receive loans, hold high posts, and enjoy educational advantages (Rothchild, 1969: 700).

Ethnic rivalries are at the center of "inside-dopester" discussions of politics. Successors to Kenyatta are categorized first in terms of Kikuyu and non-Kikuyu, and if the latter, their acceptability to Kikuyus (Ross, 1968, makes this point). Some tribes, such as the Luo and Luhya, have welfare associations that serve as agents for the tribe in some political government. Such organizations and high representation of certain groups in particular institutions, notably the Kamba in the army, reinforce ethnic interpretations of political action.[5] While "tribalism" is publicly condemned—notably by Kikuyus who have no formal tribal association—its importance is underscored by the widespread expectations that it is the most important basis for intra-elite conflict (Ross, 1968; Hopkins, 1972b).

Patron-client relationships are another base for political organization, existing primarily within tribal domains and bureaucratic structures.[6] Leaders and supporters are linked by diffuse, informal mutual obligations. Clients locate a well-placed patron and carry out functions related to his needs. These may include securing accurate information, defending his name or attacking that of enemies, and representing him to those further removed from his patronage organization. In return, clients are rewarded with jobs (now in dwindling supply as Africanization is slowed), loans, status and/or outright cash. Patron-client networks serve to maintain active links between legislators and their rural bases of support. During elections these relationships are invigorated by campaign funds and come to resemble "political machines" among factional rivals in the same constituency.[7] For many MPs, notably those who had few private resources for building or maintaining a clientist machine, the elections were a difficult task (Hyden and Leys, 1971: 24-26).[8] Seventy-seven sitting MPs were defeated in the KANU primary, the only competitive arena. These included 5 ministers and 14 assistant ministers; several others chose not to run. The turnover in the elected 158 seats in the Assembly was over half. Most of the defeats can be attributed to voters' perceptions that the incumbent had failed to support tribal positions (notably among Luos from Nyanza) or to secure sufficient benefits for constituents.

In spite of the sizable personnel change that occurred, the 1969 elections have had little impact on legislative behavior. An Africanization of high posts has continued, interlocking interests and overlapping identities have grown between the political (legislative) elite and those who run the farms, commercial firms, and foreign industry. New MPs have been accommodated by this pattern of embourgeoisment among elite. While discussion of unemployment and rural development languished in parliament, legislation to raise the salaries of MPs and ministers by 30% was passed. This occurred at the very time of a national agreement to "freeze" wages (East African Standard, 1970). In general, the emergence of a privileged elite, distributing shares in economic growth to the chosen mentors of tribal, clan, and patron-client formations was undisturbed by 1969 electoral politics; most new MPs at least tacitly supported by their actions in the legislature the embourgeoisment of Kenya.

FUNCTIONS OF THE KENYAN LEGISLATURE

Policy-making and law-making functions of legislatures are almost universally less important than constitutional doctrine or popular opinion would suggest (Loewenberg, 1971: 177-81; Packenham, 1970). The functions performed by legislatures in the political system other than these "formal" tasks are frequently more important. Such other functions in Kenya include identifying and training political leaders, facilitating communication between government and populace, articulating constituent and special interest demands and interpreting governmental responses, and legitimizing allocative decisions that are made outside the legislature. The consequences for the system of possible changes in the Kenyan legislature's actions in these regards tend to be greater than would be changes in the legislature's discretionary influence over legislation.

The law-making function of the legislature, never its exclusive prerogative, has declined since the period following independence. During 1963-65, immediately after independence, the legislature was able to block several government procedural initiatives and force revisions in others such as land policy and development allocations. In the subsequent period such discretionary influence declined. Initiatives by legislators to promote the East African Federation and reduce economic inequalities forced ministers to respond publicly to criticisms and highlighted controversies on these issues, but did not substantially affect the government's position. The fact that changes in political boundaries, an action that required Assembly approval, were made in several cases well before the Assembly was consulted indicates the ease of control over the Assembly expected by the executive. Since 1969, following the assassination of Tom Mboya, a leading non-Kikuyu leader, and the election of new MPs, the legislature has undertaken fewer initiatives such as private bills. Although in some instances individual MPs have not endorsed government proposals (such as the 1970 Succession Bill), their influence over government action remains slim. Presidential prerogative and the practice in ministries of ignoring parliamentary supremacy, notably with regard to spending money, sap much of the legislature's potential for influence. Thus, even though a tradition of criticism of the executive has been retained as populist rhetoric continued to enliven Assembly meetings in 1972, the consequences of such talk in the Assembly—not only for the law-making function but for other functions as well—have diminished.[9]

What other functions do MPs actually perform, individually and collectively within the political system? One function is legitimation of government actions which in turn promotes regime stability. Regardless of the likely negative consequences for this function from the decline in legislative autonomy from the executive, the effect of the legislature on legitimacy remains important. However, evaluating the legislature's impact on legitimacy poses a formidable analytical and evaluative task. This is because actions of legislators that affect

legitimacy of the regime as a whole relate to both direct consequences, often from symbolic acts of approving bills, and indirect
consequences generally related to other features of the legislature.
This function, for instance, involves satisfying societal demands in
rather complex ways. Legitimacy is enhanced by the legislature's
adherence to democratic forms, representation of sectional interests,
and actions responsive to perceived needs of constituents.

Stultz has argued that, by criticizing the government and ignoring
constituents, the Kenyan MPs have failed to promote fully the
legitimacy and authority of government. As a result, he believes, the
government has acted to reduce opposition and to prevent anti-
government speeches by MPs to their constituents (Stultz, 1970:
325-33). Alternatively, as the ability of the legislature to withdraw
support from government leaders became dangerous to leaders, one
expects, as in Kenya, they will act to reduce the exercise of such
ability. In this event, the Kenya legislature's influence has been
limited and the preventive detention powers that were accorded the
President have been used against selected MPs.

For the limited purposes of this paper, I will not elaborate on the
legitimation function (however, see Hopkins, 1972a: 282-90). This
function is common to legislatures in nearly all political systems. The
importance of a legislature for the legitimacy of a regime varies both
with what the legislature does and what is demanded of it by the
citizenry. In the subsequent section on citizen perceptions we will
see that few people see the legislature or any part of government as
distinctive (although citizens did have specific views about legislative
activity); one conclusion seems to be that legislative failure would
not destroy legitimacy, although its success in fulfilling expectations
can enhance it.

INTEREST BROKERAGE

Interest brokerage is one of several other consequences of
Assembly behavior that are particularly notable in Kenya's political
system. The role of the legislature in the communication of political
interests is highly visible. Assembly debates, especially during the
question hour, and public addresses abound with MPs' enunciations
of local demands and aspirations, bringing such claims directly to the
attention of the bureaucracy. This function is important in providing
an "upward" transmission of demands. Alternatively, the interests of
the cabinet members and President Kenyatta, such as the enhance-

ment of loyalty among the populace, is promoted by MPs in rather ritualized statements of fealty. In Kenya, interest articulation by the legislators is particularly salient since lobbying through "communication" is the principal method by which MPs can hope to convert electoral promises into policy.

Individually many MPs become patrons for the "clients" in their constituency; they can expect to be supported so long as they play this role well. Candidates in 1969 vying for public support frequently promoted themselves in terms of ability to secure benefits for constituents subsequent to their election. Education or close relationships with high officials were cited as attributes that would make them more effective advocates of constituency interests. National policy issues played a small role in campaign discussions. As a result, some MPs have been overwhelmed with particular demands from constituents. These range from requests for government action in large matters such as increasing the farm land available for African smallholders to the petty task of shepherding local constituents through one or another bureaucratic maze.

While local leaders and clans who assisted in an MP election tend to expect special attention, the role of the MP as a personal agent-patron is widely expected by constituents. In order to receive requests, however, the MP needs to be available locally, a pressure which generates an incentive to remain away either in Nairobi or abroad on business.[10] Since personal encounter is important, it is more difficult to disappoint those who cannot see the MP; inaccessibility after election may keep alive the illusion that MPs are influential. The assumption that a problem can be solved if only it can be presented to the MP is not challengeable if it cannot be tested. Hence, limiting accessibility has become important, and this has reinforced the distance between the political elite and the average Kenyan.

A second, less public mode for communicating interests exists in that patron-client relationships lead to mutual collaboration among leaders on issues threatening the clientist structure. The Kikuyu oathing in 1969, for instance, was an affirmation of social solidarity, a ritual that inspired allegiance and trust and exacted reciprocal promises. Most networks of elite, not only among the Kikuyu, recognize their need for mutual support and such reciprocal exchanges occur on a nationwide basis. In the last several years, delegations of local notables led by an MP have arrived at President Kenyatta's farm at Gatundu to pledge their loyalty, present donations to his personal self-help projects, and plead for one or another particular need. The face-to-face contacts, ritualized format, and acknowledgement of reciprocal obligations of these almost weekly encounters parallel on a national scale the patron-client transactions between MPs and their local supporters. Kenyatta, at least symbolically, is a national patron with MPs as his intermediaries.

MPs play important roles, therefore, in parallel structures for communicating local interests. One structure terminates with the MP who, acting as a broker-patron, addresses public groups, including the Assembly, proclaiming vociferously his conception of his clients' interests. The other structure for communicating interests is more directed and less flamboyant. Executive officials with discretionary authority, of whom Kenyatta is the most visible and potent, are approached in a suppliant manner and urged to recognize pressing problems. Contacts with ministers and influential civil servants vary considerably among MPs. Often local officials, such as town clerks, will expect the local MP to press for important budgetary allocations within the relevant ministries.[11] Satisfying local officials on this score may be more important than breaking campaign promises. However this may disappoint some constituents, it does not cut an MP's links with local elites, though it can vastly increase the distance between the "Nairobi politician" and his home base. Local elites tend to be more satisfied than average citizens and hence more conservative. For them the access provided by an MP who is *successful at the center* is important. A study in Nyeri district, for example, found that occupants of local leadership roles (headmen, cooperative and party officers, and so on) were both economically better off than random landowners and more conservative on issues, and thus more in agreement with the government. They opposed land confiscation and supported the requirement that Africans pay for plots on settlement schemes. Voters in Nyeri rejected all their sitting MPs in 1969, but over 90% (of a sample of 349 farmers) felt that MPs would give their complaints a favorable reception. Seventy-one percent felt MPs represent the "people and not other interests," but only 15% thought politicians could be trusted to keep promises that they make (Stockton, 1971).

RECRUITMENT

A second function the legislature performs is political recruitment. Since KANU is largely moribund as a party, the initial selection of national leaders is controlled by local voters. Election to the Assembly identifies potential recruits for government posts.

Once he is elected, however, the rewards available to a local notable arriving in Nairobi as an MP may induce him to conform to existing norms promoting elite cooperation and dampening agitation over dissatisfactions. In this respect, popular local leaders tend to be "system seduced," trading local loyalties for access to privilege.

In many one-party or dominant-party systems recruitment of political leadership is carefully controlled. In the Soviet Union a long period of party apprenticeship is normal. In newer states such as Tanzania and the Ivory Coast a careful review of candidates at local and national levels insures their acceptability for existing leaders and helps to maintain the strength of local party officials. In Kenya the party has used few screening controls, and service in the party has been unimportant in recruitment of leaders.

In the 1969 KANU primary, seats were contested in 148 of 158 constituencies, and in 106 locales three or more candidates stood. The qualification procedures included making a 1000-shilling "non-returnable deposit" (sic) to KANU and passing a language test in English (which less than half seem to have passed). Requirements such as these, which screen out aspirants with less education and wealth, are justified on the grounds that all debate in parliament is in English and that some token of seriousness should be required. Six months of party membership plus these "objective" requirements were the only effective hurdles faced by most aspirants, although the KANU Executive Committee had final approval. Only five nominees were rejected, all on technical grounds.[1][2]

Although the election results led to a major influx of new MPs, replacing and rejuvenating some of the leadership at the center, the key cabinet ministers were retained. As Ghai and McAuslan remark (1970: 522-23): "The elections therefore were not to provide for a new government; President Kenyatta was to continue as head of government, though individual Ministers might lose."

Existence of the legislature has required procedures for selection of popular local leaders to form a national leadership pool. Such recruitment of new ministers, assistant ministers, and other leaders by means of parliamentary election involved in turn a mutual process of selection between the executive and the local areas. Since party controls before and after selection have remained virtually non-existent, the President has become the principal force responsible for imposing cohesion and discipline on MPs. Because of the weak party organization (Okumu, 1968) the structure of opportunities offered to new leaders and the induction of new recruits into the elite of the center have become largely controlled by the president or his closest associates.

EQUAL REPRESENTATION

Leaders of the various regions and tribes of Kenya have consistently demanded a fair share of the dividends from independence and economic growth. A central feature of such demands is equal or balanced representation in the central institutions of society. Since the legislature is based on geographically distributed constituencies, such balance is assured. However, the legislature itself not only avoids resentment arising from discriminatory representation, but also it provides an important example of equity. A disproportionately large number of Kikuyu hold administrative posts, as well as enjoying greater educational, industrial, and commercial opportunities. Although criteria of merit, economy, or profit are used to justify this situation, it has not allayed antagonisms by others. Moreover, widely held views that development projects are distributed inequitably by region, a view confirmed by investment patterns, further creates resentment.[13]

The "balance" in the legislature is more *symbolic* than *effective.* Though its membership meets a general demand for equity and condemns by implication unrepresentative political institutions, these consequences have not altered the consolidation of Kikuyu power. President Kenyatta's cabinet, a far more powerful group, contains an overrepresentation of Kikuyus. The tribal composition of MPs in the government is more balanced when the 31 assistant ministers are added to the 23 cabinet members in the calculation. However, the post of assistant minister requires few skills and offers a bare modicum of influence. Nonetheless, its prestige and financial rewards are attractive. Such posts provide a large reservoir of patronage posts for the president which are useful for rewarding the faithful from peripheral areas and insuring the appearance of a fair racial and geographic balance in "government" leadership.

COMMITMENT

A fourth function of the legislature is to commit key political leaders to programs or policies designed by the bureaucracy. This is a consequence of the legislature's internal organization of its activity. Because they are called upon to answer questions and defend government policy, notably during the budgetary review of proposed expenditures, ministers and assistant ministers usually depend upon a cabinet or presidential decision over major policies, and on civil servants for minor policy clarifications. Regardless of their personal views (if they have any) or those of their constituents, their responses to parliamentary questions are expected to conform to "instructions." And since MPs lack the personal skills or staff resources to investigate problems or survey alternative policies, programs devised by the bureaucracy tend to be accepted and subsequently lauded by political leaders.

By definding "official" policy, politicians become committed to it. Ministers are often called upon to defend actions of civil servants whether they are fully in agreement with them or not. A strong and ascendant administration can thereby propel politicians to publicly share responsibility for programs beyond their actual competence to affect them.[14]

CITIZEN PERCEPTIONS

The legislative ability to perform its various functions, especially that of legitimation, is directly related to the public's perceptions of it. Public attention to legislative activity and their support of the institution provide necessary linkage between legislative behavior and system-wide functions. Perceptions congruent with activity suggest a "reality" adjustment on the part of relevant publics, while support for the legislature (indicated by congruence of predictions and preferences for legislative action) is vital for its continued performance and possible expansion of functions (Patterson et al., 1969).

In general, Kenyans have perceptions of the government and legislature which are in accord both with the socioeconomic situation of the country and with the description above of the parliament's functions. A sample of 485 Kenyans, living in or near Nairobi and Mombasa (the two largest cities) and interviewed in July-September 1971,[15] evinced expectations that closely reflected existing practices and policies. On balance their views indicated acceptance and probable reinforcement for the present pattern of political activity.

STRONG GOVERNMENT AND WEAK LEGISLATURE

The respondents generally acknowledged the potency of the central government. A comparison (Table 1) between the colonial regime and the "government today" indicates that governmental capacity was thought to have increased—65% felt that the current government was a most powerful force. This image of a strong government "able to do anything" would bolster a sense of individual vulnerability manifest by many during the interviews by concern to avoid questions evaluating the government.

Although the government was perceived as powerful, the conception of government tended not to discriminate among its parts. Two-thirds of the respondents could see no divisions in the government, but rather thought that it was all the same (see Table 2). Those who could distinguish parts were asked which one was doing its job best. The president and the administration were the branches mentioned most frequently, followed by the courts and the legislature. Clearly, parliament was not a focus of attention. This popular view of government as a single unit, rather than one composed of distinct and possibly competing branches, makes creditable Kenyatta's reference to "my government" as embracing all of its divisions and all spheres of action.

Since most citizens perceived a potent, diffuse political regime and had little awareness of the legislature as a distinctive part, few would be likely to attribute personal effectiveness to legislators. Though legislators were thought to be more approachable than civil servants, when respondents were asked to compare "who would be better able to help" a person, a politician or a civil servant, only 28% chose a politician compared to 37% who selected the civil servant (19% were indifferent). The responses suggest that the administration and the civil servant are seen as the most powerful actors in government, with more control over what individuals want, than the legislature or MPs.

TABLE 1[a]

PERCEPTIONS OF POWER OF COLONIAL AND PRESENT GOVERNMENTS (in percentages)

	Most Powerful	Powerful	Weak	Helpless	Total
Colonial Government	35	29	15	13	92
Government today	65	20	5	3	93

a. Percentages add to 100 when those not responding are included and are based on N=485. A seven-rung ladder from most powerful (uwezo) to least powerful was shown respondents who were asked to indicate where they would place each regime on the scale. The code is Most Powerful=1; Powerful=2, 3; Weak=4, 5, 6; and Helpless ("not able to do anything")=7.

TABLE 2
VIEWS OF SUPERIOR GOVERNMENT PERFORMANCE, BY PARTS

Parts Distinguished	Percent	N
President	7.8	(38)
Parliament	3.3	(16)
Courts	4.3	(21)
Administration	5.8	(28)
Local government	1.9	(9)
Don't know	8.3	(40)
Parts were not distinguished	68.6	(333)
TOTAL	100.0	(485)

THE MP AS PUBLIC REPRESENTATIVE

Interestingly, citizens were rather aware of their MPs and knowledgeable of actions to be expected of them. Although only 8% had ever personally contacted an MP on a problem (compared to 22% who had contacted politicians or government officials), 80% were able to name the MP for their current constituency, and 84% knew the MP from their "home." In contrast to civil servants, MPs were considered to be more willing and "interested" in helping the respondents, 49% to 19%. Nearly half of the respondents—44.6%— thought the MP from their "home" constituency was more representative of their interest than the one from their current area of residence, while 20% called their current MP more representative. Most respondents had moved to Nairobi or Mombasa and still thought of "home" as the area of their birth, a factor which brings out the continuing importance of rural ties. Respondents in the two cities often owned land in a rural area and some planned to retire to their ancestral area. According to a study of 1,200 urban households in 1971, nearly half of the married workers had a wife who lived apart in a rural area (Johnson, 1971). Movement between rural "home" and urban residency is frequent, even for those with permanent jobs in Nairobi and Mombasa, and it seems natural that such people should have looked to the MP from their area of birth as their representative.

Most respondents also tended to be socially mobilized, that is, educated, urbanized and exposed to mass media. While they therefore felt closer on the whole to their "home" MP, they also preferred educated men to serve as MPs. During the 1969 campaign, several candidates had campaigned with the argument that better educated men were more likely to be appointed ministers, thus were better able to help a constituency. Education was recognized as an important characteristic of MPs; although 78% of the respondents felt it was likely for an educated man to lose to a "popular" one, only 28% thought this was desirable. This discrepancy suggests that parliament was considered the rightful province of the more educated. Individual MPs thus should be qualified but also accessible.

This personal, often rural-based identification with MPs is important for the functions of legitimation and equal representation. Legislators seemed liked in spite of their relative weakness, and this positive perception of individual legislators provides needed links in performing the functions discussed earlier.

Perhaps as a result of such positive identifications; the government was close for most respondents. Only 21% felt the government was "distant, not listening or responding" to people. Bienen, drawing upon this and other studies, has concluded (1974: 124-31) that "factionalism and competition for positions and spoils among elites and restrictions on mass participation since 1963 have not destroyed support from below." Respondents were generally satisfied with those in high positions and felt the government was run for "all the people" and not a "few big interests" (Table 3).

THE LEGISLATURE AND THE FUTURE

In responding to several hypothetical situations concerning parliament, citizens felt the parliament was less likely to adopt policies

TABLE 3
SATISFACTION WITH GOVERNMENT PERSONNEL AND PURPOSES

Percentage	N=485	
		In general, how satisfied are you with those who are now in high positions of government?
8	(38)	1. Fully dissatisfied
13	(61)	2. Partly dissatisfied
34	(165)	3. Partly satisfied
36	(175)	4. Fully satisfied
9	(46)	Blank
		Would you say the government is run for the benefit of all the people, or that it is run by a few big interests (or people) looking out for themselves?
24	(116)	1. Few big interests
69	(335)	2. All the people
7	(34)	Blank

in congruence with their preferences than to follow procedures that they preferred. Predictions were solicited for each item as to how "likely" a specified action seemed and how "right" it would be. Although Kenyans tended not to differentiate parts of government when asked what parts performed best, they were generally willing to respond when asked specific questions about the operation of the legislature. Policy-related questions indicated sizable incongruence, for example, no action was expected on proposals to reduce social inequality even though these were thought to be good and right policies. Table 4 shows that over 40% think that parliament will not pass legislation to adjust income inequity, or to impose economic restrictions on themselves and other political elite, although the public favors these proposals. One carpenter whom I re-interviewed explained his reasoning on these questions as follows:

> Well, these men who sit in Nairobi, they all own land, they own cars. If they were like people who worked and who had no money, then they would want to do things like that. But the MPs have big farms so there is little land for men like myself.

Expected failure of the legislature to enact proposals which would decrease the economic gaps between the rich and the average Kenyan is understandable. For most respondents no inconsistency seemed to

TABLE 4
PREDICTIONS AND PREFERENCES CONCERNING LEGISLATORS' ACTIONS[a]

	(N)	Percentage of Respondents Who Found the Contingency:		
	(N)	Likely	Right	Incongruent[b]
1. Parliament passes rules like those in Tanzania, prohibiting politicians and government officials from earning money outside their jobs.	341	24	66	61
2. Parliament limits salaries and gives benefits to the poor.	383	24	78	64
3. Elections are held for a new parliament with more than one party allowed to put up candidates.	410	50	67	35
4. Parliament is able to change government policy on an important issue.	200	59	70	32

a. Interviewers asked respondents to choose up to 11 areas of concern from a list of 18. As a result, the number of responses to items varied considerably. More responses to an item indicates that more felt it to be important.
b. Incongruence signifies either a likely-wrong or an unlikely-right combination.

exist between their positive views of MPs and this failure. Attitudinal constraints that would reduce such apparent inconsistencies are not frequently found, even among citizenry with higher educational levels as in the United States (see, for instance, Converse, 1963). Conversations with rather sophisticated Kenyans suggested to me that MPs were not believed to be deliberately corrupt, but to live in a corrupting situation that fostered indifference to the masses and excessive concern for their own economic problems.

In some respects, the problems of "losing touch" for the upwardly mobile MP are epitomized by J. M. Kariuki, a man who was detained during the Mau Mau rebellion and subsequently wrote a well-known account of his experience (1963). Kariuki became a successful businessman within a few years of his release, is currently serving his second term in parliament, and is popular among fellow MPs who frequently ask him to speak in their constituencies. His popularity seems related in part to his practices of donating large sums for the schools and health centers he is asked to dedicate. When asked by a reporter how he could justify owning his own private aircraft, he explained that it was necessary in order to get around Kenya to meet people (Leys, 1970: 64).

The Kenyan respondents' predictions and preferences concerning the two procedural issues for the legislature indicated considerable agreement between expectations and preferences (Table 4). A majority thought that party competition and the legislature's assertion of independence vis-a-vis the government were likely and rightful future events. Awareness of the inability of the legislature to disagree with the government was not large, possibly owing to the tendency of citizens not to distinguish between legislative and executive institutions. Although the legislature since 1966 has in nearly every case acceded to government wishes, most respondents still thought it was likely that the legislature was able to change government policy. For most citizens, apparently, the degree of control exercised by the executive over legislative recruitment and action was not a source of dissatisfaction; their responses indicated ignorance or denial of this control. Moreover, a minority believed it would be wrong to end one-party control (27%) or allow the court to nullify executive actions on constitutional grounds (32%).

The collective performance expected of legislators is generally not an elevated one. As representatives of an elite by virtue of membership, they are usually expected to act in its interests rather than the interests of constituents. Although the legislature appears weak and has lost much of its "veto" power since the 1964-66 period, citizens are not motivated to strengthening it. Its perceived adequacy as a powerful body may be because the legislature contains powerful government leaders.

One seeming paradox appeared in the study. Respondents generally knew their legislator and commented freely on legislative activity (Table 3), but they had little ability or interest in assessing how the legislature did its job as a distinct political unit. This reflects low distinction among units of government. The reason for this, I believe, is that separation of powers is more readily associated with regional or ethnic cleavages than with branches of government. Checks on arbitrary or tyrannical authority therefore are founded primarily in the accumulation of such competing "political" interests, as through "balanced" representation, rather than in the separation of legislative and other powers.

Since recognition and support for MPs is not paralleled by similar attention (and presumably support) for the legislature as a whole, recruitment is a more salient function than law-making for the legislature. Recruitment *to* the government takes place *through* the availability of constituency seats in the legislature. Indeed, the failure to perceive the legislature as distinctive reflects the peripheral character of the political functions of the legislature as a whole, compared to the important role a few legislators play by virtue of their government posts. Moreover, because the formal constitution can be changed so easily, the legislature does not serve as a guarantee of countervailing power on the executive; indeed, it has only a minimum impact against arbitrary rule.

If citizens are doubtful about getting adopted policies they prefer, although they are satisfied with the rules of the political game as they see them, what are their expectations for the future? Respondents were asked what problems they considered most important for Kenya. Seventy-six percent of them mentioned unemployment; 36%, lack of education; 29%, a need for rural development; and 20%, tribalism. These problems create long-term strains on the political system, especially since there was little popular confidence that solutions to these problems could be found. When interviewers asked what political tendencies poeple thought were likely to happen in the future, a mixture of optimism and pessimism was found. Fourteen percent said the future was unsure, that anything could happen, and 16% expected some form of political strife such as a coup or civil war. In contrast, 8% foresaw either a decline in tribalism or an increase in national unity, and 36% predicted continued economic growth and little change otherwise. Twenty-three percent of the sample did not respond.

In short, though the Kenyan legislature seems to promote legitimacy and stability, it is not performing policy-making functions that are satisfying to the citizenry. By and large citizens perceive—I believe, correctly—that a diffuse governmental structure centered in the executive and the bureaucracy is responsible for policy. Because MPs are generally known and liked, however, the legislature is able to perform the secondary or complementary functions described earlier.

THE POLITICS OF INSECURITY

Insecurity can breed repression and exploitation. The Mau Mau experience, the rapid and sometimes shaky rise of Kenya's political leaders to affluence, and the recognized threats from tribal rivalry and dissident economic marginals are sources of insecurity for the political elite. Kenyatta's position, resting heavily on the fragile support he has as a heroic leader in the pre-independence period, affords few opportunities to strengthen representative institutions such as the legislature or the party. To defend such insecure positions, acquired after a costly struggle, seems natural, especially since loss of position in Kenya can carry large deprivations. The income gap between high-status positions and others held by those with about the same education or resources is extremely great. Primary education qualifies a civil servant to earn approximately $600 per year, while excluding other advantages an MP makes $6,000 to $7,000 and a minister three times that.[16] A university degree might insure a salary of $2,000, but Africans at the top of the public sector receive upwards of $13,000, not including housing, car, and other allowances.

High-income positions are not widely available, unlike the case in more industrialized societies. With unemployment estimated at 25% and the income of rural work about one-seventh or one-eighth that in the modern non-agricultural sector (Ndegwa, 1971: 42), those with high-school education are rational to seek an urban salaried job in preference to long periods of unemployment. "There is really no viable alternative to waiting around for the big money" (Johnson, 1971: 9). Incentives to secure a modern-sector, better-paying job are high and found among all strata since rural and unskilled jobs pay so little. Employees in small firms, often with low wages and insecure employment, and the peasantry have shared disproportionately in economic growth (Ndegwa, 1971: 34).

That opportunity more than skill or education rewards many elite and mid-elite while numerous Kenyans are waiting for their chance, may well account for the defensive political actions that have occurred since 1964, when backbench radicalism and attacks on tribal politics among MPs intensified. In recent years Kenyatta has repeatedly defended his government, warned students and legislators against unnecessary criticism, and reminded audiences of his long career as a freedom fighter (Mohr, 1972: 10). One example of such rhetoric was a national "Loyalty Day" held in June 1971 with rallies throughout the country. This followed the revelation that a group of thirteen Kenyans, including one MP, had been "plotting" against the government. A somber group estimated at over one million—more likely a hundred thousand, however—gathered in Nairobi to pledge their loyalty to Kenyatta.[17]

In this atmosphere the legislature is an important institution for both insecure leaders and dissatisfied followers. It meets needs of both groups not by reducing cleavages[18] but by seducing local elites into accepting the norms of the center. Continued colonial economic and administrative institutions have been instrumental in shaping this pattern. Acceptance of existing leadership has been reinforced by economic opportunities for allies and political repression for dissidents, a response to threatened security which underlines the risks inherent in political office.[19] At the same time, this pattern has operated to establish mild forms of control and to share economic gains among a diverse group of tribal and regional political entrepreneurs.

The legislature that has emerged in Kenya is more a symbol of democracy than its realization, yet this symbol is lauded by top political elite.[20] It provides "balance" in an otherwise ethnically malrepresented arena of elites and an avenue for expressing regional concerns. The representative composition of the Assembly promises a prominence to "national" considerations in decision-making and at least a concessionary distribution of values among groups. Lobbying activities of MPs to push the goals of regions and groups satisfies their concern to be heard. These activities encourage a national "patron-client" structure, although this may be rather weak in practice, and act principally to lobby for economic expansion, a necessary counter to the more intense (constant-sum) conflict that a stagnant economy might induce. Finally, members of the legislature provide symbols of "success," men whose upward mobility makes plausible the aspirations of thousands of others.

In these ways Kenya's legislature has both moderated pressures for change and provided an anchor for its insecure leadership.

NOTES

1. This claim was offered in an interview with an economic advisor in the Ministry of Finance and Economic Planning, January 1970.

2. The business ethic pervades politics to the extent that civil servants have been condemned for being too busy with their private business to work and MPs have been characterized as opportunists. See the discussion in the Ndegwa Commission report on interest conflicts in the civil service report of the Commission of Inquiry (Ndegwa, 1971: 16-19), and the description of the MP in James Ngugi's novel, Weep Not Child (1969).

3. Industry and government expanded its employees largely in low-skill, low-income positions and often did not replace those who left. Unions were willing to break the agreement, especially after they perceived its limited effects. Moreover, the publicity given the agreement seemed to induce unemployment by encouraging people who were not actively seeking work in the modern sector at the time to do so.

4. Kikuyu areas (Nairobi and the Central Province) have the highest portion of the population enrolled in school and the highest average income. Sixty-four percent of industrial loans and 44% of commercial loans made by the Industrial and Commercial Development Corporation through mid-1966 went to Kikuyus although they comprise only 20% of the population (Rothchild, 1969: 692-93).

5. The army, heavily staffed by Kamba officers (the fourth largest group in Kenya), may be the only important national institution not dominated by Kikuyus. The early retirement of the head of the army in June 1971, following accusations that he was linked with a group of anti-government plotters, increased excitement concerning Kikuyu-Kamba rivalry.

6. For a good statement of how patron-client ties develop in comparison to these other two modes of political organization in countries in Southeast Asia, see Scott (1972). For a discussion of some of the formations in Kenya, see Leys (1970).

7. At the base, the more alert populace seems to be rather calculating with respect to politicians, especially during elections. Audiences at rallies were known to exaggerate their support for a candidate in hopes he would distribute money to some of them for work on his campaign. As Hyden and Leys (1971: 24) state: "In more developed parts of the country elections were frequently seen as a kind of bargaining game between voters and candidates, in which the candidate may be awarded a license to improve his personal fortunes by becoming an MP in return for pledges and tokens of his intention to help improve the fortunes of his constituents by the most obvious means—the improvement of amenities in the area."

8. This may account for the wide popularity with which the decision to postpone local government elections for two years was greeted.

9. The decrease in number of meeting days in 1968-69 in Kenya may not continue since legislator's stipends for days in session have been increased. During 1970-71 the Assembly met with less than a quorum present on several occasions (Hakes, 1971).

10. As early as 1964 Kenyatta admonished MPs for their tendency to remain in Nairobi when the Assembly was not in session. If they wanted to "sleep in Nairobi . . . run around and see the sights," their membership in parliament would "have no value" (Stultz, 1970: 332).

11. In an interview with one town clerk I was told that local MPs were most effective when they engaged in personal lobbying with ministers or high bureaucrats. Their approach in these encounters tended to be more earnest, he thought, and bargains could be more readily struck. Noise, threats, and obstreperousness in the Assembly could even be counter-productive, he suggested.

12. The nominees also could not be civil servants (unless they resigned) or occupants of an elected post such as local councillor (Y. P. Ghai and J.P.W.B. McAuslen, 1970: 522-23).

13. Nearly all elite interviewed in Nairobi and Kisumu mentioned inequities in allocation as an issue creating resentment in disadvantaged regions.

14. I want to thank Professor Colin Leys for suggesting this function to me.

15. The respondents were selected randomly from a survey of households in Nairobi being conducted by the Nairobi City Council, and by cluster techniques in Mombasa. Four peri-urban areas were sampled by choosing every "nth" housing unit (with some deviations). The peri-urban areas were 8 to 15 miles from the major city but had country bus service to travel to it.

16. These figures include allowances but exclude income from various other sources which nearly all MPs receive (Gertzel et al., 1969: 214; Ndegwa, 1971: 56).

17. See reports in the East African Standard, June 28, 1971. The rally was heavily guarded by police, and considerable pressure was exerted for attendance. Employers were to have all workers attend, bus companies provide free transportation into the city, etc.

18. I disagree with Stultz (1970) on this point.

19. Loss of office carries a much greater risk of loss of wealth, status, and other values in the new states of Asia and Africa (Kim, 1971: 193-96).

20. Ghai and McAuslen (1970: 516) conclude in this respect: "Though the legal framework and traditions of colonial authoritarianism and partiality might remain, the independent government of Kenya is an elected government. . . . Over and above that fact, however, is the threat to legitimacy and stability of the whole political system that the continuation of the colonial approach entails."

REFERENCES

APTER, D. (1963) Ghana in Transition. New York: Atheneum.

BIENEN, H. (1974) Kenya: The Politics of Participation and Control. Princeton: Princeton Univ. Press.

––– (1970) "The economic environment," pp. 43-63 in G. Hyden, R. Jackson and J. Okumu (eds.) Development Administration: The Kenyan Experience. Nairobi: Oxford Univ. Press.

CONVERSE, P. (1964) "The nature of belief systems in mass publics," pp. 203-261 in D. Apter (ed.) Ideology and Discontent. New York: Free Press.

East African Standard (1970) Nairobi: Nov. 27-Dec. 12.

GERTZEL, C. (1970) The Politics of Independent Africa. Nairobi: East African Publishing House.

–––, M. GOLDSCHMIDT, and D. ROTHCHILD [eds.] (1969) Government and Politics in Kenya. Nairobi: East African Publishing House.

GHAI, Y. P. and J.P.W.B. McAuslen (1970) Public Law and Political Change in Kenya. Nairobi: Oxford Univ. Press.

HAKES, J. (1971) "The weakness of parliamentary institutions as a prelude to military coups in Africa." Presented to the Southern Political Science Assn. meetings, Gatlinburg, Tenn.

HOPKINS, R. (1972a) "Establishing authority: the view from the top." World Politics 24, 1: 271-292.

––– (1972b) "Codebook for Kenyan study of social mobilization and political participation," Swarthmore, Pa.: Swarthmore College, Center for Social and Policy Studies.
Mimeo.

HYDEN, G. and C. LEYS (1971) "Elections and politics in single-party systems: the case of
Kenya and Tanzania." Nairobi: University of Nairobi, Dept. of Government. Unpublished paper.

JOHNSON, G. (1971) "Notes on wages, employment and income distribution in Kenya."
Nairobi: University of Nairobi, Institute of Development Studies, Mimeo.

KARIUKI, J. M. (1963) Mau Mau Detainee. London: Oxford Univ. Press.

Kenya Statistics Division (1970) Statistical Abstract. Nairobi: Ministry of Finance and
Economic Planning.

KIM, C. L. (1971) "Toward a theory of individual and systemic effects of political status
loss." J. of Developing Areas 1, 2: 193-96.

LEYS, C. (1970) "Politics in Kenya: the development of peasant society." Nairobi:
University of Nairobi, Institute of Development Studies, Discussion paper 110. Mimeo.

LOEWENBERG, G. (1971) "The influence of parliamentary behavior on regime stability."
Comparative Politics 3, 2: 177-200.

MOHR, C. (1972) "Kenyatta, at 81, defends achievements and warns growing ranks of
critics." The New York Times (October 23): 10.

NDEGWA, D. [chmn.] (1971) Report of the Commission of Inquiry (Public Service
Structure and Remuneration Commission). Nairobi: Government Printer.

NGUGI, J. (1969) Weep Not Child. New York: Collier, African American Library.

OKUMU, J. (1970) "The socio-political setting," pp. 25-42 in G. Hyden, R. Jackson and J.
Okumu (eds.) Development Administration: The Kenyan Experience. Nairobi: Oxford
Univ. Press.

––– (1968) "Charisma and politics in Kenya," East African J. 5 (February): 9-16.

PACKENHAM, R. (1970) "Legislatures and Political Development," pp. 521-82 in A.
Kornberg and L. Musolf (eds.) Legislatures in Developmental Perspective. Durham, N.C.:
Duke Univ. Press.

PATTERNSON, S., G. R. BOYNTON, and P. HEDLUND (1969) "Perceptions and
expectations of the legislature and support for it." Amer. J. of Sociology 75 (July):
62-76.

ROSS, M (1968) "Politics and urbanization: two communities in Nairobi. Ph.D. disseration.
Evanston: Northwestern University.

ROTHCHILD, D. (1969) "Ethnic inequalities in Kenya." J. of Modern African Studies 7, 4:
689-711.

SCOTT, J. (1972) "Patron-client politics and political change in southeast Asia." Amer. Pol.
Sci. Rev. 66. 1: 91-113.

STOCKTON, R. (1971) "Aspects of Nyeri leadership." Staff paper No. 107. Nairobi:
University of Nairobi, Institute of Development Studies.

STULTZ, N. (1970) "The National Assembly in the politics of Kenya," pp. 303-33 in A.
Kornberg and L. Musolf (eds.) Legislatures in Developmental Perspective. Durham, N.C.:
Duke Univ. Press.

RAYMOND F. HOPKINS is Associate Professor of Political Science and Director
of the Center for Social and Policy Studies at Swarthmore College. He is the
author of *Political Roles in a New State,* and has contributed to numerous
journals, including American Political Science Review, Comparative Political
Studies, Social Forces, and World Politics. Currently, he is completing a book on
Attitudes and Politics in Kenya.

Chapter 9

SOME ASPECTS OF GROUP REPRESENTATION IN THE PHILIPPINE CONGRESS

R I C H A R D   A.   S T Y S K A L

Brooklyn College, City University of New York

A common problem for many of the post-colonial new states is the adaptation of traditional political institutions to Western models. After colonialism came to an end with an "amazing suddenness and finality," constitutions drawn essentially from Western models and which, formally at least, must be characterized as "modern" were just as suddenly ushered in.[1] Under such conditions a major question is how the constitutional structure is utilized, the political style in which public affairs are managed (Emerson, 1967: 244).

Cast in terms of legislative development, the problem can be defined as one of measuring the effectiveness of an "imported," relatively formalized representative body that has been juxtaposed with a less formal but nevertheless fully articulated set of indigenous norms for directing interactions between leaders and followers. Students of legislatures in the new states almost uniformly report that the main function of legislatures is to "exhibit" and "sell" government institutions and programs, and that where the representations of interests from "below" is encountered, it is characterized by personalistic rather than functionally specific, group-oriented interactions (see various studies in Kornberg and Musolf, 1970). It seems fair to say that these and other studies demonstrate a concern for the lack of development of the constituent and group representation function of legislatures and a respect for the importance of representative structures for reducing cleavage by enabling groups to obtain access to some of the authority roles.

The problem in this study is to describe some aspects of group representation in the Philippine Congress and to attempt to explain variations in (1) the experience of individual members with interests groups and (2) the use of members of two prominent interest groups of their organizations and the Congress for facilitating their demands. To guide the inquiry and to aid the evaluation of findings, some sort of benchmark is needed.

Choosing among existing paradigms, theoretical sketches and lists of functions about what deliberative bodies "do" and "should do" is difficult at best. At present, perhaps we can do no better than to adopt the two broad functions that Jewell and Patterson ascribe to legislatures. These are conflict management (with the types of conflict management being deliberative, decisional, adjudicative, and cathartic) and the integration of the polity. Both functions contribute to the maintenance of the political system (Jewell and Patternson, 1966: 8-15). Under integration of the polity are subsumed three, more specific, functions: authorization, legitimation, and representation. The latter two functions—legitimation and representation—are singled out for use in this study because they appear to be the most fundamental and comprehensive in capturing the fiduciary role of legislatures and because they have received widespread attention from developmental theorists as well as students of legislatures in the new states (Nettl, 1967).

Most definitions of the legitimation functions of assemblies stress their supportive or consensus-building nature, while definitions of representation concentrate on procedural, demand input, or linkage qualities. But recently, Wahlke (1971), drawing upon Easton's (1965) tripartite distinction of support for community, regime, and authority, urged a greater emphasis in research on the "supportive functions of representation" as against the demand input functions; and Loewenberg has made a case for certain linkage characteristics (between election results and cabinet appointments in European parliaments) associated with consensus-building (Loewenberg, 1971). Evidently, then, there is a reciprocal relationship between legitimation and representation: "Legislators are the spokesmen for, and are empowered to act for, constituencies as a result of the legitimacy of their selection as representatives," but "Legislative acts have authority and are regarded as legitimate in part because of the representative quality of the system" (Jewell and Patterson, 1966: 14).

One way of "breaking out" of this apparent circularity is to modify somewhat our conception of the legislature and the functions it performs. Instead of picturing the legislature as a body that by its existence and actions, legitimates the authority and policies of government, on the one hand, and represents the interests and demands of the populace on the other, we might: (1) conceive of the legislature as an organization that acts as a fiduciary for both the executive branch or "government" *and* citizens, including social and political groups; (2) treat representation as Garceau has suggested, as a continuum of interactions and decisions that ranges, in terms of *what* is represented, from the programs and policies of the government to the interests and demands of the people (Garceau, 1951); (3) conceive of legitimacy as a two-part variable that taps, on the one hand, the concern of citizens about "representativeness" of governments and officials (Gilbert, 1963: 616) and, on the other, the beliefs of political leaders about the appropriateness of citizens and groups participating in government. With reference to the latter type of legitimacy orientation, Wahlke and associates claim that legislators' accommodation of interest groups determines in part the effective performance of the legislative system (Wahlke et al., 1960: 206, 227). For the broad mass of citizens, on the other hand, there is no necessary relationship between their support of the government and representation of their interests. Citizens, for a variety of reasons including ignorance and manipulation, may perceive their interests to be served in a number of ways: governmental actions may be thought legitimate only if they reflect the expressed needs of citizens, or to the extent they represent the outcome of a process of conflict and compromise in which all groups have participated, or to the extent they reflect the interests of governmental institutions (Huntington, 1968: 27; Goldrich, 1966: 7). However, for the "interested" and "active" strata of the population there is probably a positive correlation between trust in the government and the use of "institutional" channels, such as the legislature, for the presentation of demands (Goldrich, 1966: 10).

Thus encounters between legislators and interest-group members or their agents (group leaders and lobbyists) are determined, in part, by their mutual perceptions of the other's legitimacy or trust. To support this claim we can turn to the definition of the *act* of representation itself. The act of representation can be defined as the communication of interests, demands, programs, and so on, from one person to another person acting as a trusted agent or fiduciary

(Pitkin, 1967: 112). While interpersonal trust may be grounded on a number of considerations—not the least of which is the calculation of the rewards and costs of the potential interaction—in most cases it would seem to be a prior condition for the development of a representational relationship. This conclusion is supported by reasearch that has found that negative interpersonal evaluations have detrimental effects on the formation of a relationship (Thibaut and Kelley, 1961: 44). This sentiment-interaction hypothesis suggests that an individual's interaction with a legislator is partially contingent on his perception of the legitimacy or trustworthiness of the legislator and vice versa. In such a reciprocal relationship, each actor's perception of the other's motives and values, whether it be in terms of an individual or a group, is especially significant (Zeigler and Baer, 1969: 9-10).

The unit of analysis for this research is the individual member of the Philippine Congress and members of the Philippine and Chinese Chambers of Commerce in Manila. The data consists of interviews completed in 1966 with 125 of the 128 members of the Congress and with random samples of the membership of the two Chambers. Before turning to the examination of the data it would be instructive to briefly trace the history and the analysis of the development of the Philippine Congress.

THE PHILIPPINE LEGISLATIVE EXPERIENCE

Until President Marcos imposed martial law in September 1972, the Philippines was widely thought to be the "showpiece" of democracy in Southeast Asia, an example of the successful transplantation of democratic institutions from the United States. The relatively extended Philippine experience with representative assemblies suggests that there should be a considerable degree of support for interest groups. Representative assemblies in the Philippines date back to the short-lived revolution of 1898-99 when the Malolos Congress was created. This attempt by Filipino revolutionaries to form a legitimate government outside the city of Manila is seen by one student of Philippine politics as establishing the idea of the legislature as an arena where conflicting opinions and interests should be openly presented and deliberated (Stauffer, 1970: 342). It was a short-lived Congress, for seven months after it convened Malolos, the capital of the Republic, fell to the American forces and the Congress was disbanded. Under the Americans, a national assembly with limited powers was formed in 1907 which lasted until 1916 when the United States passed the Jones Act creating a bicameral legislature largely patterned after the American body. Philippine leadership and opposition to American colonial policy was centered in the legislature until the 1930s when Commonwealth status brought a shift of power from the legislature to the newly created executive. The strong executive philosophy, supported to some degree by provisions of the 1946 Constitution plus a weak two-party system, continues to define executive-legislative relations, although some observers suggest that in the postwar years the legislature has grown increasingly autonomous (Grossholtz, 1964: 119).

Recent research on the legislative process in the Philippines yields inconclusive findings about the role of interest groups in the Congress. Representative of this research is the work of two students of Philippine politics, Robert Stauffer and Jean Grossholtz. Stauffer contends that the idea developed at Malolos of the Congress as a deliberative body openly considering competing opinions and interests has since gained widespread acceptance among the general Philippine population (Stauffer, 1970: 342). He claims that the Congress has remained politically strong since its inception—"probably the most independent and influential legislature in the world of developing nations"—and that this strength, together with the legislature's close electoral ties to the people dating since before independence, have established the Congress in the minds of Filipinos as "legitimately theirs": "A national political system based on mutually shared values between the political elite and its popular base has been achieved, and Congress has contributed significantly to this condition" (Stauffer, 1970: 351, 343, 358).

In contrast, Grossholtz claims that for the politician the requirements of political success, and the demands made upon him in his capacity as primarily a private citizen with the advantages of public office, raise doubts about the legitimacy of his position on policy issues and his own integrity. Political corruption is widely considered to be endemic in the Philippines. Particular demands, rather than national-interest or party or interest-group demands, become the standard for assessing legislation. Politicians are not confident that they can act as Burkean representatives. They distrust any of their members who maintain they are acting in the national interest rather than in their own interests. Politics is based on a network of private relationships that makes common interest difficult to establish and articulate, and thwarts attempts to form groups such as labor unions. While there is penetration of new styles of articulation into older modes based on primary group memberships, most congressmen deny that pressure groups exist, or they maintain that pressure groups are evil and illegitimate for they represent demands that the politicians use his public authority for private gain (Grossholtz, 1964: 166-72, 240-42).

Both Stauffer and Grossholtz agree that the "opportunity structure," both for legislators and the public at large, favors individualistic demand-making; they part company precisely over the *extent* to which groups and functional interests play a role in Philippine politics. To this question we now turn.

LEGISLATORS' ACCOMMODATION OF INTEREST GROUPS

Our task in this section is to describe Philippine congressmen's attitudes toward the role of interest groups in the political process and to explore the relationship between legislators' support of interest groups and their interaction with such groups. Overall, the legislators expressed favorable attitudes toward both specific and general roles of interest groups; in fact, their approval of interest groups in legislative activities is quite impressive compared to American state legislators' responses. Seventy-eight percent of the Philippine congressmen agreed that "legislators get valuable help from interest groups in drafting bills and amendments," compared to 55% of American state legislators who agreed to a similarly worded statement. Further, in response to the statement, "Interest groups give politicians valuable help in lining up support for their bills," 89% of the Philippine legislators agreed, compared to 69% of American state legislators (Wahlke et al., 1960: 215). This support extends to citizens' use of interest groups as the primary means for political participation. Congressmen were asked to indicate their amount of agreement or disagreement with the statement, "Working through interest groups is the best way an individual can participate in government." As Table 1 reveals, 62% of the "new" legislators—those who had been in office for a little more than three months when they were interviewed and all of whom are members of the House of Representatives—and 84% of the "old" legislators (including both House and Senate members) agreed with the statement.

TABLE 1
WORKING THROUGH INTEREST GROUPS IS THE BEST WAY AN INDIVIDUAL CAN PARTICIPATE IN GOVERNMENT (in percentages)

	New Legislators[a]	Old Legislators
Agree strongly	46	20
Agree	16	64
Disagree	25	11
Disagree strongly	11	4
No answer	2	1
TOTAL	100	100
N	(44)	(81)

a. All "new legislators" are members of the House of Representatives who had been in office for about three months at the time they were interviewed.

A reserve or surplus of support for interest groups is evident when the interactions of congressmen with groups is compared to their interactions with individuals. Although legislators considered individuals no more important than groups, 93% of the congressmen said that unattached individuals sought their help "very often"; only 26% of the legislators indicated that interest groups sought their assistance with the same frequency (Styskal, 1969: 417). The high incidence of legislators' contact with constituents is commonplace in many new states and attests to the paternalistic type of relationship that has developed historically between political leaders and their followers (for the Philippines, see Agpalo, 1962: 121; Hollnsteiner, 1964).

Table 2 presents the responses to the preceding question and two others that were put to the legislators about their contacts with interest groups. Responses are divided according to whether a legislator is "new" or "old." A third column combines the two sets of figures. The first two items in the table relate to contacts initiated by interest groups or their representatives. The emphasis here is on congressional receptivity or openness toward such contacts. For the third question—participation of interest groups in legislators' campaigns—the dependency relationship implied by the preceding two items is reduced, and we can assume that a greater number of contacts are legislator-initiated ones.

The relatively slight differences between the two sets of legislators in reports of electoral support (item 3)—an activity for which time in office was not a factor—suggests that the differences between the two groups on the first two items is the result, at least partially, of differences in time spent in office. Note too, that requests from groups for assistance (item 1) outnumber specific policy demands

TABLE 2
LEGISLATORS' INTERACTION WITH INTEREST GROUPS

	Representatives: Less Than 2 Yrs. in Congress	Representatives and Senators: 2 or More Yrs. in Congress	Representatives and Senators: Combined (Cols. 1 & 2)
1. Frequency groups seek aid on group-related problems (in percentages)			
Very often	7	36	26
Somewhat often	25	30	28
Not too often	27	23	25
Very seldom	23	7	13
Never	18	3	8
TOTAL	100	100	100
N	(44)	(81)	(125)
2. Frequency group members ask legislator to vote pro/con on an issue (in percentages)			
Very often	7	34	25
Somewhat often	9	16	14
Not too often	11	5	7
Very seldom	5	5	5
Never	55	9	25
Depends	2	27	18
No answer	11	4	6
TOTAL	100	100	100
N	(44)	(81)	(125)
3. Frequency group support in campaign for office (in percentages)			
Yes, recently	59	68	65
Yes, in part	7	7	7
Never	32	20	24
Don't know/no answer	2	5	4
TOTAL	100	100	100
N	(44)	(81)	(125)

(item 2), an indication perhaps that groups, like unattached constituents, may be less interested in a congressman's formal, legislative role than in his role as a power broker vis-a-vis other government agencies (on legislators as "interveners" see Mohapatra, 1971).

Viewing these data, can we say that Philippine legislators' interaction with groups is high or low? In absolute terms it is difficult to tell: still, the congressmen's rate of interaction compares favorably with recent reports of American state legislators' contact with lobbyists and interest groups (Zeigler and Baer, 1969; Wahlke et al., 1962). For example, 72% of the Philippine congressmen said they had received support in their campaigns for election, compared to 58% of Oregon legislators and 62% of Utah legislators; both American states were classified as "strong lobby states." The significant point, as Zeigler and Baer (1969: 115-16) note, is that electoral support by interest groups creates feelings of obligation on the part of the legislator that groups may profit from once the legislature is in session. This generalization is not lost on the Philippines where reciprocity is a customary norm in political and social transactions (Hollnsteiner, 1964).

The combined categories for each of the items in Table 2 show considerable variation among the legislators in their dealings with interest groups. This prompts the question, what other variables in addition to tenure in office account for this variation in experience with groups? Our major hypothesis is that legislators' interaction with interest groups is a function of the legitimacy accorded to those groups as a class of significant actors in the legislative process. To inquire into this question, a Group Interaction Index was constructed by scoring legislators' responses to the three items in Table 2 and then adding the scores. Freshman representatives were given an extra point if they answered item 1 positively and an additional point if they answered positively on item 2. Index scores ranged from a low of 0 to a high of 11. Collapsing the index into terciles, 24% of the legislators had low experience with groups, 36% medium, and 40% high experience. The degree of association between the Index and two criterion variables provides a rough check of the validity of the Index. Legislators were asked, "How often do you communicate (talk to, write to, and so on) with: (1) Filipino businessmen; and (2) Chinese businessmen, about their business problems." The question was designed to gauge legislator-initiated interactions with a particular constituency. The association between the Index and the two items is .44 and .33, respectively, suggesting that those legislators who had a substantial degree of experience with groups also had initiated more contacts with businessmen constituents than legislators whose experience with groups was minimal.[2]

To account for variations in legislators' interaction with groups, six independent variables were examined: legitimacy accorded to groups, age, education, tenure, number of leadership positions held in the legislature, and previous government positions held.[3]

Legitimacy accorded to groups was measured by scoring legislators' response to three statements supportive of groups and one statement supportive of direct rather than mediated citizen participation in government.[4] It is important to note that the perceptual object in each case was not the congressman in his role as a facilitator or resister of groups, but the generalized interest group as a participant in the political process.[5] Two of these items were considered earlier. They are, "Working through interest groups is the best way an individual can participate in government" (Table 1), and "Interest groups give politicians valuable help in lining up support for their bills." The other two items were: "The democratic way of conflict resolution in the legislative decision-making process is to include the opinions of outside competing groups," and "Under our form of government, every individual should take an interest in the government directly and not through interest group organizations."[6] Each respondent was given a score of from one to six points on each item. The scores were then summed, forming a simple index that ranged from a low of 10 to a high of 23.

The variable, number of leadership positions (floor leaders, whips, standing, sub, and special committee chairmen and vice-chairmen, and various other positions), was included on the assumption that legislators whose positions have become sufficiently important might attract the attention of interest groups and their spokesmen more than those congressmen who do not hold leadership positions (Zeigler and Baer, 1969: 150-51). For the same reason, age and number of previous government positions held should be related to support of interest groups. Wahlke and his colleagues (1960) have argued that a more educated legislator should be more supportive of pressure groups on the premise that education promotes open-mindedness and a greater awareness of the environment. Their results tended to confirm this hypothesis. They have also argued (1962: 341) that tenure is directly related to support of interest groups. Davidson, however, reports (1969: 168-69) that among representatives in the United States Congress, seniority is inversely related to receptivity to group claims, reasoning that the inexperienced congressman, lacking the necessary expertise for gathering information, must turn to outside sources of assistance. All of these variables in one way or another have been seen as determinants of legislator behavior with groups.[7]

Our major concern is to determine the combined and relative contribution of the six independent variables to variation in the level of legislators' experience with interest groups. Multiple regression is the technique used for this purpose. The independent indicators, again are: X_1 = Age, X_2 = Education, X_3 = Tenure, X_4 = Number of Leadership Positions in the Legislature, X_5 = Previous Government Positions, and X_6 = Legitimacy Accorded to Interest Groups. The relative importance of each of these indicators can be given by the normalized b coefficient, usually called the beta weight. The beta weight indicates how much change in standard units is produced in the dependent variable with one standard unit change in one of the independent variables when the others are controlled.

The multiple regression equation for the six indicators with the beta weights in parentheses below the coefficient is:

$$Y' = -1.13537 + .28778(X_6) = .32077(X_3) + .36131(X_1) - .23301(X_5) +$$
$$\qquad\quad (.86) \qquad\qquad (.20) \qquad\quad (.34) \qquad\qquad (-.11)$$
$$.1000(X_4) + .01567(X_2)$$
$$(.04) \qquad\quad (.02)$$

The multiple correlation coefficient (R) is .47. The coefficient of multiple determination (R^2) is .22, indicating that the combined effects of the six indicators account for 22% of the variation in the legislator scores on the Group Experience Index. The amount of variation explained is not great; neither, however, is it small given the relatively crude level of measurement of the variables and the fact that an attitudinal construct accounts for a disproportionate share of the variation. The intercorrelations between the independent variables were all below .38 (the mean correlation was .12), indicating that multicollinearity is not a problem here (Blalock, 1963: 233-37).

As the beta weights indicate, the most important predictor variable is legitimacy accorded to groups, with a value of .86. The next two most important variables are age with a value of .34, and time in office with a value of .20. Education and number of previous governmental positions held have little predictive value. By squaring the beta weights we can determine the percent that each of the independent variables contributes to the dependent variable. Legitimacy accorded groups, it turns out, predicts seven times more of the variation in legislators' experience with groups than does age and 18 times more than tenure.

The findings up to this point reveal several important, though tentative, conclusions that build upon the work of Wahlke and his associates and on Zeigler and Baer's extension of that work for American state legislators. It was shown that compared to American state legislators, a substantial majority of Philippine congressmen hold favorable opinions about the role of groups in the political process. Grossholtz's statement (1964: 242) that Philippine politicians view interest groups as evil and illegitimate because they represent demands that he uses his public authority for private gain appears doubtful in light of this finding. Certainly legislators' support for groups was not unqualified; during the course of the interviews many legislators remarked that their main concern was to represent the "public" or "general" interest. However, there is no evidence to suggest that categorical demands do not reflect the "public interest," however that is defined. As one legislator put it:

> If I believe that a member of a group represents the interests of people, he would be more important to me than an ordinary individual. However, if in a particular instance, I believe he represents the partisan and selfish interests of his group, I would not favor his positions.

The rate of Philippine congressmen's interactions with groups was fairly substantial compared to American data on state legislators. There were, however, significant differences in the extent of interaction. More important, these different patterns of behavior correlated with basic differences in affective attitudes. Among six variables and as many hypotheses singled out in the literature to account for legislators' interaction with groups (five of the variables were non-attitudinal or background), only legitimacy accorded to groups showed any significant predictive value. The amount of variation left unexplained in legislators' experience with groups is vexing; but clearly, the Philippine legislator sample provides evidence supporting the sentiment-interaction hypothesis.

Wahlke and his colleagues (1960: 210) note that the extent and manner of any given legislature in taking into account the demands of significant interest groups is no more than a reflection of the behavior of legislators, and interest group members obviously take this behavior into account when deciding when or if to press their claims on legislators. However, necessity may also be a factor in such decisions, for it is clear that in most relationships between legislators and interest groups or their representatives, the former have more freedom and greater power than the latter; that is, the interest group member has certain constraints born of his dependency on the legislator (Zeigler and Baer, 1969: 82). Thus, in their decisions about whether to contact legislators, necessity may outweigh group members' attitudes about the integrity of politicians. To this question, as it relates to the activities of members of two businessmen's associations in Manila, we turn to next.

TWO INTEREST GROUPS: LEGITIMACY ORIENTATION AND STRATEGIES OF INFLUENCE

Two businessmen's associations, the Chamber of Commerce of the Philippines and the Federation of Filipino-Chinese Chambers of Commerce (hereafter referred to as the CCP and the FECCOP) were chosen for study.[8] These two groups do not exhaust nor do they represent the full spectrum of interest associations in the Philippines; however, alongside the typical Filipino interest group—often a one-man organ—they are conspicuous for their size and organization (Agpalo, 1962: 274). Moreover, they represent two dominant economic interests in the Philippines—the indigenous Filipino and the "alien" Chinese—whose conflict and antagonisms have had, and probably will continue to have, profound implications for economic growth and political stability in the Islands. Further, as primarily economic organizations, the CCP and the FECCOP represent many of the issues and problems that congressmen deemed salient and about which they were most pressured (see Table 3).

Including the Chinese Chamber also provides an opportunity for assessing the sentiment-interaction hypothesis under conditions where the relationship between the legislator and the interest group member might be better described as defensive rather than depend-

TABLE 3
PUBLIC PROBLEMS LEGISLATORS SAID THEY WERE MOST CONCERNED ABOUT (in percentages)

Economy and development	19
Provincial problems	15
Unemployment	13
Poverty and crime	12
Public works	10
Other	31
TOTAL	100
N	(125)

ISSUES WHICH LEGISLATORS SAID THEY RECEIVED MOST GROUP PRESSURE (in percentages)

Economic	28
Taxation	23
Self-service	13
Retail trade	10
Education	9
Other	17
TOTAL	100
N	(78)

ent. Members of the FECCOP enjoy substantial economic strength, great familial and extra-familial solidarity, but relatively weak political and social status. As the most visible and longstanding minority group in the Philippines, the Chinese have long been the object of restrictive legislation and "shakedowns" by petty officials (Agpalo, 1962; Liao, 1964; Wickberg, 1965). Because of their political vulnerability, we may assume that FECCOP members, in their dealings with the legislature, are more concerned with defending their interests than promoting them, the latter being realized through the extensive economic organization of the Chinese community. What implications this has for our findings will be considered below.

Our major hypothesis is that interest group members' interaction with legislators is a function of their generalized support and trust of political authorities (Easton: 1965). Measuring group members' rather than lobbyists' interactions with legislators presents a knotty problem. The lobbyist presumably is a bona fide representative of his interest group. The same is not necessarily true of the ordinary group member. The group member who desires to direct a demand to a legislator has basically two options: he can deal with the legislator indirectly through his interest group, utilizing the group as an intermediary or agent by which to transmit his demands; or he can deal directly with the legislator. The difficulty with the first measure is our uncertainty as to whether or not the interest group (its leaders or lobbyists) does (or should) in fact communicate with the legislator once it has received the member's demand. Interest groups exist to resolve independently, members' government-related demands, as well as to channel them to public authorities. The problem with the second measure is our doubt about whether the interest group member approaches the legislator as an unattached citizen or in his role as a member of an interest group. Grossholtz (1964: 245) mentions the tendency of group members to utilize their own personal relations to advance their interest to the detriment of the group. The distinction is an important one if we are interested in interest group members instead of Filipinos and Chinese, or citizens in general.

There is no easy solution to the problem. For this study we rely primarily on members' interaction with their group as an indirect measure of their communication with legislators. In choosing this influence strategy, it is assumed that a major function of interest groups is to resolve members' demands by applying collective pressure on the government and, through their good offices, to assist members in dealing with politicians and public officials, particularly, the legislator. A member will direct his request of demand to his interest group if he is satisfied that it will be communicated to the legislator and if he trusts the legislator or political authorities to give it a fair hearing.

A second measure taps interest group members' choice of influence strategies (including going directly to politicians) when faced with a government-related problem. Here, the object of concern changes from chamber member to individual businessman faced with a hypothetical problem.

Our initial goal is to explain the variation in members' use of their association as a means of communicating with legislators and the government. For the dependent variable, a 13-point index was constructed from chamber members' responses to four questions. An attempt was made to choose those items that elicited information about members' use of their interest group as a linkage between themselves and politicians. The items were the following: (1) "How often does your chamber help you in dealing with politicians?" (2) "How often do you discuss government-related problems with your chamber?" (3) "How are 'connections' in government usually made?" (4) "What is the best way for businessmen to deal with the government?" The distribution of responses to the four items are given in Table 4. The scores for members of the Philippine Chamber of Commerce ranged from a low of 4 (Low utilization of the chamber) to a high of 11 (high utilization of the chamber). The mean group utilization was 6.5. Scores for members of the FECCOP ranged from a low of 4 to a high of 13. The mean was 7.7. The mean index scores suggest that members of both chambers of commerce use their associations moderately for demand facilitation.[9]

Six variables were considered as being possibly significant in explaining group utilization. Besides legitimacy accorded politicians, these were: satisfaction with the lobbying activities of the chamber; the necessity of the individual member to meet with government officials, political efficacy, education, and age.

Perceived trustworthiness of politicians was used as an indicator of legitimacy.[10] Five Likert-type statements were used to measure trustworthiness (the items are from Agger et al., 1961). Together the statements yielded a 30-point Trust in Politicians Index, with possible scores ranging from a low of 5 (cynical) to a high of 30 (trusting).[11] The statements together with the mean scores of CCP

TABLE 4

CHAMBERS: GROUP UTILIZATION INDEX ITEMS
(in percentages)

	CCP	FECCOP
"How often does your chamber help you in dealing with politicians?"		
Often	9	9
Sometimes	19	22
Hardly ever	19	21
Never	50	47
Don't know	3	1
TOTAL	100	100
N	(264)	(104)
"How often do you discuss government problems with your chamber?"		
Often	23	28
Sometimes	41	40
Never	34	25
Don't know	2	7
TOTAL	100	100
N	(264)	(104)
"Connections in government are mostly made through . . .?"		
Personal friends	50	65
Family and relatives	6	3
Chamber of commerce	8	12
Social clubs	21	10
Other, Don't know	15	10
TOTAL	100	100
N	(264)	(104)
"What is the best way for businessmen to deal with the government?"		
Make friends with people well known in government circles	14	18
Establish friendship with politicians	19	16
Establish friendship with public administrators	25	15
Join a business organization such as your chamber of commerce	29	28
Depend on family and relatives	2	11
Other, Depends, Don't know	11	12
TOTAL	100	100
N	(264)	(104)

and FECCOP members are presented in Table 5. The scores of the two chambers are compared with those of residents in two American communities reported in a study by Agger and his colleagues (1961).

Overall, the chamber members' attitudes reveal substantial distrust of politicians. The Filipinos and especially the Chinese are considerably more cynical about their leaders than the respondents of two American communities are about theirs. Time and again Chinese respondents echoed the sentiments of a 48-year-old textile importer who said that Philippine legislators are more "lawbreakers" than they are "lawmakers." Similar statements were encountered among CCP members, such as the comment from a 45-year-old assistant manager of a retail store that if you deal individually with politicians you "first have to corrupt them," and only then will you get assistance. We might note that while these results are limited to particular subgroups in the Philippines, they cast doubt upon the contention that the Congress has gained widespread acceptance and legitimacy among the Philippine population (Stauffer, 1970: 342).

The sharp contrast between legislators' support of groups and the distrust of politicians shown by group members is revealing, for it suggests in broad terms that politicians have been unable to mobilize political support among an important sector of the society, even though they themselves (the legislators) evince accommodating attitudes toward groups and citizens. It is possible that distrust of

TABLE 5
CHAMBERS: COMPARISON OF MEAN SCORES ON
ITEMS IN TRUST IN POLITICIANS INDEX

	CCP	FECCOP	Two American Communities
1. In order to get nominated, most candidates for political office have to make basic compromises and undesirable commitments	2.35[a]	1.93	3.62
2. Politicians spend most of their time getting reelected or reappointed	1.89	1.75	3.53
3. Money is the most important factor influencing public policies	2.13	1.94	3.02
4. A large number of politicians are unqualified for their jobs	1.98	2.32	3.29
5. People are frequently manipulated by politicians	2.03	2.22	3.28

a. Means were calculated from responses that ranged from "agree strongly, somewhat, or slightly" to "disagree strongly, somewhat, or slightly." The lower the score, the higher the cynicism.

authority in the Philippines is a "cultural trait"; Bulatao (1964: 69) presents some evidence supporting this claim. Interesting as it is, such a thesis remains inconclusive until further evidence is amassed. The significant point is that in the minds of chamber members, the actions of politicians (frequently associated with venality and corruption) apparently weigh heavier than their appeals to democratic norms.

As mentioned above, a members' decision to use the resources of his group for demand-facilitation may hinge, in part, on his satisfaction with his group in initiating and applying pressure on legislators. Members of both chambers indicated substantial dissatisfaction with their respective chambers' lobbying activities: 76% of the FECCOP and 69% of the CCP were dissatisfied. Although the level of dissatisfaction is quite high, it is variable enough to be included in the analysis.

Utilization of one's interest group for demand-facilitation may also depend on how frequently the group member needs to meet with government officials on government-related business problems. One would expect that as this need increases, the probability of utilizing the chamber increases. Fifty percent of the members of the CCP and 37% of the FECCOP sample said that it was "very" or "somewhat" necessary to meet with government officials.

Efficacy refers to the degree to which a citizen believes that he has a say in government and the extent he believes that government recognizes and cares about what he says. Studies dealing with the relationship between efficacy and participation have found that individuals who believe they have influence are more likely to use it, and are more likely to be politically active in a variety of settings, including secondary associations (Maccoby, 1958; Almond and Verba, 1963). A single measure, "People like me don't have any say about what the government does," was used.

Education and age have been found in numerous studies to be positively related to participation, including the use of one's interest group for demand facilitation.

Stepwise regression was used to examine the predictive value of the six indicators. Variables are entered into the equation one at a time on the basis of their "success" in accounting for variation in the dependent variable. The results for members of both chambers of commerce are given in Table 6. The first column provides the cumulative multiple correlation coefficient. The second column is the square of the first column and indicates how much of the

TABLE 6
STEPWISE REGRESSION OF SIX PREDICTOR VARIABLES
ON MEMBER UTILIZATION OF CHAMBER

	Multiple R	R Squared	Beta
FECCOP			
Trust in politicians	.738	.545	.74
Necessity meet gov't officials	.747	.559	−.12
Political efficacy	.755	.571	−.11
Satisfaction chamber lobbying	.757	.575	−.06
Education	.757	.576	.04
Age	.757	.576	−.00
CCP			
Necessity meet gov't officials	.133	.017	−.10
Satisfaction chamber lobbying	.146	.022	−.08
Trust in politicians	.155	.024	−.05
Political efficacy	.163	.026	−.06
Education	.167	.027	−.04
Age	.172	.027	−.01

variation in the dependent variable is explained each time a new independent variable is added to the regression equation. The adjusted partial slopes or beta weights in the third column provide an indication of the direction of the relationship.[1][2]

For members of the FECCOP, the six independent variables together predict over 57% of the variation in members' use of their chamber for demand-facilitation—an impressive result. More important is the fact that members' trust in politicians accounts for over 54% of the variation in the dependent variable, a finding that lends support to our hypothesis. This result must be viewed within the context of a decidely distrustful group of businessmen; therefore, the correct generalization is that among a group of politically cynical chamber members, there was an inverse relationship between cynicism and members' use of chamber in their dealings with politicians. The remaining five variables combined accounted for little more than 3% of the variation. Among the intercorrelations of the six independent variables only age and education showed a sizable correlation (r = −.45); the remaining correlations were all below r = +.17.

By contrast, the predictive value of trust in politicians for members of the CCP was very weak, as was the remaining five independent variables. The data in Table 6 reveal that the six variables combined accounted for about 3% of the variation in member utilization of their chamber. That is, other (unknown) variables account for 97% of the variation in the dependent variable. Perhaps Filipino businessmen utilize their chamber more or less randomly or largely for non-political reasons, while Chinese businessmen rely on their Chamber more consistently for assistance in the resolution of their demands. Given the predominance of individualized demand-making in the Philippines, access to political authorities in Manila may be easier for the Filipino businessman than it is for his Chinese counterpart.

Is, then, businessmen's trust in politicians a factor in their direct interaction with them? To inquire into this question, both sets of group members were asked: "If you had a difficult business problem that resulted from government regulations, who would you go to first, second, third, etc., for advice and help?" The question is designed to place the individual in a "challenging political situation" in order to find out to whom he would turn for support.[13] The most favored strategy of influence by Filipino businessmen was to go directly to the government. This was followed by turning to relatives and friends and by turning to the chamber. For the Chinese, it was relatives and friends first, chamber second, and lawyer third (Styskal, 1971: 414).

Respondents were given three points if they mentioned turning to the government first, two points if government was a second choice, and one point if government were the third choice. In each case an extra point was added to the total score if politicians were specifically mentioned, as they frequently were. The cross-tabulation between this dependent variable and the Trust in Politician Index is given in Table 7. There is a moderate relationship between the two variables for the Chinese businessmen, strengthening the earlier

TABLE 7
TRUST IN POLITICIANS BY STRATEGY OF INFLUENCE (in percentages)

Political Strategy Favored	FECCOP Trust in Politicians			CCP Trust in Politicians		
	Weak		Strong	Weak		Strong
Indirect	53	48	26	38	20	25
	20	36	18	40	41	37
Direct	27	16	56	23	7	18
TOTAL	100	100	100	100	100	100
N	(30)	(25)	(34)	(101)	(68)	(80)

$\gamma = .36$
$\chi^2 = 14.05(4), p < .01$

relationship found between attitudes toward politicians and member utilization of the chamber as a means of access to politicians. Once again, however, the data indicates no relationship between trust and interaction for Filipino businessmen.

As a final measure of interaction with legislators, Philippine Chamber of Commerce members were asked if they had ever asked a congressman to sponsor a bill, a request that is considerably more significant than, say, a request for a legislator to vote a certain way on an issue.[14] Surprisingly, 32% of the chamber members said they had made such a request of congressmen, which attests to the relatively easy familiarity that exists between congressmen and businessmen in Manila. But is this familiarity based on mutual trust? In Table 8, measures of association between a number of independent indicators and interaction with congressmen are given. Included in the former are a number of the predictor variables in the regression analysis reported above. Overall, the measures of association are weak, with only one, necessity to meet government officials, showing any sizable significant relationship. Trust in Politicians shows a weak relationship in the expected direction, but the relationship is not significant. It appears justified to conclude that Philippine interest group members' initiated interaction with politicians is more or less random with perhaps the *need* to meet with government officials a modest factor in predicting interaction. Although we can only surmise at this point,

TABLE 8

CCP: ASSOCIATION BETWEEN SELECTED INDEPENDENT VARIABLES AND RESPONSE TO QUESTION: "HAVE YOU EVER PERSONALLY ASKED A CONGRESSMAN TO SPONSOR A BILL?"[a]

1. Necessity meet gov't officials and politicians (N = 240)	−.23	χ^2 = 9.94 (3) $p < .02$
2. Legitimacy Index (N = 248)	.19	ns
3. Education (N = 248)	.18	ns
4. Political efficacy (N = 246)	.16	ns
5. Age (N = 248)	.16	ns
6. Taken active part in local politics last three years (N = 224)	.14	χ^2 = 4.31 (1) $p < .05$
7. Difficult to predict policies and regulations that the Congress may pass that may affect your business (N = 234)	.09	ns
8. Success of CCP in influencing politicians (N = 235)	.08	ns
9. Difficult to personally see legislators (N = 242)	.05	ns
10. Satisfied with CCP lobbying activities (N = 248)	.02	ns

a. The measure of association for items 1, 2, 3, 4, 5, 8, 9 is Cramer's V; for items 6, 7, and 10, the measure is Phi.

one factor that may account for this result is the random nature of the political environment as perceived by the Filipino businessmen: over 70% of the businessmen stated that they were unable to predict the actions of the legislature which might in some way affect their business.

CONCLUSION

We began this inquiry by describing the dual nature of the legislature's representative function: as a body of elected leaders, the legislature serves to represent the interests and ameliorate the grievances of its constituents; it is also mandated to air and represent the programs and policies of the government. For new states with imported constitutions and a desire to move toward representative democracy, a key problem of legislative development has been the top-heavy role of executive and bureaucratic representation and the "underdevelopment" of organizations such as parties and interest groups that link citizens to their representatives. It was posited that an important determinant of the inclusion and power of interest groups in the legislative process is the mutual acceptance by legislators and interest group members of the other's legitimacy.

The data clearly revealed a pronounced *discongruence* in the mutual evaluations of legislators and interest group members: group members were highly distrustful of legislators; legislators were, by contrast, quite supportive of interest groups. The expressed needs of Filipino and Chinese businessmen to meet with politicians, coupled with their high degree of mistrust of such leaders, suggest that at least part of their interactions with legislators may be entered into unwillingly or with reservations. Whether deliberate or not, such a linkage is more coercive than representative and, by Western democratic standards, corrupts the role of interest groups. Under such conditions interest groups may become defensive or reactive organizations, non-political social clubs, or merely spokesmen for the government rather than contributing participants in the legislative process.

Whether legislative support for interest groups is, in fact, genuine is a matter of conjecture; the consistency of congressional receptivity or openness toward groups together with the relationship found between congressional attitudes and behavior suggest that it might be. The problem, then, may be one of diffusing group representative norms throughout the more organized sectors of the society. On the other hand, such support by legislators may simply be part of a strategy for developing and maintaining profitable relationships. No one would contest the fact that the emoluments of political office are one of the primary marketable items in the Philippine society. "Politics," as one member of the CCP put it, "is the best industry in the Philippines. It has to do with every affair in life." For the Philippine congressman, the development of optimum conditions for "influence peddling" may be more important than the representation of interests.[1 5]

The sentiment-interaction hypothesis has demonstrated significant predictive value in a number of psychological and sociological studies, and has been usefully employed to explain legislator interactions and potential interactions with interest groups and lobbyists (Thibaut and Kelley, 1961; Homans, 1950; Zeigler and Baer, 1969; Wahlke et al., 1962). Our findings lend qualified cross-cultural support to this hypothesis as applied to both legislators and interest group members. We have shown that knowledge of legislators' attitudes toward interest groups is helpful in predicting their interactions with such groups. A major qualification, of course, is that much of the variation in legislators' contacts with groups remains to be explained. This, however, should not diminish the very important fact that legislators' affective orientations toward groups appreciably outweighed other explanations of differences in legislators' interaction with groups. Further, we have shown that among members of an economically powerful but politically and socially subordinate group of entrepreneurs, knowledge of their feelings of trust toward political leaders were useful in predicting the extent to which they utilized their group to aid them in dealing with politicians. This finding, together with the assumption that interest groups will play a more active role in legislative politics the more their members press them with government-related demands, strongly suggests that at least a partial determinant of the activity of an interest group in legislative politics will be the members' belief that politicians can be trusted.

The failure of the sentiment-interaction hypothesis in the case of the CCP presents a more difficult problem of interpretation. Why the different outcome for Chinese and Filipino chamber members? A satisfactory answer to this question would require another study; we can, however, briefly speculate on the difference. One reason for the difference may be that the Filipino businessman is uncommonly

said they listened to no one or relied on their conscience (N = 43); those who listened to all comments (N = 50); and those who responded to interest groups and their political party (N = 31). This typology proved to be so uniformly unrelated to a large array of variables, including the Group Interaction Index, that it was dropped from further consideration. Incidentally, this distribution of representational types cases some doubt on Grossholtz's generalization that Filipino politicians are not confident they can act as Burkian representatives (Grossholtz, 1964: 172).

4. Measures of legitacy orientation have been numerous and varied. As Gurr has remarked, "A dense thicket of concepts and distinctions" have developed out of attempts to understand the attitudes of citizen and ruler toward one another, including legitimacy, political community, political myth, support, authoritativeness, political trust, system affect, political allegiance, and loyalty (Gurr, 1970: 183-92).

5. This distinction was not made in Wahlke and associates' (1960) typology of legislators' role orientations toward interest groups.

6. The last item, "Under our form of government . . . ." is reversed so that agreement with it indicates lack of support for groups. All four items had a response format of six alternatives ranging from three degrees of agreement through three degrees of disagreement. For each of the first three items, respondents were given a 6 if they "agreed strongly," a 5 if they "agreed somewhat," and so on. This process was reversed for the fourth item. The scores of each respondent were then summed. The power of the items to discriminate between respondents of high and low support (upper and lower quartiles were compared) was greater than 1.0 in each case, which is considered sufficient enough to include the item in the Index.

7. The following are the frequency distributions for these five variables. Number of Leadership Positions: none = 42%, one = 28%, two = 14%, three = 8%, four or more = 6%, Don't Know/No Answer = 2%; Age: 25-34 = 5%, 35-44 = 19%, 45-54 = 42%, 55-64 = 29%, 65 and over = 3%; Number of Previous Government Positions Held: n one = 20%, one = 32%, two = 22%, three = 10%, four or more = 14%; Education: grade school = 2%, business school = 8%, four years college = 13%, one or two years beyond bachelor's degree = 9%, one or two years law school = 6%, law graduate = 65%; Tenure: three months = 36%, one to three years = 2%, four to six years = 22%, seven to nine years = 10%, ten to fifteen years = 15%, sixteen years and over = 14%.

8. The Federation of Filipino-Chinese Chamber of Commerce is an organization of local and regional chambers of commerce and trade associations as well as individual memberships. Twelve trade associations were randomly selected and respondents were randomly selected from these twelve. These were supplemented with a random selection of respondents who held direct membership in the Federation. A total of 104 Chinese businessmen were interviewed. Two hundred sixty-four members of the Chamber of Commerce of the Philippines out of a total membership of 759 (all in Manila) were interviewed.

9. For item one, 5 points were given for "very often," 4 points for "often," and so on. For item two, "very often" was scored 4, and so on. For item three, "chamber of commerce" was given a 2 and all others were given a one. For the last item, 2 points were given for "join a business organization such as a chamber of commerce," and all others were scored a one.

10. The primary concern was to measure group members' attitudes toward politicians as a generic class. For the most part, politicians in Manila means legislator; the two terms are often used synonymously.

11. The power of the items to discriminate between both Filipino and Chinese respondents of high and low trust (upper and lower quartiles were compared) was greater than 1.0 in each case, which is considered sufficient enough to include the item in the Index.

12. Because of "don't know" responses, the total number of respondents for the

FECCOP dropped from 104 to 97. For the CCP the number of respondents dropped from 264 to 251.

13. This question is a revised version of one used by Almond and Verba in The Civic Culture (1963: chapter 7).

14. Unfortunately, members of the FECCOP were not asked this question.

15. On the "pakiusap" and "pabagsak" system and influence peddling in the Philippines, see Agpalo (1962: 121).

REFERENCES

AGGER, R. E., M. N. GOLDSTEIN, and S. A. PEARL (1961) "Political cynicism: measurement and meaning." J. of Politics 23 (August): 477-506.

AGPALO, R. E. (1962) The Political Process and the Nationalization of the Retail Trade in the Philippines. Dilman, Quezon City: NEC-AID, U.P. Development Project.

ALMOND, G. and S. VERBA (1963) The Civic Culture. Princeton: Princeton Univ. Press.

BLALOCK, H. M. (1963) "Correlated independent variables: the problem of multicollinearity." Social Forces 42: 233-37.

BLONDEL, J. (1969) An Introduction to Comparative Government. New York: Praeger.

BULATAO, J. (1964) "The Manileno's Mainsprings," pp. 50-86 in F. Lynch (ed.) Four Readings on Philippine Values. Quezon City, Phil.: Ateneo de Manila Univ. Press.

DAVIDSON, R. H. (1969) The Role of the Congressman. New York: Pegasus.

EASTON, D. (1965) A Systems Analysis of Political Life. New York: John Wiley.

EMERSON, R. (1967) "Political modernization: the single party system," pp. 238-66 in R. Macridis (ed.) Political Parties. New York: Harper & Row.

GARCEAU, O. (1951) "Research in the political process." Amer. Pol. Sci. Rev. 45 (March): 69-85.

GILBERT, C. E. (1963) "Operative doctrines of representation." Amer. Pol. Sci. Rev. 57 (September): 604-18.

GOLDRICH, D. (1966) Sons of the Establishment. Chicago: Rand McNally.

GROSSHOLTZ, J. (1964) Politics in the Philippines. Boston: Little, Brown.

GURR, T. R. (1970) Why Men Rebel. Princeton: Princeton Univ. Press.

HOLLNSTEINER, M. R. (1964) "Reciprocity in the Lowland Philippines," pp. 22-49 in F. Lynch (ed.) Four Readings on Philippine Values. Quezon City, Phil.: Ateneo do Manila Univ. Press.

HOMANS, G, C. (1950) The Human Group. New York: Harcout, Brace & World.

HUNTINGTON, S. P. (1968) Political Order in Changing Societies. New Haven, Conn.: Yale Univ. Press.

JEWELL, M. E. and S. C. PATTERSON (1966) The Legislative Process in the United States. New York: Random House.

KORNBERG, A. and L. D. MUSOLF [eds.] (1970) Legislatures in Developmental Perspective. Durham, N.C.: Duke Univ. Press.

LIAO, S.S.C. (1964) Chinese Participation in Philippine Culture and Economy. Manila: Univ. of the East.

LOEWENBERG, G. (1971) "The influence of parliamentary behavior on regime stability: some conceptual clarifications." Comparative Politics 3 (January): 177-200.

MACCOBY, H. (1958) "The differential political activity of participants in a voluntary association." Amer. Sociological Rev. 23 (October): 524-32.

MOHABATRA, M. K. (1971) "Administrative value patterns of legislators in an Indian state: conflicting demands on bureaucracy in Orissa." Presented at annual meeting of the American Political Science Assn., New York.

NETTL, J. P. (1967) Political Mobilization. New York: Basic Books.

PITKIN, H. F. (1967) The Concept of Representation. Berkeley: Univ. of California Press.

RIGGS, F. W. (1964) Administration in Developing Countries. Boston: Houghton Mifflin.

STAUFFER, R. B. (1970) "Congress in the Philippine political system," pp. 334-65 in A. Kornberg and L. D. Musolf (eds.) Legislatures in Developmental Perspective. Durham, N.C.: Duke Univ. Press.

STYSKAL, R. A. (1971) "Citizen influence strategies in the Philippines: the use of primary and secondary groups." Social Science Q. 52 (September): 409-16.

——— (1969) "Philippine legislators' receptions of individuals and interest groups in the legislative process." Comparative Politics 1 (April): 405-22.

THIBAUT, J. W. and H. H. KELLEY (1959) The Social Psychology of Groups. New York: John Wiley.

WAHLKE, J. C. (1971) "Policy demands and system support: the role of the represented," pp. 141-71 in G. Loewenberg (ed.) Modern Parliaments. Chicago: Aldine-Atherton.

——— , H. EULAU, W. BUCHANAN, L. C. FERGUSON (1962) The Legislative System. New York: John Wiley.

——— (1960) "American state legislators' role orientations toward pressure groups." J. of Politics 22 (May): 203-27.

WICKBERG, E. (1965) The Chinese in Philippine Life, 1850-1898. New Haven, Conn.: Yale Univ. Press.

ZEIGLER, H. and M. BAER (1969) Lobbying: Interaction and Influence in American State Legislatures. Belmont, Calif.: Wadsworth.

RICHARD A. STYSKAL is Associate Professor of Political Science at Brooklyn College of the City University of New York. He has written numerous journal articles on the Philippine Congress and on economic interest groups in the Philippines. He is currently completing a panel study of legislative-executive relations in the Legislative Assembly of Puerto Rico, and has recently finished a study of power in innovating organizations.

Chapter 10

POLITICAL REPRESENTATION IN THE
KOREAN NATIONAL ASSEMBLY

C H O N G   L I M   K I M
University of Iowa

B Y U N G - K Y U   W O O
The Korean National Assembly

In recent years there has emerged an impressive amount of research on legislative behavior.[1] Most research has, however, focused primarily on the Congress (Davidson, 1969), state, and local legislatures in the United States (Wahlke and Eulau, 1962; Sorauf, 1963; Bell and Price, 1969), and some legislatures in developed Western nations (Kornberg, 1967; Hunt, 1969; Gerlich, 1972). In contrast, systematic study of legislative behavior in the developing nations of Asia and Africa has been largely ignored.[2] The main reason for this is probably the general tendency that legislatures of the developing nations occupy relatively insignificant positions in their political process. Decisions on key political issues and important shifts in power often take place elsewhere in the political system. The constitutions of these developing nations formally guarantee, with but few exceptions, the existence and authority of a legislative body. However, the power of the legislature is almost

AUTHORS' NOTE: An earlier version of this chapter was published in The Midwest Journal of Political Science 16 (November 1972). Reprinted by permission of the Wayne State University Press.

alwasy circumscribed by the executive, the bureaucracy, the military, or a dominant ruling party.

Overshadowed by the predominant power of the executive or other political institutions, legislatures in the developing nations may not function the same way they do in developed Western nations. Nevertheless, members of the legislature in these Asian and African nations may perform an important role in political representation. The critical role of legislators in the process of representation may be highlighted by a few observations. First, there are few effectively organized interest groups in most of the developing nations (Pye, 1962; Almond and Powell, 1966). Where such groups do exist, they are often organized by the government or a dominant ruling party. As a result, these organized groups tend to have little autonomy and often function as the agents of the government or a political party rather than representing the interests of their constituency.

Secondly, political parties of the developing nations tend to be what Apter (1965) has called "parties of solidarity." The party ideology and organizational structure are often geared explicitly to the twin national goals of political integration and rapid economic development. Consequently, political parties in the developing nations tend to show little tolerance for any opposition parties and their main emphasis tends to be to mobilize the population in support of policy goals set by the party leadership rather than to aggregate the divergent interests of the citizenry. Due to their monopolistic and directive nature, political parties in these developing nations are not likely to be sensitive to the demand of political representation.

Thirdly, the bureaucracies of the developing nations retain much of their traditional or colonial attitudes toward the citizenry (LaPalombara, 1965; Eldersveld et al., 1968). In general, bureaucrats tend to have an excessive sense of self-importance, tend to be indifferent to the feelings and the needs of the masses, and often lack the notion of "the public servant." Thus the bureaucracy remains largely unresponsive and unwilling to recognize the public demands. In the absence of the interest groups, political parties, and bureaucracies capable of responding to the public demands, members of the legislature in these developing nations may assume the major burden of political representation.

The purpose of this study is to examine empirically the nature of political representation in the *Kukhoe* or the Korean National Assembly. The major questions are as follows:

(1) What ideas do Korean assemblymen have as to their representative roles?

(2) What actions do they take as the incumbents of representative roles?

(3) What are the determining factors of their representative role orientations and behavior?

The primary source of data for this study is derived from a larger study of Korean legislative elites which contains interviews with 112 legislators of the 7th National Assembly.[3] The interviews were conducted from July 1968 to March 1969 in Korea, and include data on the assemblymen's social background characteristics, their adolescent and career politicization, their recruitment experiences, and their legislative role orientations and behavior.

REPRESENTATIVE ROLE ORIENTATIONS AND BEHAVIOR

The concept of political representation resists easy definition. Although the term "representation" has occupied a central part of political discourse in Western democratic thought (Pitkin, 1967), there remains a great deal of ambiguity in its meaning. To understand political representation in the developing nations is even more difficult. The institution of representation has been only recently transplanted in these nations, often as a mere mark of modern statehood. Moreover, their traditional culture lacks the institutional bases or practices which can reinforce the new institution of representation. Thus both representatives and their constituencies tend to have disparate or more often amorphous conceptions of representation.[4]

In order to study representation in the Korean National Assembly, we have adopted the functional view of representation proposed by Eulau and Wahlke (1959). According to this view, representation is essentially an issue pertaining to the relationship between the representative and the represented. This relationship may be fruitfully investigated by focusing on the questions as to "who" and "how" of representation. We have approached these questions through the use of role concept. Analytically, two aspects of role need to be distinguished: role orientations and role behavior. Representative role orientations refer to the individual legislator's own ideas as to how he ought to behave, whereas role behavior is his action as a representative. Role orientations indicate therefore the normative aspect, while role behavior the empirical aspect of role.

REPRESENTATIVE ROLE ORIENTATIONS

Representative role orientations can be explored in terms of the *style* (how) and the *focus* (who) of representation. The style refers to a legislator's own idea or conception concerning the manner in which he ought to represent, while the focus is his own idea as to whom he ought to represent. Table 1 presents data on representative role styles of Korean national assemblymen.[5] It is clear that an overwhelming majority of Korean assemblymen (78%) perceived their roles as "Delegates": they felt that they should act upon the instructions from their constituents. The remaining 23% adopted the role of "Trustees," emphasizing the importance of their own mature and enlightened judgments rather than their constituency's instructions in the performance of their duties.

Representative roles are defined and measured somewhat differently in the studies of different legislatures. Therefore, a direct comparison of the Korean data with the findings in other countries calls for considerable caution. Nonetheless, the predominance of Delegate roles among Korean assemblymen is striking as compared to studies conducted elsewhere. For example, the Davidson study (1969: 117) of the 88th U.S. Congress reported that 28% of American legislators could be classified as Trustees, 56% as "Politicos," and 23% as Delegates. In a study of Colombian congressmen, Hoskin (1970: 15) found that 28% were Trustees, 52% Politicos, and 20% Delegates. Because of hierarchical social relations rooted in the pre-modern Korean traditions which was reinforced further in the colonial period of Japanese domination, we would expect to find the elitist view of representation among Korean assemblymen—the view

TABLE 1
COMPARISON OF REPRESENTATIVE ROLE STYLES
(in percentages)

Role Style	Korean Assemblymen N=112	Japanese Assemblymen N=193	U.S. Congressmen N=87	Colombian Congressmen N=219	Canadian MPs N=165
Delegate	77.5	56.9	23	20	49
Politico	0.0	2.6	46	52	36
Trustee	22.5	38.4	28	28	15
Not ascertainable		2.1	3		
TOTAL	100	100	100	100	100

SOURCES: Data are derived from: Davidson (1969: 117), Kornberg (1967: 108), Hoskin (1970: 15), and Kim (1973).

that a legislator should act upon his own mature and enlightened judgments rather than upon the instructions of his constituency.[6] Contrary to this, most of the assemblymen considered the latter as the primary basis of their representative actions. This finding suggests that Korean assemblymen tend to subscribe, at least in their normative conceptions of representation, to the notion of "direct democracy" as evidenced by the prevalence of Delegate roles.

The total absence of Politico roles among Korean assemblymen is also intriguing. Politicos, a role style characterized by the mixture of a legislator's own independent thinking and the constituency influence, have been found more or less typical among American (Davidson, 1969: 117), Canadian (Kornberg, 1967: 108), Colombian (Hoskin, 1971: 15), and Dutch legislators (Daalder and Rusk, 1972: 162). Although a conclusive explanation for this phenomenon requires a comparative analysis of representative roles in many different political systems, we might suggest two lines of speculation.[7] The first explanation is that the Confucian ideology, still an important part of the Korean political culture, has emphasized the importance of *chicho,* or being a man of principle in personal political conducts (see Kim, 1969; Woo and Kim, 1970a). The role of Politico, which involves frequent shifts in role style, may be considered as blatantly opportunistic and therefore incongruent to the Confucian norm. There is some evidence to support this argument. A study of representative role orientations among Japanese prefectual assemblymen (Kim, 1973) has also indicated that the role of Politicos was seldom perceived as legitimate in Japan. If one can argue that the Confucian norms are still salient parts of both Korean and Japanese political culture, it is probably this set of norms which discourages Korean and Japanese assemblymen from adopting Politico roles.

The second explanation has to do with the lack of bargaining culture in the Korean National Assembly. The pattern of conflicts in the Assembly has been characterized by the frequent recourse to violent and obstructionist tactics of both the government and the opposition legislators (Henderson, 1968: 273-311; Oh, 1968: 23-50; Han, 1069-70: 446-64). A few examples would suffice to illustrate this. The 1968 budget bill was passed after only three minutes of deliberation by the ruling party members, while the entire opposition membership categorically refused to participate. Systematically planned violence, both on the floor and in the corridor of the National Assembly building, has frequently occurred over issues of major importance, such as the decision to send armed forces to Vietnam, the conclusion of the Korea-Japan treaty, and the constitutional revision of 1969. Where the bargaining norm is pervasive, Politico is an appropriate role, for it calls for actions such as compromise, accommodation, and conciliation (Dahl and Lindblom, 1953: 333-34). The absence of the bargaining norm may therefore discourage Korean assemblymen from adopting the Politico role.

The focus of representation is the reference group that structures a legislator's ideas of representation. There are a variety of such foci, including both formal and informal groups such as political party, social class, region, interest group, district constituents, local elites, and the nation as a whole. As shown in Table 2, Korean assemblymen chose the nation, their parties, or district constituents as their primary focus of representation. Fifty-four percent indicated the nation as their primary focus. Another 19% chose their own parties, whereas only 4% felt that they ought to represent the constituents in their districts. A considerable number of Korean assemblymen were, however, unable to name a specific reference group for representation. When those assemblymen who named a vague collectivity such as the nation and those incapable of naming a specific reference group are combined, they constitute an overwhelming 77.5% of all assemblymen. Thus it seems safe to conclude that Korean assemblymen tend to be unclear in their representative focus.

The fact that Korean assemblymen hold unspecific role foci contrasts dramatically with their choice of Delegate roles. Because Delegates are those assemblymen who see their roles as "errand boys," they must have clear ideas as to whom they ought to represent. Despite this, a majority of Korean assemblymen were Delegates and, at the same time, were highly unspecific in their role foci. This seemingly inconsistent conception of representative roles

TABLE 2
FOCUS OF REPRESENTATION IN THE KOREAN ASSEMBLY
(in percentages)

Role Focus	N=112
District	3.6
Political party	18.9
Nation	54.1
No specific focus	23.4
TOTAL	100

reflects, in our opinion, the particular stage of development of the legislative institution in Korea.[8] The history of political representation is relatively short and there are no complementary traditional institutions or practices in Korean culture which can help the new system of representation take root. As a result, legislative roles are not yet highly institutionalized. This may in part account for the inconsistent ideas held by Korean assemblymen of their representative roles.

REPRESENTATIVE ROLE BEHAVIOR

While representative role orientations reveal the individual legislator's own ideas as to how he ought to behave, role behavior indicates his actions as the occupant of a representative role. In order to investigate role behavior, we asked our respondents to indicate whether they had taken any direct actions to represent the interests of any groups, both formal and informal, during the legislative term covered by this study.[9] In Table 3 we find that 49% of Korean assemblymen had not taken representative actions of any kind during the entire term. Among those who had taken some actions, 25% acted in behalf of their districts, 19% of their parties, and only 5% of the interest groups. Negligibly few assemblymen acted for the interests of their primary groups such as personal friends and relatives.

Several major conclusions emerge from the preceding analysis. First, in comparison to the legislators of other political systems, the role of Politicos is completely absent among Korean assemblymen. This finding suggests that bargaining as a modus operandi is not an important part of the legislative norms in the Korean National Assembly. Second, Korean assemblymen tend to have highly "unstructured" representative role orientations in the sense that they hold Delegate roles while having no clear ideas as to whom they

TABLE 3
REPRESENTATIVE ROLE BEHAVIOR (in percentages)

Actions Taken For:	N=112
District	25.0
Party	18.7
Association	5.4
Relatives and friends	1.8
No action taken	49.1
TOTAL	100

ought to represent. This may be related to the low institutional-ization of legislative roles in Korea. Finally, Korean assemblymen tend to be highly unspecific in their foci of representation. About four-fifths of them were unable to indicate a specific reference group which they felt they ought to represent. Similarly, over one-half of Korean assemblymen had not taken direct actions of any kind to represent the interests of any groups. Thus it is clear that a majority of Korean assemblymen do not seek actively to represent the interests of any specific social groups.

CORRELATES OF REPRESENTATIVE ROLE ORIENTATIONS AND BEHAVIOR

In this section we shall investigate the variables which affect representative role orientations and behavior. Previous studies have identified many different variables as important sources of repre-sentative roles and behavior.[10] For conceptual clarity, these variables may be ordered into five distinct groups: social background characteristics, adolescent politicization, career politicization, recruitment experiences, and relevant "political" variables.

The dependent variables are representative role style, role focus, and role behavior. All these variables are treated as dichotomous variables. In the data we have already identified two role styles, Delegate and Trustee, and we have considered them as polar types.[11] Role focus is classified in terms of its specificity. When an assemblyman could name a specific group such as his party, his district, or an interest group, his role focus was taken to be specific. Otherwise, he was considered to have an unspecific role focus. Role behavior was measured by whether an assemblyman had taken direct actions to represent the interests of any group. Accordingly, we have classified them into those who had taken such actions and those who had not.

SOCIAL BACKGROUND VARIABLES

One major assumption implicit in many background analyses of legislators (Sorauf, 1963: 63-94) is that background characteristics influence legislators' attitudes and behavior. We have selected six background variables for analysis because of their particular rele-vance in the Korean political context. These include respondent's age, place of birth (rural-urban), region of birth (South-North), level of education, occupation (prestige ranking), and social status (subjective rating).[12] Simple Pearsonian correlation between the independent and the dependent variables are presented in Table 4. It is clear that the background variables are correlated significantly neither with role focus nor with role behavior. Although role style shows some relationship to place of birth (r = −.19), the overall evidence strongly suggests that the background variables bear no significant relations with role orientations and behavior. This finding is generally consistent with the evidence reported in several other studies. Searing (1969: 471-500) has, for example, demonstrated that the background characteristics do not significantly determine elite political attitudes. Another study (Kim, 1974) of the attitudinal effects of legislative recruitment among Japanese prefectural assemblymen showed that the background variables such as age, education, occupation, place of birth, and social status are not related to the attitudes of prefectural assemblymen.

ADOLESCENT POLITICIZATION

Despite recent interest in political socialization, there have been relatively few studies which relate different socialization to representative roles. Nevertheless, the socialization literature (Dawson and Prewitt, 1969: 105-26) suggests that the family and school environments are important arenas for the politicization of the individual. It is probable that legislators grow up in the family and school environments more politicized than do most of the citizens. Moreover, differences in adolescent politicization may lead to different role orientations and behavior. It seems likely that legislators who grew up in a highly politicized environment would acquire political interest early in their life and would place more confidence in their own judgments by adopting Trustee roles.[13] Similarly, an early politicization may be associated with a relatively long exposure to a variety of active social groups, and therefore legislators politicized early in their life are more likely to exhibit a specific role focus and are more likely to take representative actions than others.

Our respondents were asked about the frequency of political discussion in their homes while growing up, the frequency of political discussion at school, and whether they had been politically active at school.[14] Considerable differences were found among

TABLE 4

CORRELATES OF REPRESENTATIVE ROLE ORIENTATIONS
AND BEHAVIOR (Simple Pearson Correlations)

Variables	Role[a] Style	Role Focus	Role Behavior
Respondent's age[b]	.01	.17	.01
Place of birth (urban-rural)	−.19[c]	.01	.02
Region of birth (South-North)	−.03	.12	−.13
Level of education	−.02	.02	−.12
Occupation (prestige ranking)	−.06	−.09	−.04
Social status (subjective rating)	−.12	.01	.03
Political discussion at home while young	.09	.04	.05
Political discussion at school	.08	.10	.14
Political activity at school	.11	−.13	*.24*
Initial political interest	.07	.07	*.32*
Length of time in politics	−.10	−.03	*.29*
Length of time in party	−.08	.02	*.27*
Experience of holding public office	.14	−.07	*.23*
Political ambition (high-low)	−.03	.01	*.21*
Sponsorship (sponsored-unsponsored)	*.19*	.08	.07
Winning margin	−.21	−.06	*−.30*
Party affiliation	.01	−.04	*.28*
District type (urban-rural)	*−.27*	.06	−.14
Election type (regular versus district at large)	.10	−.05	*.31*
Legislative tenure (number of terms served)	−.08	.07	*.21*
Role style (Delegate-Trustee)	1.00	*−.29*	.08
Role focus (specific-unspecific)	*−.29*	1.00	.09

a. The three dependent variables are coded as follows:
Role styles, 1=Trustee, 2=Delegates
Role focus, 1=specific, 2=unspecific
Role behavior, 1=performed some representative action, 2=did not perform such an action

b. The independent variables are scored as follows:
Age, 1=25-30, 2=31-35, 3=36-40, 4=41-45, 5=46-50, 6=51-55, 7=56-60, 8=61-65, 9=66 or older
Place of birth, 1=farm, 2=town, 3=city
Region of birth, 1=South Korea, 2=North Korea
Education, 1=primary school, 2=middle school, 3=high school, 4=college, 5=graduate college
Occupation (Hollingshead's social position index), 1=higher officials and owners of large business, 2=managers of large business, 3=professionals, 4=semi-professionals, 5=clerical workers, 6=farmers, 7=skilled workers
Social status, 1=upper class, 2=upper middle class, 3=middle class, 4=lower class
Political discussion at home, 1=often, 2=occasionally, 3=never
Political discussion at school, 1=often, 2=occasionally, 3=never
Political activity at school, 1=many times, 2=several times, 3=one or two times, 4=never
Initial political interest, 1=during boyhood, 2=during middle school, 3=during high school, 4=during college, 5=after college
Length of time in politics, 1=all my life, 2=20 years or more, 3=10-19 years, 4=5-9 years, 5=2-4 years
Length of time in party, 1=since 1945, 2=since 1950, 3=since 1960, 4=since 1961, 5=since 1963, 6=since 1967
Experience of holding public office, 1=yes, 2=no

TABLE 4 (continued)

Political ambition, 1=high, 2=medium, 3=low
Sponsorship, 1=present, 2=absent
Winning margin, 1=30,000 votes or more, 2=20,000-29,999 votes, 3=10,000-19,999 votes,
    4=5,000-9,999 votes, 5=1,000-4,999 votes, 6=1-999 votes
Party affiliation, 1=Democratic Republicans, 2=New Democrats
District type, 1=rural, 2=mixed, 3=urban
Election type, 1=regular assemblymen, 2=assemblymen-at-large
Legislative tenure, 1=one term, 2=two terms, 3=three terms, 4=four terms, 5=five terms,
    6=six terms or more

c. The italicized correlations are significant at the .05 level. N=112.

Korean assemblymen in their adolescent politicization. Over one-half of the assemblymen recalled that politics was discussed "often" or at least "occasionally" in their homes. Roughly 18% reported that politics was "never" discussed. In regard to school political activities, almost 52% replied that they had been actively involved in such activities at least one time or more.

The adolescent politicization variables show, however, no significant relationship with role style or with role focus. Representative role behavior is also unrelated with all but one politicization variable, namely political activity at school. The level of political activity at school shows a significant positive association to role behavior ($r = .24$), which lends some support for the hypothesis that legislators politicized early in their life are more likely to take representative actions than others. On the whole, the data make it evident that the adolescent politicization variables do not strongly affect either representative role orientations or the behavior of Korean assemblymen.

CAREER POLITICIZATION

The process of career politicization is closer in time and thus is more salient to legislators' attitudes and behavior than their adolescent political experiences. To test the relationships between differences in career politicization and representative roles, we have examined four variables: the time an assemblyman first became interested in politics, the length of time he had been active in politics, the length of time he had been active in political parties, and the experience of holding public office prior to his legislative career. The data reported in Table 4 show that the four career politicization variables are not significantly related to either role style or role focus. However, the same politicization variables show strong relationships with representative role behavior, with the correlation coefficients ranging from .32 to .23. This suggests that the assemblymen who had highly politicized careers tend to engage in representative actions more frequently than do others.

RECRUITMENT VARIABLES

Differential recruitment of legislators may affect their representative role orientations and behavior (Jewell and Patterson, 1966: 528-30). For the measurement of differential recruitment of Korean assemblymen we have relied on three items: level of political ambition, presence or absence of sponsorship, and winning margin. As Schlesinger (1966) has suggested, the level of political ambition that a legislator has may be related to his roles, for he is likely to structure his legislative actions in a manner consistent with his ambition. The relationship between the level of ambition and role behavior is significant ($r = .21$), which suggests that the higher the level of ambition, the greater the likelihood that an assemblyman would take representative actions. Obviously, highly ambitious assemblymen must appeal not only to the constituency of their present positions but also to the potential constituency of the higher office to which they aspire. Therefore, they are more likely to take representative actions than are others with low ambition.

Legislative recruitment engages a number of recruiting agents or sponsors. Political parties, interest groups, and other social groups often sponsor a legislator's political career. They instigate a potential candidate to seek office, and provide both organizational and financial resources to his campaign. As a result, a candidate's obligation and loyalty become closely intwined with the interests of his sponsoring group. We have classified our respondents into two groups: those whose careers were sponsored and those without such sponsors. The presence or absence of sponsorship shows a significant relationship with role style ($r = .19$). The assemblymen whose careers were sponsored tend to take Delegate roles more than others.

Several studies (Jewell, 1970a: 478-83) have indicated that legislators elected by a slim margin tend to be more sensitive to their constituency demands than others elected by a substantial margin. Thus it might be hypothesized that the smaller the winning margin, the greater the likelihood that a legislator would take a Delegate role and a specific role focus. He would also take more representative actions than others elected by a large margin. The evidence presented in Table 4 lends some support for these hypotheses. Sponsorship is significantly related to both role style and role behavior (r = .21, −.30). It appears that the "big" winners tend to take Trustee roles and act less frequently in behalf of their constituents than other assemblymen who won by a slim margin.

RELEVANT "POLITICAL" VARIABLES

For lack of a better label, we have grouped variables such as party affiliation, type of district, type of election, and length of legislative tenure together and called them "political" variables. There are now two major political parties in the Korean National Assembly: the ruling Democratic Republican Party and the opposition New Democratic Party. The data indicate that the difference in party is strongly correlated with representative role behavior (r = .28). In comparison to the opposition members, the Democratic Republican assemblymen tend to take representative actions more frequently. The Democratic Republican Party is in fact the government party and therefore its assemblymen would have an easy access to and influence upon the bureaucracy. This fact may account for a greater degree of representative actions among the Democratic Republicans.

The urban-rural characteristics of the district that an assemblyman represents may affect his role orientation and behavior. Voters in urban districts are generally better educated and more knowledgeable about politics than voters in rural districts in Korea (Lee, 1970). As a result, the expectations and demands of urban and rural voters in regard to their representatives may be significantly different. The type of district shows a negative relation with role style (r = −.27), indicating that the urban assemblymen are more likely to be Trustees than are the rural assemblymen.

Korean assemblymen are elected by two different methods. The majority are elected in single-member districts by popular votes. Other assemblymen are elected from the party list: each party receives a certain number of assembly seats based on the number of assemblymen it elects from single-member districts.[15] The electoral system in Korea combines therefore elements of both geographical and proportional representation. Because Korean assemblymen are elected by different methods, they are likely to exhibit different role orientations and behavior. The data in Table 4 indicate a strong association between the type of election and role behavior (r = .31), and also a moderate relationship between the type of election and role style (r = .10). It appears that the regular assemblymen, as compared to the assemblymen-at-large, tend to take Delegate roles and act more frequently in behalf of their constituents.

Korean assemblymen differ considerably in the length of their legislative tenure. About one-half of them have served more than ten years in the legislature. However, 45% were freshmen legislators. Such differences in legislative tenure may influence a legislator's ideas about his job and his actions as a representative. The data show that length of legislative tenure is not related to role style or role focus. But it is positively correlated with representative behavior ($r = .21$). It is evident, then, that the veteran assemblymen tend to take representative actions less frequently than others who have a relatively short legislative tenure.

In summary, the preceding analyis of bivariate relationships between representative roles and some selected variables suggest several tentative conclusions. First, despite the popular assumption that the background characteristics affect legislators' attitudes and behavior, we have found little evidence to support this. The background characteristics of Korean assemblymen show no significant relationships with their representative role orientations and with their representative actions. Secondly, the level of adolescent politicization is not related in any important way to representative roles. Although adolescent politicization variables are strongly correlated with career politicization variables, they do not appear to exert direct influence upon the representative roles and actions of Korean assemblymen. Thirdly, the independent variables which affect representative roles and actions most strongly are career politicization, recruitment, and relevant "political" variables.

MULTIVARIATE ANALYSIS

Most studies of representative roles have considered only a limited number of variables and have reported simple bivariate relationships. In this section an attempt is made to consider a wide variety of variables simultaneously, and to determine the relative importance of each of these variables as sources of representative roles and behavior. A stepwise multiple regression program was employed to analyze the data.[16] This program ranks each independent variable in terms of its explanatory capacity, that is, the amount of variance explained in the dependent variable.

Table 5 presents the results of analysis. Considering representative

TABLE 5

CUMULATIVE MULTIPLE CORRELATIONS BETWEEN SELECTED
VARIABLES AND REPRESENTATIVE BEHAVIOR

Variables	Multiple R	Increase in R^2
Initial political interest	.32	.10
Winning margin	.43	.08
District type (urban-rural)	.48	.05
Length of time in politics	.53	.05
Respondent's age	.56	.03
Political ambition (high-low)	.58	.02
Sponsorship (sponsored-unsponsored)	.59	.01
Level of education	.60	.01
All other variables[a]	.63	.05

a. These variables include (1) place of birth, (2) region of birth, (3) occupation, (4) social status, (5) political discussion at home, (6) political discussion at school, (7) political activity at school, (8) length of time in party, (9) experience of holding public office, (10) party affiliation, (11) election type, (12) legislative tenure, (13) role style, and (14) role focus. These 14 variables independently account for less than a 1% increase in R^2.

behavior first, it should be noted that the full set of 23 independent variables can account for 40% of the total variance. Four variables emerge as the most important sources of representative behavior, each capable of explaining at least 5% or more of the total variance. These variables are: initial political interest, winning margin, district type, and length of time in politics. Thus we can conclude that the representative behavior of a Korean national assemblyman is significantly determined by the time he first became interested in politics, his winning margin of votes, the urban-rural characteristics of his district, and finally the length of time he has been active in politics.

Why do some assemblymen choose Delegate roles while others Trustee roles? What variables might account for such difference in representative role style? Table 6 ranks the independent variables in terms of their respective explanatory power. It is clear that four variables stand out as the most important determinants of representative role style: district type, sponsorship, winning margin, and length of time in politics. These four variables explain in combination roughly 20% of the total variance in role style. With the addition of other 16 variables, the explained variance increases from 20% to only 24%. The choice of representative role style (Delegate or Trustee) among Korean assemblymen appears to depend in large part on the urban-rural characteristics of their districts, the presence or absence of career sponsorship, their winning margin of votes, and the length of time they have been active in politics.

Role focus which we have operationalized in terms of its

TABLE 6

CUMULATIVE MULTIPLE CORRELATIONS BETWEEN SELECTED
VARIABLES AND REPRESENTATIVE ROLE STYLE

Variables	Multiple R	Increase in R^2
District type (urban-rural)	.27	.07
Sponsorship (sponsored-unsponsored)	.35	.05
Winning margin	.40	.04
Length of time in politics	.45	.04
All other variables[a]	.49	.04

a. These variables include (1) respondent's age, (2) place of birth, (3) region of birth, (4) level of education, (5) occupation, (6) social status, (7) political discussion at home, (8) political discussion at school, (9) political activity at school, (10) initial political interest, (11) length of time in party, (12) experience of holding public office, (13) political ambition, (14) party affiliation, (15) election type, and (16) legislative tenure. These 16 variables independently account for less than a 1% increase in R^2.

specificity is another aspect of representative role orientations. The multivariate analysis reported in Table 7 reveals that the full set of 20 independent variables fails to explain a substantial amount of the total variance in representative role focus (11%). This finding suggests that there are important variables other than those considered here which might affect representative role focus. Nonetheless, among the variables analyzed several seem to exert more influence on role focus than others. For example, the respondent's age, length of his legislative tenure, frequency of political discussion while going to school, and region of birth (South-North) can explain some variations in the dependent variable—whether he is specific or unspecific in his representative role focus. However, the overall evidence strongly suggests that none of the variables examined in the present paper can explain a significant proportion of the variance in representative role focus.

TABLE 7

CUMULATIVE MULTIPLE CORRELATIONS BETWEEN SELECTED
VARIABLES AND REPRESENTATIVE ROLE FOCUS

Variables	Multiple R	Increase in R^2
Respondent's age	.17	.03
Legislative tenure	.21	.02
Political discussion at school	.24	.01
Region of birth (South-North)	.26	.01
All other variables[a]	.33	.04

a. These variables include (1) place of birth, (2) level of education, (3) occupation, (4) social status, (5) political discussion at home while young, (6) political activity at school, (7) initial political interest, (8) length of time in politics, (9) length of time in party, (10) experience of holding public office, (11) political ambition, (12) sponsorship, (13) winning margin, (14) party affiliation, (15) district types, (16) election type. These 16 variables independently account for less than a 1% increase in R^2.

The stepwise multiple regression analysis has allowed us to select a relatively small subset of variables, and thereby to identify the most powerful explanatory variables for representative role orientations and behavior. We have found that certain variables appear to have a powerful explanatory capacity for various aspects of representative role such as role style, role focus, and role behavior. For example, the urban-rural characteristics of district, the length of time assemblymen have been active in politics, and his winning margin were found to be most important variables in both cases of representative role style and behavior. Other variables appear, however, to act upon only one aspect of representative role. This finding suggests that sources of representative role style, role focus, and role behavior of Korean national assemblymen are not completely identical.

CAUSAL LINKAGES BETWEEN ROLE ORIENTATIONS AND BEHAVIOR

One further step of data analysis needs to be taken. This concerns the problem of relating representative role orientations to representative behavior. Jewell (1970a: 487) has recently stated in his extensive review of the literature on legistive behavior:

> An analysis of the sources of roles is not an end in itself, nor is it enough to describe the patterns of roles that are found in a legislature. The value of role analysis for most political scientists lies in its potential for improving explanation and prediction of legislative behavior. As yet, this is a potential that remains largely unrealized in practice. The problems of relating roles to behavior need to be understood in order to define both the limitations and potential of role analysis.

Although representative role orientations are analytically distinguished from role behavior, the common assumption implicit or explicit in many representative role analyses has been that role orientations are related to role behavior. We now subject this assumption to testing.

We have discovered earlier in a simple bivariate analysis (Table 4) that certain career politicization, recruitment, and "political" variables are strongly correlated with representative role behavior. We now postulate that the causal relationships between these variables and representative role behavior can be traced through the inter-

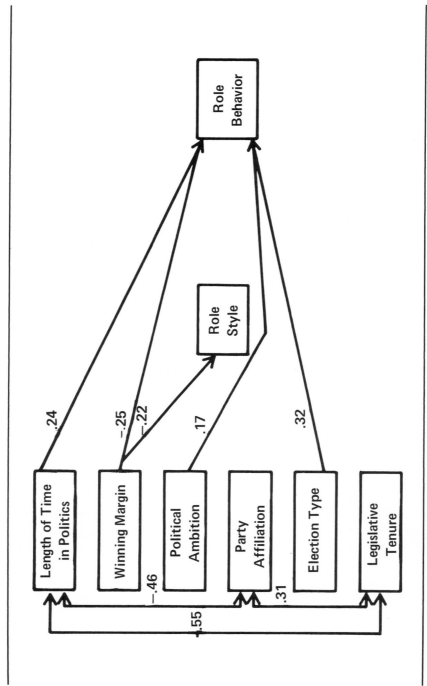

Figure 1: A PATH DIAGRAM OF REPRESENTATIVE BEHAVIOR: ROLE STYLE

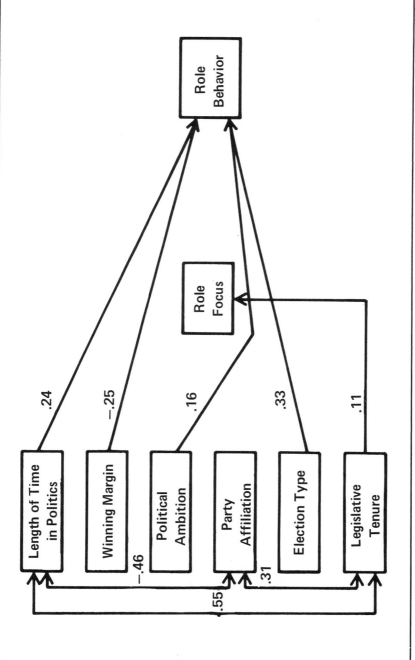

Figure 2: A PATH DIAGRAM OF REPRESENTATIVE BEHAVIOR: ROLE FOCUS

vening representative role orientations. To test this, we have used path analysis (Duncan, 1966). Figures 1 and 2 present path diagrams in which only significant path coefficients are indicated by arrows.

The basic finding is simple but dramatic. The relationships between length of time in politics, winning margin, political ambition, party affiliation, election type, and legislative tenure, on the one hand, and representative role behavior, on the other, *are not explained at all* by either of the two variables, role style or role focus, which we have presumed to be the intervening variables. In short, this means that the impacts of the independent variables upon representative role behavior are direct and do not operate through representative role orientations. The evidence is thus not supportive of the commonly assumed linkages between role orientations and role behavior. A perfect fit between a normative conception of a role and its behavioral manifestation is unlikely in real-life situation, for some important constraints may intervene such as role expectations, personality, and specific context in which a role is enacted. However, the extent to which role orientations are congruent with behavior may indicate the degree of institutionalization of a role. In a developing legislature such as the Korean National Assembly, the role of a representative may not be highly institutionalized, and this may be reflected in the weak linkages found between representative role orientations and behavior among Korean assemblymen.

Several other points are also worth commenting. The path coefficients in the diagrams indicate that representative behavior of Korean national assemblymen is determined in large part by the length of time they have been active in politics, their winning margins of votes, and whether they are assemblymen-at-large or regular assemblymen. Also the level of political ambition that assemblymen exhibit exerts moderate influence upon their representative role behavior. Party affiliation and legislative tenure, which showed initially strong zero-order correlations with role behavior ($r = -.28, .21$), lose their significance when considered together with other variables. Because political parties are important sources of legislative norms and voting cues, we have expected that Democratic Republican and New Democratic assemblymen would act quite differently in their representative roles. However, it is clear in the data that party difference does not exert a direct influence on representative behavior among Korean assemblymen. This finding is consonant to the popular view (Henderson, 1968: 308-11; Woo and Kim, 1971) that a principal reason that sustains a party organization in Korea is its office-seeking activities, and that no significant difference exists between the two parties in their ideology or their positions on key political issues. Therefore, party difference is not likely to lead to different representative actions in Korea.

SUMMARY AND INTERPRETATION

The purpose of this paper has been to investigate representative role orientations and behavior among Korean national assemblymen. Another research objective was to explore the key variables which explain differences in role orientations and behavior. We now summarize major findings and discuss their theoretical implications.

First, one striking aspect of representative role styles among Korean assemblymen is the total absence of Politicos. Studies of representative roles in Western nations have consistently shown that Politicos are important role orientations. We have suggested that the absence of Politicos in the Korean National Assembly may be associated with the Confucian norm of *chicho,* on the one hand, and with the lack of a bargaining culture, on the other. The Confucian norm, still a salient part of Korean political culture, emphasizes the virtue of being a man of principle in personal political conducts, and thereby tends to discredit the opportunistic attitudes such as those associated with Politico roles. The pattern of legislative conflicts in the Korean National Assembly has been characterized by frequent violence—the use of obstructionist and extraparliamentary tactics by both the government and the opposition assemblymen. Compromise, accommodation, or conciliation does not appear to be an important part of the legislative norms. This fact seems to account for the absence of Politicos—a role style most congruent with a bargaining culture—among Korean assemblymen.

Second, Korean assemblymen saw the nation, political parties, and electoral districts as their prime foci of representation. However, a considerable number of them also indicated *no specific foci* (23.4%). Combining those assemblymen who named vague collectivities such as the nation and others incapable of giving specific foci, we have found that more than three-fourths of Korean assemblymen had highly unspecific role focus.

Third, focusing upon representative actions, we have found that over half of the Korean assemblymen had not taken any direct actions to represent the interests of any group during their entire legislative term. It is then apparent that a significant number of Korean assemblymen seldom act in behalf of any specific social groups.

Fourth, the use of multivariate analysis revealed several key variables which affect representative role orientations and behavior in the Korean National Assembly. In general, we have found that career politicization, recruitment, and "political" variables are most salient to the assemblymen's own ideas as to how they ought to behave and how they actually act as representatives. In particular, the urban-rural characteristics of the district, size of the winning margin, presence or absence of sponsorship, and length of time in politics proved to be most important determining factors for representative role style and behavior. The assemblymen who represent rural districts, who win by a precarious margin, who have been active in politics for a relatively short period, and whose careers were sponsored by political parties or other organized groups, tend to be generally Delegates in their role style and tend to act in behalf of the interests of their constituents more frequently than other assemblymen.

Fifth, the most important finding is perhaps the absence of significant linkages between representative role orientations and behavior. As Wahlke and Eulau (1962: 8-11) have asserted, the utility of role analysis rests upon the assumption that legislators' role orientations influence their legislative behavior. To test this assumption, we have proposed a path model of representative behavior in which legislators' role orientations were considered as the intervening variables. The evidence indicated that the impacts of the selected independent variables upon representative behavior are *direct* and do not operate through either role style or role focus. This finding suggests that the ideas that Korean assemblymen have as to their representative roles are totally unrelated to the way they actually act as representatives.

The democratic institutions of the West, such as Constitutionalism and the system of popular representation, came to Korea relatively recently, following the conclusion of the Pacific War in 1945. However, these institutions were adopted not on a wave of popular support but rather as a result of what might be called "the diffusion of world culture." Like leaders of other Asian and African countries, political leaders of Korea were committed to the assimiliation of modern science and technology, modern organizations, and modern political institutions, one of which was the legislature. Despite the limited role that the legislature has been permitted to play, Korean leaders appear to be quite sincere in their assertion that they seek a democratic political order and see the legislature as an essential step toward this goal. The fact that most of Korean assemblymen were Delegates in their role style indicates their strong commitment to the notion of popular representation. However, Korean assemblymen are themselves also a product of the Korean political environment in which the concept of representation has been totally unknown until recently. As a result, they seem to fully subscribe to the ideas of popular representation, on the one hand, and act quite differently, on the other. The point is that the ideas that Korean assemblymen have about their representative roles are not integrated into their representative actions.

Speculatively, the legislatures of the new states of Asia and Africa may operate in the political environment similar to that of Korea. Most of their legislative bodies were established in the past few decades, and their social and political environments are generally adverse to the development of the legislative institution. Although legislators of these new states may genuinely subscribe to the principle of popular representation, they may not reflect such normative commitment in their day-to-day representative actions. Thus, a significant discrepancy may exist between the normative conceptions that legislators hold as to their representative roles and the ways in which they actually behave. For this reason, the analysis of role perceptions may have limited value for understanding legislative behavior in developing political systems such as Korea.

NOTES

1. An excellent review of the literature on legislative behavior appears in Jewell (1970a/b).

2. A few systematic studies of legislative behavior in the developing countries have recently appeared. See, for example, Hopkins (1970), Mezey (1970), Hoskin (1970), and Woo and Kim (1970b).

3. The 7th Korean National Assembly had 175 seats. Of these 129 were the Democratic Republican, 45 were the New Democrats, and one was an independent at the time of the interviews.

4. The disparate conceptions of representation held by Korean Assemblymen were discussed in our earlier report (Woo and Kim, 1970b).

5. Representative role styles of the assemblymen were classified on the basis of their responses to the question: "What do you think your representative duties entail?"

6. The elitist attitude of Korean assemblymen was also revealed in their responses to a Likert-type question: "Politics must be guided by the enlightened and experienced leaders rather than by the will of the masses." For a general discussion of the elitist character of Korean politics, see Henderson (1968: 195-224) and Woo and Kim (1971).

7. Obviously, systematic explanation for such an issue requires two levels of inquiry. One is the investigation of the determinants of representative role style, which would indicate why some legislators take politico roles. Another is a comparative analysis of role style in a wide variety of political systems which would identify systemic factors that account for the difference in the pattern of distribution of role styles.

8. We have presented this line of interpretation in a previous study (Woo and Kim, 1970b). When we cross-tabulate representative role styles and the specificity of role focus, more than two-thirds of the Delegates (71%) were unable to indicate a specific representative focus. The following tabulation shows the degree of role specificity by representative role styles:

CROSS-TABULATION OF ROLE STYLES AND FOCI (in percentages)

Role Focus	Trustees	Delegates
Specific focus	8	29
Unspecific focus	92	71
TOTAL	100	100
(N)	(25)	(87)

9. The question was: "Have you taken any direct action during this legislative term to represent the interests of any groups?"

10. Previous studies (Wahlke and Eulau, 1962: 21-24; Jewell, 1970a: 465-83) have identified many different variables which might affect legislators' role orientations. They have suggested individual demographical characteristics, ecological characteristics of political units, personality characteristics, recruitment experiences, and legislative experiences as the most probable sources of legislative roles.

11. We are aware of the controversy over the question as to whether we should conceive representative roles such as Delegate, Trustee, or Politico as a continuum or as discrete role categories. However, since Politico roles did not appear among Korean assemblymen, this particular issue does not seem relevant to our study (Francis, 1965: 567-85).

12. Age is an important surrogate variable for changing socialization experience, for Korea has undergone a series of drastic changes in its recent history from Japanese rule to the period of American Military Government, to political independence in 1948, to the three-year-long Korean War, and to the Student Uprising of 1960 followed by another military coup d'etat in 1961—all of these in less than a quarter of a century. Region of birth is also important because those who were born in North Korea do not have the advantages of local ties based on the length of residence, family, or clan name which still determine the result of election significantly in many rural districts. Thus the northern-born candidates may behave differently from others born in South Korea (Woo and Kim, 1970c).

13. Jewell (1970a: 473) suggested a similar hypothesis.

14. The questions were: (1) "How often was politics discussed in your family while you were growing up?" "How often did you discuss politics with your friends while you were going to school?" (3) "How many times did you participate in political clubs or groups while you were a student?"

15. Under the election law at the time, each political party could elect one-third of the total legislative seats that it won in single-member districts from its party list (Park, 1963: 195-202).

16. The particular program used here was the stepwise multiple regression analysis included in Statistical Package for the Social Sciences (Nie et al., 1970: 174-95).

REFERENCES

ALMOND, G. A. and G. B. POWELL (1966) Comparative Politics. Boston: Little, Brown.

APTER, D. E. (1965) The Politics of Modernization. Chicago: Univ. of Chicago Press.

BELL, C. G. and C. PRICE (1969) "Pre-legislative sources of representational roles." Midwest J. of Political Science 13: 254-70.

DAALDER, H. and J. G. RUSK (1972) "Perceptions of party in the Dutch Parliament," pp. 143-98 in S. C. Patterson and J. C. Wahlke (eds.) Comparative Legislative Behavior. New York: John Wiley.

DAHL, R. E. and C. E. LINDBLOM (1953) Politics, Economics, and Welfare. New York: Harper.

DAVIDSON, R. H. (1969) The Role of the Congressman. New York: Pegasus.

DAWSON, R. E. and K. PREWITT (1969) Political Socialization. Boston: Little, Brown.

DUNCAN, O. D. (1966) "Path analysis: sociological examples." American J. of Sociology: 1-6.

EDINGER, L. J. and D. D. SEARING (1967) "Social background in elite analysis: a methodological inquiry." Amer. Pol. Sci. Rev. 61: 428-45.

ELDERSVELD, S. J., V. JAGANNADHAM, and A. P. BARNABAS (1968) The Citizen and the Administrator in a Developing Democracy. Glenview, Ill;: Scott, Foresman.

EULAU, H. and J. C. WAHLKE (1959) "The role of the representative." Amer. Pol. Sci. Rev. 53: 742-56.

FRANCIS, W. (1965) "The role concept in legislatures: probability model and a note on cognitive structure." J. of Politics 27: 567-85.

GERLICH, P. (1972) "Orientations to decision-making in the Vienna City Council," pp. 87-106 in S. C. Patterson and J. C. Wahlke (eds.) Comparative Legislative Behavior. New York: John Wiley.

HAN, Y. C. (1969-70) "Political parties and political development in South Korean." Pacific Affairs XLII, 4: 446-65.

HENDERSON, G. (1968) Korea: The Politics of the Vortex. Cambridge, Mass.: Harvard Univ. Press.

HOPKINS, R. F. (1970) "The role of M.P. in Tanzania." Amer. Pol. Sci. Rev. 64: 754-71.

HOSKIN, G. (1971) "Dimensions of representation in the Colombian National Legislature," in W. Agor (ed.) Latin American Legislative Systems: A Comparative Reader. New York: Praeger.

HUNT, W. H. (1969) "Legislative roles and ideological orientations of French Deputies." Presented to the annual meeting of the American Political Science Assn., New York.

JEWELL, M. E. (1970a) "Attitudinal determinants of legislative behavior: the utility of role analysis," in A. Kornberg and L. D. Musolf (eds.) Legislatures in Developmental Perspective. Durham, N.C.: Duke Univ. Press.

--- (1970b) "A reappraisal of the legislative system." Prepared for the annual meeting of the American Political Science Assn., Los Angeles.

--- and S. C. PATTERSON (1966) The Legislative Process in the United States. New York: Random House.

KIM, C. L. (1974) "Attitudinal effects of legislative recruitment: the case of Japanese assemblymen." Comparative Politics (October): 109-126.

--- (1973) "Consensus on legislative roles among Japanese prefectual assemblymen," pp. 398-420 in A. Kornberg (ed.) Legislatures in Comparative Perspective. New York: David McKay.

KIM, T. G. (1969) "How to harmonize the traditional moral values and present-day needs," pp. 12-31 in C.I.E. Kim and C. Chee (eds.) Aspects of Social Change in Korea. Kalamazoo, Mich.: Korean Research and Publications.

KORNBERG, A. (1967) Canadian Legislative Behavior. New York: Holt, Rinehart & Winston.

LaPALOMBARA, J. [ed.] Bureaucracy and Political Development. Princeton: Princeton Univ. Press.

LEE, Y. H. (1970) "Social change and political participation in Korea." Presented at the Conference on Tradition and Change in Korea, Seoul, Korea.

MEZEY, M. L. (1970) "The functions of a minimal legislature: role perception of Thai legislators." Presented to the annual meeting of the American Political Science Assn., Los Angeles.

NIE, N. H., D. H. BENT, and C. H. HULL (1970) Statistical Package for the Social Sciences. New York: McGraw-Hill.

OH, J.K.C. (1968) Korea: Democracy on Trial. Ithaca, N.Y.: Cornell Univ. Press.

PARK, I. K. (1963) Shinhunpub Haeu (A Commentary on the New Constitution). Seoul: Jinmyung Moonhwasa.

PITKIN, H. (1967) The Concept of Representation. Berkeley: Univ. of California Press.

PYE, L. W. (1962) Politics, Personality, and Nation-Building. New Haven, Conn.: Yale Univ. Press.

SCHLESINGER, J. A. (1966) Ambition and Politics. Chicago: Rand McNally.

SEARING, D. D. (1969) "Comparative study of elite socialization." Comparative Political Studies 1: 471-500.

SORAUF, F. J. (1963) Party and Representation. New York: Atherton.

WAHLKE, J. C. and H. EULAU (1962) The Legislative System. New York: John Wiley.

WOO, B. K. and C. L. KIM (1971) "Intra-elite cleavages in the Korean National Assembly." Asian Survey 11: 544-61.

——— (1970a) "Daeu jungchi wa Kukhoe Euwon (Representative Politics and the National Assemblymen)" Jungkyung Yungu 68: 23-32.

——— (1970b) "Legislative recruitment and political representation in South Korea." Laboratory for Political Research, Report No. 35. Iowa City: University of Iowa.

——— (1970c) "Social and political background of Korean National Assemblymen." Laboratory for Political Research, Report No. 38. Iowa City: University of Iowa.

CHONG LIM KIM is Associate Professor of Political Science and Associate Director of the Comparative Legislative Research Center at the University of Iowa. His publications include a co-authored book, *Patterns of Recruitment: A State Chooses Its Lawmakers* (1974), and numerous journal articles in American Political Science Review, Midwest Journal of Political Science, Comparative Political Studies, Comparative Politics, and Journal of Developing Areas.

BYUNG-KYU WOO is a Senior Staff member in the Home Affairs Committee of the Korean National Assembly, and Lecturer of Political Science at Choo-Ang University, Seoul, Korea. He has published books and articles on the politics of contemporary Korea.

INDEX